EDITIONS SR

Volume 8

Of God and Maxim Guns
Presbyterianism in Nigeria, 1846-1966

Geoffrey Johnston

Published for the Canadian Corporation for Studies in
Religion/Corporation Canadienne des Sciences Religieuses
by Wilfrid Laurier University Press

1988

Canadian Cataloguing in Publication Data

Johnston, Geoffrey.
  Of God and maxim guns

(EdSR, Editions in the study of religion ; 8)
Includes index.
ISBN 0-88920-180-3

1. Presbyterian Church − Nigeria − History.
2. Nigeria − Church history. I. Title. II. Series:
Editions SR ; 8.

BX9162.N5J64 1988   285′.2669   C86-094302-X

56,437

© 1988 Canadian Corporation for Studies in Religion/
        Corporation Canadienne des Sciences Religieuses

88 89 90 91 4 3 2 1

Cover design by Michael Baldwin, MSIAD

Order from:
Wilfrid Laurier University Press
Wilfrid Laurier University
Waterloo, Ontario, Canada   N2L 3C5

TABLE OF CONTENTS

Acknowledgments iv

Introduction 1

Chapter 1
Expansion on the Cross River 8

Chapter 2
Arochuku and Beyond 32

Chapter 3
The Government of the Church 72

Chapter 4
A Learned and Godly Ministry 104

Chapter 5
Neighbours in the Gospel 132

Chapter 6
Religion and Literature 160

Chapter 7
To Heal the Sick 191

Chapter 8
The Mothers in Israel 221

Chapter 9
The Church and Civil Power 242

Chapter 10
The Authority of the Word 273

Chapter 11
The Prophets and the People 303

Index 308

Map
**Principal Centres of the Presbyterian Church
of Nigeria, 1846-1966** 322

ACKNOWLEDGMENTS

I must express my sincere thanks to the many people who have shared in this book's preparation. First must be my wife, who has shared all the ups and downs of this project over the last thirteen years and put up with the numerous domestic upheavals that research seems to entail. The staff of the Overseas Council of the Church of Scotland has been most hospitable, providing not only access to material but also the use of an office. Second must be Dr. A. H. Johnson, his colleagues, and successors, and the Board of World Mission of the Presbyterian Church of Canada, whose interest and support made the research possible. Thanks are also due to Professor A. F. Walls of Aberdeen for his encouragement and support in the early stages and to Dr. Ogbu Kalu of Nsukka for his many perceptive and useful comments. Last but not least, I must mention my many friends in the Presbyterian Church of Nigeria who answered my endless questions and provided an indispensable antidote to the missionary sources. This book has been published with the help of a grant from the Canadian Federation for the Humanities, using funds provided by the Social Sciences and Humanities Research Council of Canada.

INTRODUCTION

In January 1964 the Presbyterian Church of Nigeria appointed me as its representative on the staff of Trinity College, the college that trained ministers for the Presbyterian, Anglican, and Methodist churches in the old Eastern Region of Nigeria. Since the college lacked an historian, I turned my hand both to the basics of church history and to the study of the church of Africa, a subject almost as new to me as it was to the students.

This book was born in the search for source material. After a year of working with missionary biography and mission society history, it was abundantly clear that no real understanding of the history of the church in Africa was possible without extensive research. When I left the college in May 1966, I started on the long road which has led twenty years later to the appearance of this book.

In the meantime, other scholars have been at work: Turner, Webster, and Peel have written on the independent churches; Ayandele and Ajayi, on the missionaries of the nineteenth century; and Ekechi, on the Catholics and Anglicans around Onitsha. This book adds a further piece to the puzzle. Ayandele and Ajayi, because they were writing on southern Nigeria as a whole, could spend only a limited amount of time on the Presbyterians. Because Ekechi concentrated on Onitsha, he left aside the Presbyterians and the people of the Cross River valley: the Efiks, the Ibibios, some Igbos,

and the numerous small tribes which live along both
sides of the river. Furthermore, unlike the
earlier studies, this book continues to the late
1960s, past the years of pioneering and
consolidation down to the end of the missionary
period.

I have decided to handle the material
topically rather than chronologically. Each
chapter deals with a specific aspect of the
church's life to the end of the period. While the
method enables the reader to get a clear picture of
the development of educational or medical work, it
does not provide an overall picture of the church's
history. In the next few paragraphs, therefore,
the history of the church as a whole will be set
out in terms of the book's title, Of God and Maxim
Guns. Such an introduction should help the reader
see how all the pieces of the puzzle fit together.

The impetus which led to the founding of the
Presbyterian Church of Nigeria came from the
enthusiasm of the young church in Jamaica. When
the Scottish Missionary Society revived its lagging
work in Jamaica in 1824 it became part of a great
movement into Christianity, which has permanently
coloured the life of the West Indies. Associated
with this movement into the church was the campaign
for the abolition of slavery. In response to these
two events, the coming of Christianity and the
coming of freedom, the Presbyterians in Jamaica,
missionaries and converts alike, conceived the idea
of starting a mission to the homeland, to the
shores of West Africa from which so many Jamaicans
had come.

The first mission party arrived in Calabar in 1846 and quickly settled into a routine which did not change a great deal until the coming of the British Empire after 1890. The missionaries were never numerous. They preached, they taught school, they visited among the women, they engaged in periodic campaigns for social reform; in the 1850s and again in the 1890s they practised medicine, and they did a certain amount of ministerial training.

The early church had three principal characteristics. First, it was in the main a church among the Efiks, the people of Calabar. The principal congregations were in the major Efik communities of Creek Town and Duke Town; the minor stations were in Efik settlements further up the Cross River. Second, the church was small, comprising no more than a few hundred members. Most Christians came from two major sources: the dispossessed of Duke Town and the family of King Eyo of Creek Town. King Eyo, alone among the major figures in Calabar in the 1840s and 1850s, was sympathetic to the mission; because of this, his family connections were sympathetic as well. Creek Town, therefore, though the smaller of the two major Calabar communities, was the centre of the church. Third, the church was governed without discrimination based on race. All its activities were managed by a single presbytery in which black and white sat as equals.

The coming of the British Empire introduced far-reaching changes. With the extension of the British government, a new generation of missionaries succumbed to a kind of colonial mentality; they came to believe that they alone

were capable both of deciding what was good for the
church and of putting their ideas into action.
Hence they took over the management of the church
altogether, vesting in their assembly, the Mission
Council, all effective power and relegating the
presbytery to minor functions. They let the
training of a Nigerian leadership lapse and
accepted the colonial regime, despite its
ambiguities, with hardly a murmur, abandoning the
campaigns for social reform which their
predecessors had taken up with such enthusiasm.

The Nigerian response to the conquest had even
more dramatic results. Because Nigerians came to
the missionaries for answers to the questions the
new situation posed, the church grew by leaps and
bounds. In 1900, it was a Calabar church with a
few struggling outstations; in 1920, it was a
network of churches and schools extending up both
sides of the Cross River as far as the great bend
and beyond. To manage this enormous growth, the
missionaries changed from being pastors of
congregations to being administrators of districts
--more like Anglican bishops or Methodist
superintendents than Presbyterian ministers.
Because more people were going to school and the
colonial government had become interested in
education, the informal, unregulated schools of the
nineteenth century became units in a system of
public instruction. Since girls as well as boys
wanted some kind of education, the women expanded
their work from the few girls they could handle in
their backyards into a system of boarding schools.
With the number of Christians having increased so
dramatically, the missionaries had to resume the

systematic training of Nigerian ministers. About
the only aspect of the church's life not
dramatically affected by the British conquest was
medicine. It was not until the appearance of new
treatments for yaws and leprosy that the hospitals
began to grow.

The church of the colonial period was barely
established when signs of its transformation began
to appear. By 1930 the church had developed a
fairly large corps of trained teachers and a
smaller body of trained ministers. In the 1930s
these men began to assert their independence, and
by 1950 the nationalist period had begun.

The nationalist period was marked by a rapid
growth in sophistication rather than an increase in
numbers. Few new primary schools were opened, but
teacher training colleges and secondary schools
appeared in abundance. Only one new hospital was
built, but it was larger, better equipped, and
better staffed than the old ones. Instead of
relying on junior staff taught on the job, the
doctors instituted systematic training for nurses.
Instead of waiting for well-educated people to
offer their services, the church began awarding
scholarships. The one-man theological college
which had served in the colonial period was
replaced by Trinity College, an interdenominational
project with a more sophisticated curriculum. Most
important of all, the system which had concentrated
power in Mission Council was dismantled and the
various aspects of the church's life were
integrated under a Synod representative of the
church as a whole.

The shift from the colonial to the nationalist era was accomplished without serious difficulty, not because of any great wisdom or foresight on anybody's part, but because the older generation of missionaries--the men of the colonial period-- simply had retired. In 1960 the church, much expanded but still recognizable, was back where it had started. Its affairs were regulated by a court in which black and white sat and argued as equals.

Thus, along with many changes, there were many constant factors. Hope Waddell, the first missionary, was both a preacher and a schoolmaster. One hundred and twenty years later the Presbyterian presence in village after village was at once church and school. If King Eyo was instrumental in rooting the church in Creek Town in 1846, so was Chief Nwancha Otuma in giving it a firm foundation in Ikwo in 1960. If the women missionaries divided their time between work among mothers in their homes and girls in the schools in the nineteenth century, they still did so in 1965. There are striking similarities between the message of the pioneers and that of a modern evangelist like Ulu Eme. It is to these constant factors, the prophetic tradition of the Presbyterian Church, that the title refers.

The prophecy of one generation is the tradition of the next. Prophetic preaching is fresh, immediate, direct. It deals, not with God's nature, but with his word for the here and now. If the preacher has understood the Lord his message is relevant, and because it is relevant, it can be accepted or rejected, but not ignored. Once accepted it becomes the tradition, the established

pattern of thinking and doing. The tradition may
continue to be prophetic; as the church moved out
of Calabar at the beginning of this century it
often was. But it was still tradition, the
inherited package of things to do and things to
say. Although the details might vary, the
substance remained the same. That tradition is the
constant in the church's life. Nigerians within
and without the church responded to it, and the
tradition in its turn, with varying degrees of
flexibility, responded to the response. The
history of this church is the history of the
interplay between the prophetic tradition and the
peoples' response.

Chapter 1
EXPANSION ON THE CROSS RIVER

The Presbyterian Church in Nigeria began with the enthusiasm of freed slaves in Jamaica. For centuries Europeans, especially the British, had scoured the West African coast for slaves to be marketed in the West Indies. These slaves formed one of the earliest mission fields of the British evangelical churches, the Methodists, the Baptists, and the Presbyterians of the Scottish Missionary Society. The Scots had begun work in Jamaica as early as 1800, but it was not until 1824 that they really began to build up their staff. Among the pioneers was Hope Masterton Waddell, whose arrival in 1829 coincided with the great years of church growth in Jamaica. In the middle of those busy years came one of the most momentous events in West Indian history, the abolition of slavery. The slaves expressed their gratitude in terms of their newly found faith:

The eve of freedom was spent by the people in their places of worship, to praise the Lord for the peaceable termination of their weary slavery; and that night the hospitals were emptied of patients whose ailments were all miraculously cured. The song of jubilee from every village awoke the next morning's sun, and soon processions with appropriate banners were seen in all directions, wending their way with the voice of sacred melody to the central point of attraction, the church.[1]

Characteristic of Jamaican Christianity in the years following emancipation was a concern for the land of their fathers, for taking the gospel to

Africa. Before 1838 was over the Presbyterians were taking up a collection for a mission[2] but their plans did not really begin to take shape until the appearance of a book by the well-known British abolitionist Thomas Buxton, entitled The African Slave Trade and its Remedy.

Although slave trading was made illegal for British subjects as early as 1808, the traffic went on; the Royal Navy had to keep a squadron of ships patrolling the coast in an effort to suppress the activities of other Europeans and renegade Englishmen. It was difficult, dangerous, and not very successful work. Buxton argued that the slave trade could only be abolished by providing an equally profitable alternative. His suggestion was the Bible and the Plough--the substitution of agricultural exports for the trade in people and the rebuilding of African society on Christian principles. In reply to the objection that European missionaries could not live in West Africa, Buxton pointed to the West Indian missions where, he assured his readers, converts who were ready, willing, and able to undertake the work could easily be found.[3]

Before the appearance of Buxton's book, none of the Scots in Jamaica had very clear ideas about Africa, nor did they even know the first principles of an African mission. Buxton provided both. In 1841, just before a meeting of the Jamaica Mission Presbytery, the bookstores in Kingston were ransacked for every available copy. With the confidence that Buxton's ideas provided, the missionaries proposed to open from Jamaica a mission to West Africa staffed largely by

Jamaicans, but supervised by missionaries "inured to a tropical climate."[4]

The Scottish Missionary Society regarded this idea with considerable scepticism. Buxton's first major attempt to put his ideas into practice had been the Niger Expedition of 1841, launched with great fanfare in the presence of the Prince Consort. Unfortunately, the Niger Expedition lost a third of its European staff in three months on the Niger River. News of this grisly debacle was still ringing in Scottish ears when the Jamaican mission, small and dependent though it was, proposed a permanent establishment in the same "pestilential district." The directors of the society, with commendable tact, praised the Jamaicans' zeal, but did not think such a mission was "expedient at present."[5]

Though official doors in Scotland might be closed for the time being, much could still be done. Contacts were established in Liverpool, which carried most of the West African trade, and through them an invitation was received from the king and chiefs of Duke Town. John Beecroft, Her Majesty's informal representative on the coast, had spoken to them about a mission, as had Commander Raymond of the Royal Navy when he signed the antislave trade treaty with them in 1841. Eyamba II was prepared to accept a mission even then:

Now we settle treaty for not sell slaves, I must tell you something I want your queen to do for we. Now we can't sell slaves again, we have too much man for country, and want something for make work and trade, and if we could get seed for cotton and coffee, we could make trade, and plenty sugar cans live here, and if some man come teach we way for to do it we get plenty sugar too, and then some man should come for teach book proper and make we all saby God like white man and then we go on for same fashion.[6]

By the middle of 1844, the invitation was on hand with Beecroft's approval attached. In the meantime, a certain amount of publicity had made the idea more familiar, and the society was willing to listen. At this point one of the many reunions of nineteenth-century Scottish Presbyterianism intervened. The new United Secession Church adopted the mission, appointing Hope Waddell to raise the necessary money. He proved an effective propagandist. In a few months he had 3,000 in hand, plus a coasting vessel and a schooner for trips to and from Africa.[7] In April 1846 Hope Waddell, Samuel Edgerley, catechist and printer (with his wife), Andrew Chisolm, assistant, Edward Miller, carpenter, and G. B. Waddell, the founder's houseboy, arrived before Calabar to open the mission. Operations began at once in Duke Town and Creek Town, and when a second party arrived the following year a new station was opened in Old Town, the third of the Calabar communities.

CALABAR IN 1846

Calabar is <u>obio efik</u>, the Efik town. The Efiks are a tribe, part of a linguistic group which includes the Anang, Oron, Enyong, and Ibibio. Originally the Efik were fishermen living at Uruan in Ibibio country near Itu. When they migrated to the mouth of the Cross River, they settled first at Creek Town on a stream joining the Cross and Calabar rivers, and a few decades later at Old Town, near the head of navigation on the Cross River delta. Meanwhile a daughter of one of the

founding fathers had the misfortune to bear twins.
Because twins were an abomination they were usually
destroyed, but an uncle managed to have them moved
to an island in the river where they grew up to be
the founders of Duke Town, the most important of
the Calabar communities.[8]

The date of Calabar's founding is difficult to
establish with certainty. Calculations from the
genealogies suggest that Creek Town was founded
late in the sixteenth century, Old Town early in
the seventeenth, and Duke Town a few decades later.
Since it is unlikely that the Quas, the original
inhabitants of the area, would have allowed the
Efiks to take over the Atlantic trade without a
fight that would have been remembered in the
traditions, the settlement must have taken place
before the slave trade began in a serious way, an
event which does not seem to have happened before
the third quarter of the seventeenth century.[9]

The Efiks then came to the mouth of the Cross
River as fishermen, bringing with them the
traditional social structure of an Ibibio village,
but within a few decades of their arrival the
became involved in the Atlantic slave trade, an
activity which required a much more centralized
organization than a fishing community to which
trade was only marginal. By the time the
missionaries arrived in 1846, Calabar was no longer
a typical West African community but a trading
state, in which the inherited social structure had
been profoundly modified by the necessities of the
Atlantic trade. The basic unit was the ufok, or
house, consisting of a number of closely related
families and their slaves. Each of the communities

was made up of a number of such houses who
recognized a common authority in the obong, or
chief. The whole tribe was held together by the
Ekpe fraternity, a secret society consisting of the
leading men, which formed an assembly where the
common affairs of Calabar were regulated.[10]

The slave trade in Calabar lasted from the
third quarter of the seventeenth century until
1841. Originally slaves had been acquired by war,
but as the trade developed, it became more common
to buy them in upriver markets like Umon, but more
commonly Itu. Not all were sold; some were
retained to man canoes, handle miscellaneous
domestic duties, and provide sacrifices at
funerals. Hence the Efiks continued to buy slaves
even after the trade was abolished, to the point
where the slave population far outnumbered the
free. But Efik slavery was a very different
institution from that known in the West Indies.
Like the free born, the slaves were members of an
ufok; to them as well as to the free, the head of
the house was ete, the father. An enterprising
slave could work his way from paddler to trader,
buy slaves of his own, and purchase his way into
the lower ranks of the Ekpe society and a measure
of protection. Although it is true that there was
little respect for human life and little restraint
on the sinfulness of the ruling class, it is also
true that there was opportunity for the energetic.
Perhaps the classic illustration of this point is
that none of the leading families of the 1840s came
from impeccable origins. The Eyos in Creek Town
originated from a foreign soldier of fortune who
married into the Efik aristocracy, and in Duke Town

the Dukes, the Archibongs, and the Eyambas were all
descended from twins.

When the slave trade ended, the Efiks shifted
to the collection and export of palm oil. The oil
palm grows wild in a wide belt across southern
Nigeria, especially in places which have been
cleared for farming. The fruit was cut and the oil
extracted from the berries and sent off to Britain,
where it was used in tin-plating or as a vegetable
oil. Since Itu, the major slave market was also in
the palm-oil belt, it was not difficult for the
Efiks to switch from one commodity to the other.
As Eyamba pointed out, the major consequence of the
change was unemployment. Slaves continued to be
bought, but they could not be sold in significant
numbers. For the aristocracy slaves were a source
of power, but they also had to be fed. The obvious
solution was to settle surplus retainers on vacant
land, in Akpabuyo, east of Duke Town, and in the
country back of Creek Town, the district which
provided the first outstations of the Creek Town
church.

THE FATHERS OF THE CHURCH

Three men dominate the early years of the
mission: Eyo Honesty II, Hope Waddell, and William
Anderson. Eyo Honesty was a descendant of Eyo Nsa,
the adventurer who married into the Efik
aristocracy and founded the leading family in Creek
Town. As a young man Eyo Honesty learned the palm-
oil business from Duke Ephraim of Duke Town, and
when he set up on his own account in Creek Town, he
soon became the wealthiest and most influential man
in Calabar. He was a typical Victorian

businessman--honest, shrewd, and industrious. Unlike most of his contemporaries he avoided recourse to magic, relying instead on the secular methods common to entrepreneurs everywhere. He supported the mission from the beginning, even translating at the early Sunday services. Although he never became a Christian, and although friction between Eyo and Hope Waddell was not uncommon in the later years of the king's life, Eyo's public support of the mission was a decisive factor in the formative years.

His closest associate was Hope Waddell, the founder of the mission and minister in Creek Town from 1847 to 1858. Hope Waddell was an Irishman who decided to be a missionary with the Scots. After some time at the Secession Church's theological college, he went off as part of the Scottish Missionary Society's attempt to revive the moribund Jamaica mission. All his working life he was a missionary pioneer--no scholar, but a careful observer and an expert propagandist. With the possible exception of Mary Slessor, no one was more adept at selling the Calabar mission than Hope Waddell, but he is not the most attractive person in the church's annals. He was careful, prudent, and austere: "I hate anything flashy," he once remarked. His relations with his more tempestuous colleagues in Duke Town were cordial but rarely warm.

William Anderson is the third of the trilogy. Anderson was a Scot who never had the advantage of a formal theological education. With little more than a primary school education and what his active mind could pick up, he went as a catechist to

Jamaica in 1839. After four sessions with William
Jameson, the theological tutor in the Jamaica
mission, he was ordained in 1845. Anderson was the
minister in Duke Town for forty years, fighting all
the while with his colleagues and the Efik
aristocracy. Nevertheless, towards the end of his
life the Calabar people came to regard him with the
trust and affection they gave to ete, the head of
the house. Although he was turbulent and short-
tempered, there was a charm about him that Hope
Waddell lacked. Commenting on one of the numerous
kings of Duke Town whom he had known, he noted in
his diary: "I know of no man in Calabar less
fitted to rule himself or anyone else. . . . He is
however, very modest; he informed me that there was
no man in Calabar fit to rule other than himself,
which, for all I known, may well be true." Hope
Waddell would not have permitted himself this kind
of levity; hence it is not surprising that Anderson
admitted that "everything that Mr. Waddell writes
annoys me somewhat." The missionary quarrels which
dot the early years of the church were founded as
much on personality as on principle.

The Presbyterians did not choose Calabar
because of some far-reaching policy discussion
which identified the Cross River as the key to
evangelizing Africa; they came because they were
invited. However, once established they were
prepared to argue enthusiastically for the
possibilities of the Cross River. Even in modern
times, the literature of the mission has insisted
on the Cross River as the means whereby the church
might advance into the interior. It comes as
something of a surprise to find that the first

attempt to open a station outside Calabar was not
in the Cross River valley, but in the Niger Delta
at Bonny.

BONNY, IKUNETU, AND IKOROFIONG

Bonny was the most important state in the
Niger Delta. From their town in the mouth of the
river, now used as the harbour of Port Harcourt,
the Bonny people had built up an extensive network
of trading contacts in the delta and in Igbo
country. From the British government's point of
view, it was a more difficult town than Calabar,
and it may well be that the greater receptiveness
of the Calabar people to British policy was
influential in Bancroft's recommending Calabar as a
mission station. But when Hope Waddell visited
Bonny in 1846, King Pepple asked for a missionary.
Hope Waddell referred the matter to Scotland, which
replied by launching an appeal and asking for more
information, particularly regarding the location of
a missionary's house. Hope Waddell's second report
suggested that the only possible procedure was to
use an abandoned ship anchored in the harbour. The
Foreign Mission Board was not impressed, and as
there was no answer to its appeal, it let the
matter drop. Pepple revived it in 1860 when he
wrote to Scotland asking for a missionary and
offering to pay 500 a year towards his expenses.
The board replied that it had no missionaries
available; and even if some had been, the board was
not sure a European could live in Bonny. However,
the board did suggest that a few young men might be
sent to the missionaries at Calabar for training

with a view to their returning to Bonny as
Christian teachers.

A few people were actually sent to Calabar and
trained for a while with Alexander Robb. But
Pepple was not satisfied with anything less than a
proper missionary. In 1864 the Anglicans began
work in Bonny, and from Bonny they expanded to
other Delta towns. There is reason to believe that
the Delta people with their Sierra Leone ministers
were the most successful missionaries in
southeastern Nigeria, being responsible for the
penetration, not only of the delta itself, but also
of wide stretches of Igbo country. So aggressive
were they that they reached Arochuku, a town but a
few miles from the Cross River, before the
Presbyterians. That so many of the clans in
Igboland are Anglican is partly a consequence of
the Presbyterians' failure to respond to Pepple's
invitations.

The expeditions to Bonny were something of a
sideline. The mission's natural line of advance
was the Cross River, and on its wide and tempting
waters it concentrated its attention.
Unfortunately, the river was not the open highway
the missionaries had first thought. In 1851 Hope
Waddell recorded a conversation with King Eyo in
which the latter requested that he be notified of
any expeditions the missionaries might want to
make. Waddell was reluctant to give the king an
opportunity to object and the question remained
open. He added, however, that this hesitation had
been present from the beginning.[12]

The reason is not hard to find. The Efiks
held a monopoly on trade on the Cross River from

Umon to the sea. If the Europeans broke that monopoly and traded directly with the producers of palm oil, Efik prosperity was finished. Where one white man went, another could follow. The missionaries insisted that they had nothing to do with trade, and on the whole their actions suited their words. But some mistakes were made and it was many years before sufficient confidence was built up to allow them to travel the river at will.[13]

Some advance on the lower Cross River was possible. As early as 1849 Eyo was suggesting a station at Ikorofiong, an Efik settlement near Itu.[14] In 1852 a sum of over 2,000 was on hand from an anonymous donor for expansion.[15] Waddell drafted a proposal for the Foreign Mission Board including a variety of places within a few miles of Calabar. When a new station was opened in 1855, however, it was in none of these places, but at Ikunetu, an Efik settlement on the left bank of the river between Creek Town and Ikorofiong. Ikunetu is not now, and was not then, a very important place, but it was a step up the river and gave access to the Okoyong people immediately to the east. Hugh Goldie was appointed to open the station in 1855 and actually settled there in 1856.

This step seems to have been accomplished with Eyo's support and against some opposition from Duke Town, which had not unreasonable fears about its commercial position.[16] When the next advance was made in 1858 to Ikorofiong, Eyo required an agreement from the missionaries that they would allow no trading on the premises, either by themselves or by anyone else.[17] Total abstinence

from direct or indirect participation in commerce
was the condition upon which missionary advance and
indeed missionary residence in the country
depended.

The year 1858 marks the end of the first
period of the church's expansion. In the twelve
years from the founding of the missions, five
stations had been established: Creek Town, Duke
Town, and Old Town in Calabar itself, and Ikunetu
and Ikorofiong in Efik settlements up the river.
Ikorofiong was the last major advance for over
twenty years. Even though the Cross River lay
before it, tempting it into what was thought to be
a healthier interior, the Presbyterian Church
remained tied to Calabar until the 1880s.

Two reasons for this long pause may be
suggested. In the early 1860s W. C. Thomson, the
minister at Ikunetu, tried to establish direct
trading connections between the suppliers of palm
oil at Umon and the European buyers in Calabar.
The reaction of the Calabar aristocracy was so
violent that in 1862 Anderson had to deny publicly
any sympathy with Thomson's activities in order to
keep his station open. Thomson was eventually
officially repudiated, and while the significance
of the affair is hard to gauge, it is probable that
it seriously impaired the confidence men like Hugh
Goldie and William Anderson had tried so hard to
build.[18]

Of more importance, however, was the fact that
once it had reached Ikorofiong, the mission had no
place to go until one of the major communities
further up the river opened its doors. The most
important town seemed to be Umon, on an island just

above Itu, which controlled trade on the river as far as Akunakuna. Until Umon could be brought around no passage up the river was possible, and its broad sweep remained tempting but unusable. When Alexander Robb moved to Ikorofiong in 1869, he talked to everyone he could in an effort to find out what to do when the river opened, but for the time being further advance was impossible.

THE LONG PAUSE, 1858-1880

With the main avenue closed the missionaries turned their attention to other possibilities, particularly in Creek Town. Eyo Honesty's successors were mediocrities; before long the town had ceased to be of commercial importance and people retreated to the farms. Since most of them belonged in one way or another to the house of Eyo, and since this house was the most promising field for converts in Calabar, there was nothing to do but follow them.

In 1862 the Presbytery of Biafra, the local governing body of the mission at the time, proposed locating a missionary among the farms, but the Foreign Mission Board turned the suggestion down because it could not afford another mission house.[19] In 1863, perhaps anticipating the board's decision, Robb and the senior Creek Town teacher, E. E. Ukpabio, began making regular Sunday visits to the farms and in August of that year the first outstation was opened. In 1866 a further advance was made to Ikot Mbo on the Calabar River, and when Edgerley and Goldie divided the affairs of Creek Town between them in 1870, it was decided that the former should devote much of his time to

supervising the outstations. Ten years later the
work had almost doubled and the most advanced
community, Adiabo, was erected as a congregation,
with Ukpabio as its minister.

From the Creek Town farms it was a short step
across the Calabar River to the forest country the
missionaries called Ekoi. Men were actually
stationed there from 1875 to 1880, but for the most
part the district was important to the mission, not
in itself, but as a way to circumvent Umon.
S. H. Edgerley and Ukpabio were the most
enthusiastic explorers, making a series of trips in
an attempt to find a way to the Cross River above
Umon. They had almost succeeded when the Umon
people changed their minds and the overland route
was abandoned for the river. Ekoi country, the
subject of much discussion in the 1860s and 1870s
was henceforth left alone for almost a century.

The most celebrated advance of this period was
into Okoyong, a clan north of Creek Town and east
of Ikunetu. In the nineteenth century they were a
rather warlike people; battles with their principal
trading partners in Calabar were not uncommon.
When Hugh Goldie first went to Ikunetu he called on
them, returning with a polite but evasive reply.
He held out little hope in that quarter. They were
visited again in 1862, and then left alone until
the late 1870s when the received two visits, one
from a Creek Town missionary in 1878 and the other
from the two senior Efik preachers in 1879. By
1881 Ukpabio was pressing for a "practical
interest" in Okoyong, and after some hesitation
Asuquo Ekanem, the minister in Ikunetu, agreed to
live there. He was relieved by a Creek Town elder,

but when one of the periodic quarrels between Creek
Town and Okoyong broke out, he was forced to
withdraw.

Meanwhile Mary Slessor was chafing at the bit.
She had come to Calabar in 1876 and was by this
time a seasoned missionary who, as the Old Calabar
Mission Committee tactfully observed in 1885, would
give "her services more comfortably and more
efficiently by having a sphere of her own." After
the usual hesitations and considerations, she was
recommended for Okoyong and sent off in 1888 to
start the work that made her famous.

She was not, strictly speaking, a pioneer.
The gospel had been preached next door in Ikunetu
for thirty years and missionary visits had become
increasingly frequent since the late 1870s. But
hers was a permanent appointment, and one of great
significance for the clan. Okoyong lacked any
central authority which could handle the inevitable
disputes between villages; even if one discounts a
good deal of her biographer's lurid language, there
is little doubt that Okoyong suffered from a
combination of unemployment and a lack of general
leadership. By encouraging legitimate trade, Mary
Slessor took the beginning steps towards solving
the first problem, but her great contribution to
Okoyong was in providing the leadership that no
local man could have given at the time. As her
host at Ekenge remarked: "We are all weary of the
old customs . . . but no single person or house
among us has the power to break them off, because
they are all part of the Egbo system."[20]

Mary Slessor was part of no house and was not
subject to Egbo. But, above all, she possessed the

essential qualifications of a good chief--she could
and did settle disputes. As her skill and justice
became known, her influence spread, and it was
entirely appropriate that the protectorate made her
president of the Native Court. She was not so much
an evangelist as a reforming chief. She founded
few churches and left behind her only a rudimentary
Christian community, but she fostered the
conditions in which a church could grow. It fell
to her successor, Mina Amess, to preside over the
rooting of Christianity in Okoyong.

BREAKTHROUGH AT UMON

In December 1880 Edgerley heard that Umon was
wavering. As son as he could, he had his canoe
loaded and headed up the river, taking with him
Prince Eyamba, an elder in the Duke Town Church.
Eyo VII, the first Christian king of Creek Town,
would have gone himself, but since he could not he
asked Eyamba to go and sent a canoe ahead to warn
Umon of the impending visit. Eyamba acted as
sponsor to the missionary, introducing him to the
king and chiefs and adding a few well chosen words
about the benefits of church and school. The
meeting was sympathetic but asked for time to
consult the whole town. Edgerley agreed and went
on to ask for permission to travel further up the
river. On this point they were more hesitant, but
finally allowed him to visit Ikot Ana. Edgerley
was quick on his toes. By March he made temporary
arrangements for both Umon and Ikot Ana and had
visited Akunakuna, the furthest point of Umon
commercial penetration, which he found willing to
receive a teacher. The presbytery called on the

Foreign Mission Board for more staff, but all they got was a promise to help. By 1882 African teachers were posted at both Umon and Ikot Ana, but the following year Edgerley died, and further progress was held up for the time being.[21]

In the meantime, Jamaica had entered the picture again. The last appointment from Jamaica had been Alexander Robb, who left Calabar in 1875 when his health deteriorated and returned to Jamaica to take up ministerial training. In 1882 two of his students, H. G. Clerk and E. W. Jarret, appeared in Calabar. Clerk stayed in Creek Town to replace Edgerley, but in 1885 Jarret was posted to Ikot Ana. For three years he was the only missionary above Ikorofiong until James Buchanan, the new secretary of the Mission Board, began pressing for an opening at Unwana, an Igbo town well up the river on the right bank.[22] When the Presbytery replied that Akunakuna was closer and more important, Buchanan suggested it open both and provided the men, Luke and Gartshore, to do so. Both stations were opened in the course of 1888. In the twenty-three years between 1858 and 1881 the church opened one major station, Adiabo. In the next seven years they opened four: Okoyong, Ikot Ana, Akunkuna, and Unwana.

But the advance was more apparent than real. For the upriver missions the last years of the nineteenth century were dreary ones indeed. The stations were lonely and remote for both Africans and Europeans. Death and sickness were the order of the day, and of the many appointments to these stations, only one remained on the job. In 1893 a young Ikorofiong teacher, Akpan Essien Uwa, was

sent to Ikot Ana with the new missionary. The
missionary lasted five years but Uwa, ordained in
1905, lasted for forty. Otherwise the stations
were forever falling vacant. Umon proved to be on
stony ground and was abandoned. Akunakuna was a
notoriously unhealthy place for missionaries and
was finally closed. Only Unwana survived as a
missionary location, but it was not till 1900, with
the arrival of W. A. J. Gardiner, that it received
any kind of continuous attention.

Nor did the inhabitants show much enthusiasm
for the faith. In 1901 they mustered a grant total
of twelve communicants, including the teachers.
Despite an impressive extension of ground occupied,
the church in 1900 was a Calabar church, with only
the slightest of holds on the middle reaches of the
Cross River. It was not until the British took
over the country after 1901 that the church really
took root outside of Calabar.

Some general observations may be made on the
expansion of the church in the nineteenth century
before going on to consider the changed conditions
of the twentieth. In the first place, every
advance was made by a combination of African and
missionary initiative. In the early extensions of
Ikunetu and Ikorofiong this is not so clear, but
there is reason to believe that both these openings
were dependent on Eyo II. In Creek Town the
missionaries only supervised the work on the farms.
Men like Ukpabio and Okon Nyamse were associated
with the work from the beginning and made up the
teaching staff. When the breakthrough came at Umon
it was in part because of the support of Eyo VII
and James Eyamba. Throughout the long and dreary

years in the upriver stations the Efik teachers, just as often as the missionaries, kept the flag flying in conditions which were at least as trying for them as for the Europeans.

In the second place, it has been suggested that the Presbyterians were really not interested in expansion, but in building up a solid base before attempting any serious advance.[23] On the face of it, the argument appears sound. Throughout the 1860s and 1870s there were, on the average, nine or ten men in the five stations, plus four or five women, plus a varying number of Efik teachers. They would hardly appear to have been understaffed. Further, there was little theoretical compulsion to expand. In 1868 Hugh Goldie, by this time one of the acknowledged leaders of the mission, argued in a letter to The Record (The Missionary Record of the United Presbyterian Church) that their primary task must be to develop a native agency, concentrating on the thorough conversion of the Efiks, and only when that was accomplished should they begin to move out, relying for the most part on Efik preachers.[24]

This letter is the nearest thing to a reasoned statement of mission policy that one finds. It envisages a slow and careful building, line upon line, precept upon precept, as Hope Waddell would say, rather than any dramatic sorties into the interior. The point is a valid one, but it can easily be carried to extremes. Advance was so slow in the 1870s that the board undertook a review of the mission, fortunately deciding against closing it.

The missionaries were not altogether
consistent, for when they were charged with a lack
of dynamism they replied, not with variations on
Goldie's careful building theme, but with "lack of
staff." Ten missionaries for five stations may
seem ample, but turnover was rapid, and when a
foreign language must be learned, they are not much
use on their first tour. Besides, someone was
always sick or on leave, and the mission did not
have anything comparable to the numerous and well-
trained Sierra Leonians. The Presbytery called
repeatedly for reinforcements in the 1860s and
1870s but it was not till the 1880s that they began
to appear.

However, it seems that the real reason for
lack of advance is that there was no place to go.
Missionaries can only go where they are invited,
and small places like the Creek Town farms did not
impress the board as worthy of the capital outlay
that a missionary and a house involved. But theory
or no theory, staff or no staff, when the
opportunity came in 1880, the Presbytery jumped at
it. It is true that there were missionaries in the
offing, but it would be some time before they
appeared, if they appeared at all. Nevertheless,
despite the uncertainties, the Presbytery did not
hesitate. Theory and staff might have been of some
importance, but the main point is that serious
expansion was not possible without a major opening,
either at Umon or behind Ikorofiong. The first
have already been discussed: while it was long on
heroism, it was short on converts. The second is
the subject of the next chapter.

Chapter 1

EXPANSION ON THE CROSS RIVER

[1] H. M. Waddell, Twenty-Nine Years in the West Indies and Central Africa, 146.

[2] The Scottish Missionary Register, June 1839.

[3] T. F. Buxton, The Slave Trade and its Remedy, 281-491.

[4] The Register, February 1845.

[5] Minutes of the Scottish Missionary Society, November 19, 1841.

[6] Eyamba to Raymond, December 4, 1842, in Waddell, Twenty-Nine Years, Appendix II, 663. An agricultural mission was considered at one time but was dropped as of secondary importance.

[7] J. McKerrow, History of the Foreign Mission of the Secession and United Presbyterian Church, 373. A regular mail service began to Calabar in March 1854 and made the mission ship obsolete. Its disappearance was a blessing, for the vessel and its crew took up an inordinate amount of missionary time.

[8] A. J. H. Latham, Old Calabar, 1600-1891, 9-10. Calabar's origins are a disputed question. For alternative explanations, see A. K. Hart, Report of the Enquiry into the Dispute over the Obongship of Calabar, official document 17 of 1964, Enugu, Government Printer.

[9] Ibid., 10, 17.

[10] Ibid., 36-37.

[11] H. M. Waddell, Diaries, December 1849;
Andrew Somerville to Hope Waddell, July 6, 1850;
Minutes of the United Presbyterian Mission Board,
November 7, 1848, and October 2, 1860; and
Somerville to Pepple, October 3, 1860. Andrew
Somerville was secretary of the Mission Board.

[12] The Missionary Record of the United
Presbyterian Church, January 1852.

[13] The river was actually divided into three.
Below Umon the Efiks were in control. Umon traded
as far as Akunakuna, and Akunakuna controlled the
rest. Hence the missionaries could describe, in
1888, Akunakuna as the key to the river.

[14] Hope Waddell, The Record, January 1850.

[15] McKerrow, History of the Foreign Mission,
387.

[16] Somerville to Goldie, February 22, 1856.

[17] Minutes of the Presbytery of Biafra,
October 6, 1858. The undertaking was signed by all
the senior missionaries.

[18] On this point, see Somerville to John
Baillie, June 18, 1861. The Thomson affair is
discussed more fully in chapter 9.

[19] Somerville to Goldie, July 3, 1863; and
UPMB, June 30, 1863.

[20] W. P. Livingstone, Mary Slessor of Calabar,
104.

21 S. H. Edgerley, _The Record_, June 1881; _Presbytery_, January 19, 1881.

22 James Buchanan to Goldie, July 2, 1888. Buchanan became secretary of the Mission Board in 1881.

23 J. F. A. Ajayi, _Christian Missions in Nigeria_, 23-95.

24 _The Record_, October 1868. See also Andrew Somerville, _Lectures on Missions and Evangelism_.

Chapter 2

AROCHUKU AND BEYOND

THE AROCHUKU EXPEDITION

At the beginning of the twentieth century, Europeans knew next to nothing about the country between the Niger and the Cross river apart from the waterways themselves and the trading states along the coast. It was not until 1885 that the British staked out a paper claim to southern Nigeria, and not until 1891, with the appointment of Claude Macdonald as high commissioner, that serious penetration began. Throughout the 1880s Macdonald, his subordinates, and successors went probing along the rivers, conciliating or burning as circumstances and the temperament of the officers seemed to suggest.

The more they probed, the more conscious they became of a mysterious people known as the Aros. So ubiquitous were the Aros that the British came to believe that they must be absolute masters of the interior and therefore would have to be destroyed before effective occupation could take place.

In fact they exaggerated, a normal failing for colonial officers making a case for a particular line of action. Igbo and Ibibio government is based on villages ruled by assemblies of lineage or family heads. While they normally recognize the existence of village groups or clans, effective authority in these bodies is rare; each village is

an autonomous republic. Improbable as it seems at
first sight, the system worked reasonably well, but
that such a wide area could have so little
government was a concept that the British mind at
the beginning of this century could not grasp. The
British concluded that the interior was either in a
state of anarchy or under the domination of the
Aros.

But the Aro hegemony was purely commercial.
They are an Igbo clan living on the edge of Ibibio
country north of Itu. Like most border communities
they are of mixed origins, and since one of the
founding groups, the Akpa, were a trading people,
the Aros took to commerce and were soon found doing
business all across southeastern Nigeria. They
were well established by the middle of the
eighteenth century and their power peaked with the
slave trade a few decades later. But even in the
nineteenth century their influence spread across
the Niger and the Cross rivers, and from the valley
of the Benue in the north to the coastal states in
the south. Their principal commodity was slaves
collected for the export trade until the nineteenth
century and for the internal market after exports
were cut off. At the same time, they monopolized
the distribution of imported goods and established
themselves as the sole organizers of long distance
trade based on the two great markets at Bende, near
Arochuku and Uburu, some forty miles to the north.[1]

Aro hegemony rested on competence and an
alliance with their northern neighbours, the Abam,
Ohafia, and Edda clans. These clans laid great
stress on achievement. In precolonial days, no
young man was considered important until he had

taken part with honour in a raid. The Aros found
these clans enormously useful, for if a village
proved stubborn they could simply turn to their
friends. Igbo oral tradition is full of the
terrors of the Abam warriors.

Parallel to their normal commercial activities
was the shrine known as Ibinukpabi, or the Long
Juju. This oracle was not part of traditional Aro
theology; the Aro people marketed its services as
they marketed anything else. Chukwu, the god of
the oracle, provided both arbitration and
divination. It settled disputes and solved
problems which could not be handled by normal
means. To some extent the oracle was connected
with the slave trade, for while it was claimed that
the deity "ate" those who lost their case, most of
them disappeared into the slave markets at Itu or
elsewhere. But the Aros obviously could not
exploit this source of slaves too heavily or people
would stop using the oracle. A man who was a small
boy at the time of the British conquest estimated
that about half the suppliants ended their days at
the oracle or were sold as slaves. The other half
presumably went home happy with the decision.[2]

The success of both normal commercial
activities and the oracle depended on the network
of Aro settlements, which can still be found
throughout Igboland. The settlers handled regular
trade and acted as agents for the oracle,
encouraging people to refer cases to Ibinukpabi and
briefing the priests before the litigants arrived.
Tying this system together was a network of roads,
that is, paths through the bush which were big
enough to take parties of 200 people at a time and

which provided the only form of overland transport in the region.

By 1900 the British had become very much aware of the Aros and were sufficiently impressed that some have said they developed a real obsession with the clan. In fact Aro power was declining; the erosion of traditional forms of government on the coast and the penetration of British traders and missionaries up the Niger were cutting the Aros off from the extensions of their empire. They knew the British were their enemy and were not averse to a fight. Ralph Moor, who succeeded Macdonald as high commissioner, insisted that the Aros would have to go. His administration rested on revenue from trade and the Aros could stop trade, it would seem, more or less at will. At the end of 1901, therefore, he launched a campaign into the interior aimed at destroying the power of Arochuku and establishing the British presence throughout Ibibioland and among the southern Igbos.

Two columns converged on Arochuku, one from the south along Enyong Creek and the other from the west. The southern column reached the town first and had some hard fighting before the second detachment arrived and the Aros gave up. After destroying the oracle, the force divided again, one part making a wide sweep to the west through Igbo and Ibibio country and the other heading north through Ohafia and up the left bank to the Cross River. The principal objective was to disarm the villages, and it was this attempt that gave them the most trouble. If a village cooperated, it was left alone; if not, it was burned.[3]

The Aro Expedition marks the beginning of the British presence in what is now the Cross River and Imo states, but it was only a beginning. While government stations were immediately established in some places, northern Igboland was left to subsequent expeditions; even the people who had known the Aro field force were not always convinced that the British had come to stay. Uprisings continued; the latest one developed among the Ikwo clan near the Cross River as late as 1918.[4]

THE BOOM YEARS

At much the same time as the Arochuku Expedition, but for entirely different reasons, the structure of the church in Nigeria underwent a profound change. The earlier Mission Committee was reorganized as the Calabar Mission Council, a meeting of ordained and medical missionaries which soon took over effective control of the church's affairs. The new Council was quick to respond to the opportunities British arms had provided. In July 1903 it appointed a committee to reconnoitre the state of affairs. The Council received its report the following November, along with a pair of unsolicited suggestions from Mary Slessor. The Council Committee recommended transferring the flagging station at Akunakuna to Itigidi, where the people were more enthusiastic, and opening a new station at Itu. From these two bases, new stations could be opened up in a kind of pincer movement until they met somewhere in the middle.[5] Mary Slessor argued the case for Itu in some detail. It was, she said, "incomparable," being only a day's journey from Calabar, having a good beach, offering an opening into Ibibio country and, via the Enyong Creek, into Arochuku itself. Furthermore, and of more immediate significance, she suggested that she take her furlough, not in Britain, but on the Enyong Creek travelling up and down at her own expense to see what she could get started.[6]

The Calabar Mission Council referred the last idea to the Women's Foreign Mission Committee, noting only that it was beyond the Council's authority. It took no action on the long-range scheme, but it did endorse moving the Akunakuna station to Itigidi and opening a new station at Itu, with the proviso that since the medical work in Calabar had become redundant with the establishment of a government hospital, the new station should be a medical one.[7]

It was not a good time to ask the United Free Church for money. The Women's Foreign Mission Committee overspent its 1903 budget by nearly £2,000. The Foreign Missions Committee showed a deficit of £4,300 in 1901 and a further £2,230 in 1902. In 1903 there was a surplus of some £5,000, but the whole church was living in the shadow of a court case. The Free Church and the United Presbyterian Church had combined in 1900 to form the United Free Church, but the dissenting minority in the Free Church, the "Wee Frees," had taken them to court, successfully claiming all the property that had belonged to the pre-union Free Church. Consequently, the only suggestion that the people in Edinburgh would accept was Mary Slessor's "busman's holiday" on the Enyong Creek, provided, they stressed, that it did not commit them to any extension of the mission.[8]

Two years later, in 1905 the Foreign Missions Committee found it had money in hand. The Calabar account had been underspent the previous year, and in addition, the students at New College had raised almost £400 for the purchase of a steam launch on the Enyong Creek. The balance in hand from 1904 plus the students' gift would go a long way towards opening a station at Itu; the Committee authorized the mission to go ahead in the hope that the outstanding balance could be made up from gifts and the expected under-expenditure in 1905.[9] In the course of the year David Robertson, the doctor at Creek Town, moved himself and his house to Itu to begin a new phase in the medical work and to undertake the supervision of the burgeoning Enyong churches.

But the really significant event of these years was a change of heart among the Ibibios. Ikorofiong had been a mission station since 1858, but it had made so little impact on the community that a day school of the Calabar type had proved impossible. From 1861 the Ikorofiong missionaries had been operating a boarding school on the premises, filling it with whomever could be collected, rescued, or induced from the surrounding villages. Other mission stations used this method, but Ikorofiong had more success than most. Alexander Cruickshank, who was in the station from 1881 to 1935, was responsible for the training of more Nigerian leaders than almost any other missionary. But the day of the "Ikorofiong yard," as it was called, did not really dawn until after the British conquest. In 1901 Cruickshank had only thirty-six communicants and a few struggling stations in nearby villages.

After the Arochuku Expedition, the clans suddenly came to life. People flocked to church and requests for teachers poured in from every side. The Ikorofiong yard came into its own, for from it Cruickshank was able to supply the claimant villages with something in the way of a ministry. The big years were from 1910 to 1920. Of twenty-seven churches returning questionnaires on this subject, two were founded in the nineteenth century, four between 1900 and 1909, twenty between 1910 and 1919, and one in 1920.[10]

How the churches were started is a more complicated matter. Sometimes a trader, a native of the village, or a stranger would become converted in the course of his business and begin agitation for a school. Sometimes the agitator would be a schoolboy, sometimes the Christians from Ikorofiong would be the first to arouse interest, but in every case there was no school until someone had built up a party in favour of it and the village, or part of it, had agreed to contribute to the teacher's salary.

North of Cruickshank's district, in the Enyong valley in Ibiono and Ediene, the story begins with Mary Slessor's travelling holiday. In the course of her visits she met Chief Onoyom Iya Nya, a prominent trader in the valley whose support gave the new cause the kind of prestige it needed. Until Chief Onoyom's death in the early 1920s he was a leading figure in the Enyong churches, building the sanctuary at Akani Obio and using his

time and influence to open churches in many of the
Enyong and Ibiono villages.

In 1905 the Council moved Mary Slessor to Ikot
Obong in Ibiono, which became a woman's station
and, in the hands of her successor, Martha Peacock,
it provided the same service for Ibiono and Ediene
as Ikorofiong had for Itam and Uruan. Again the
big years were between 1910 and 1920, again the
mission school provided the staff, again no school
was possible without village support, first to ask
for a school and second to pay for it.

Enyong seems to have experienced something
like a mass movement into Christianity. In 1909,
after a visit to Asang to take communion,
Cruickshank noted in his diary:

> Weekend at Asang. Blessed 67 marriages,
> baptized 71 adults and 20 children. New
> church seats 625, crowded morning and
> afternoon. Membership now 245. Asang killed
> twins and sometimes twin mothers, many
> abiaidiongs much drink, Ekpe. Now no
> abiaidiongs, some in church few sell drink,
> Ekpe dead. School, care for the sick bury the
> dead poor even outside the church, family
> worship, evangelism.[11]

In 1912 the Council observed "with awe" that the
membership of the Enyong churches was nearly a
thousand. Clearly they had outgrown the part-time
supervision of the doctor at Itu and the Council
placed the first of many requests for additional
missionary staff in Ibibioland.

In Arochuku itself a similar development was
taking place. The government, fearing a spiritual
vacuum after the destruction of the Ibinukpabi
oracle, had encouraged a Christian presence in the
clan, and the first man on the scene was a Mr.
Jumbo, an Anglican from the Niger Delta. But the

decisive event was the conversion of six chiefs, prominent Aros who were members of the Native Court. These men began taking services from quarter to quarter according to the Book of Common Prayer, and at the same time made repeated requests to the Presbyterian Church, with which some of them had become acquainted during their imprisonment in Calabar.

The United Free Church was still husbanding its pennies and might have lost Arochuku altogether had it not been for Anglican forbearance. In 1904 Bishop Tugwell and Dandeson Crowther, the leading spirit in the Anglican Niger Delta Pastorate, came to Calabar to discuss two questions: the opening of an Anglican church in Calabar as a kind of chaplaincy to Anglicans who had migrated there in search of work; and the formal occupation of Arochuku by the Niger Delta Anglicans. The Presbyterians had no objection to the first, but the second would cut them off from the very country they were anxious to occupy.

It was two years before the Presbyterians moved on Arochuku and the Anglicans did not intervene. In 1906 John Rankin, a Calabar missionary who was thinking of a move upriver and who had already met some of the Aro chiefs, went on a tour to Arochuku and made a stirring speech in Missions Council when he returned. Mary Slessor commented that, if anything, Rankin had been too cautious, and A. W. Wilkie, the secretary of the Council, capped the discussion by reporting that he had a letter from Bishop Johnson of the Niger Delta Pastorate saying that if the Presbyterians didn't occupy Arochuku, he had a man ready to move on a

moment's notice. The Council took the bit in its
teeth and appointed Rankin to Arochuku, telling the
Council that if they didn't accept the decision,
which would cost them nothing but Rankin's salary,
they would have to resign Arochuku to the
Anglicans. Creek Town Church had just raised 200
in its fiftieth anniversary celebrations and the
money went to a temporary house. Rankin was ready
to start work pending the Foreign Missions
Committee's confirmation. It agreed, but with the
typical rider that it understood it was not
expected to replace Rankin in Calabar.[12] In 1907
Arochuku was safely in Presbyterian hands.

Once a station was established in Arochuku,
extension into the surrounding country was
relatively easy. Even before Rankin's arrival in
1906, a member of the Aro Native Court from the
nearby clan of Iwerre followed the example of his
colleagues by starting a church in his own village.
Within a few years a number of other churches had
sprung up, mainly from the normal connections
between Arochuku and Iwerre. By 1908 the Aro
Christians were taking Rankin to a friend of theirs
in Amakofia, in Ututu, who was persuaded to come to
church in Arochuku. Before long he had put up a
small shed in Amakofia and the church in Ututu had
begun. Within ten years the church had spread
throughout the clan, mainly by people coming into
touch with the work at Amakofia or through their
connections with Arochuku itself.

Rankin had hardly unpacked when a delegation
appeared from Chafia, a clan some twenty miles to
the north. The clan was having trouble with its
court clerk and proposed that if Rankin would help

get rid of him it would allow the opening of a
school. Rankin was sufficiently impressed to take
the case up with the District Officer in Bende and,
whether because of his intervention or not, the
clerk disappeared and the way to Ohafia was opened.
The usual delays ensued, but by 1910 the Council
was able to build a house out of its reserves, and
the following year Robert Collins moved from
Ikorofiong to begin over twenty years of a
singularly successful ministry.

The development of the church in Ohafia has
been described elsewhere.[13] We need only note here
that again the first ten years were decisive. By
1921 all the important villages and a number of
minor ones had been opened, all of them relying on
half-trained teachers whom they paid themselves.
Ohafia differed from Ibibio country, however, in
that the elders, who were not normally teachers,
took a very active part in the affairs of the
church. In Ibiono people speak of the teachers; in
Ohafia they speak primarily of the elders, most of
whom came from leading families.

Collins' district included more than Ohafia.
Immediately to the west is a large town called
Abiriba, whose founding is worth recounting in some
detail as it illustrates many of the factors at
work.

The first contact between the mission and
Abiriba seems to have been in 1906 when two Abiriba
lads "escaped from trading" and turned up at Hope
Waddell Training Institution in Calabar. Since
J. K. Macgregor, the principal, was always on the
look-out for such people he took them in and set
them to their lessons. The following year he

himself visited the town but found the elders, the
leaders of the community, "not ready," as they put
it, for a school. When Rankin, Collins, and
Robertson passed through in 1910, the elders said
they would accept a school and within a few months
the two lads appeared in town to begin the work.
The first sermon was right out of Isaiah, a
critique of idolatry and an appeal for faith in the
God who made heaven and earth. Most of the
audience walked out, but Chief Agwu Otisi said, "Go
on with your message, for I am listening to you."

Early in 1911 Collins visited Abiriba and
began to get a school organized. Before it was
finished some Abiriba men who had been trading on
the Cross River warned the elders that church and
school would mean such things as the destruction of
shrines and the abolition of discrimination against
mothers of twins. The elders changed their minds,
and when Collins came next to Abiriba he found he
was forced to start afresh.

Agwu Otisi set out to bring the elders round
again. He seems to have been convinced of the
value of a school when he had won a court case a
few years earlier by paying £20 to get his argument
written down. Hence he contended that if Abiriba
had no school and Ohafia did, Abiriba was sure to
lose any disputes it might have with its
neighbours. When Collins returned, Otisi's own
section of the town, Agboji, was ready for a school
and produced the necessary twenty pounds. The
others were adamant, and Collins asked the District
Officer to use his good offices. When he came to
Abiriba, the District Officer found his rest house
falling down. Orders were sent out to have it

repaired, but only Agboji showed up. The elders of
the other sections of the town were punished for
not fixing the roof and concluded that while those
who accepted the schools got off easily, the others
did not. They agreed. Work was begun in 1912 and
by 1918 the congregation was strong enough to have
its own session.[14]

Beyond Abiriba on the road to Umuahia is
Igbere. The church entered Igbere in a variety of
ways: through elders from Abiriba; because of a
man who had been a court messenger in Ohafia; and
through a man who had worked in Bende in the days
of F. W. Dodds, the Methodist. The first teacher
in Igbere was actually a Methodist from Bende, but
under the boundary arrangements Dodds did not press
a claim to the clan, referring the teacher
henceforth to Collins in Ohafia. This appears to
have occurred during 1916-1917.

South of Igbere and Abiriba lives the Abam, a
clan lying across the boundary between the
Methodists and Presbyterians. Its ecclesiastical
development came a little later, the earliest
schools dating from 1919 with the rest of the clan
following suit in the twenties. Although Collins
was responsible for their supervision, not all the
churches were started from Ohafia. Abiriba
influence is noticeable, as is that of Calabar. In
Amuru Abam, for example, the first Christian heard
the gospel while he was in Calabar on business.

North of Ohafia is a group of clans, the Edda,
the Unwana, the Amaseri, and the Afikpo, none of
which has ever been very enthusiastic about
Christianity. They have not lacked exposure. The
Unwana station was opened in 1888, but even after

the British conquest the church made little
progress. In Edda territory, for example, while
the first church was opened in 1893, by 1920 there
were only three or four churches. Christianity did
not begin to spread in Edda until the 1930s. Even
now, the church in these four clans is small
compared to that in the district immediately to the
south. North of Ohafia, the church found its
warmest welcome among the small clans along the
Cross River.

The centre of this most northerly expansion
was not the mission station or Unwana, but the town
of Itigidi. Once again, the key is a leading
layman. Chief Eja Esega was a prominent man in one
of the Itigidi wards who around the turn of the
century formed a friendship with Mkpanam, a Calabar
man trading up the now pacified Cross River.
Mkpanam took Eja to Calabar for a visit. There he
saw a church, a subject of much interest to him,
and palm nuts being sold for good money. In
Itigidi, they were thrown away. On his return, he
began trading in palm nuts. Since he was breaking
new ground, he soon became wealthy, with
connections as far up the river as Okuni (Ikom).
He also tried, but without success, to start public
worship in his own house.

At this point Mkpanam suggested that one or
two Itigidi boys might be sent to Calabar for
schooling. Eja offered two of his wards, but the
families objected probably because of Mkpanam's
reputation as a part-time slave trader. But
Gardiner, the missionary in Unwana, stood as
guarantor for them and off they went.

One of them was Ejemot Ecoma. Ecoma became a
Christian at Hope Waddell Training Institution and
during his vacations held the first promising
services in Eja's compound. When he left school he
entered the government service as an interpreter
and came in the course of his work to Mkpani on a
punitive expedition. By this time he had decided
to become an evangelist, and in November 1904
Mission Council appointed him to Itigidi. He began
one of the most successful ministries in the
history of the church.

Ecoma was a good teacher and an outstanding
preacher. His attention was first concentrated on
the new work at Itigidi, but within eight or ten
years he was drawn further afield. In 1911 the
reputation of his school brought a number of young
men from Ugep, across the river, who returned to
start the churches in Yakurr. In 1912 an
evangelistic tour started the church in Ediba, and
from there throughout the rest of Bahumuno. In the
same year Eja's connections led to an opening at
Okuni near Ikom. These churches, plus another one
at Apiapum dating from 1918, gave Gardiner more
than he could handle. In 1915 Ecoma was relieved
of his duties at Itigidi school and set free to
devote his full time to church work. He was
ordained in 1918 and died in 1920.[15]

RESISTANCE TO GOSPEL

With Ejemot Ecoma the success stories come to
an abrupt end. North of Edda is a broad plain
occupied by the people known as the North East
Igbos. To them in the dry season of 1911-1912 came
a young doctor named Hitchcock in search of a

station. He was very impressed by Uburu, the site
of the Aro market, a town of some 4,500 souls, a
day-and-a-half journey west of the Cross River. It
was not a particularly big town nor were the chiefs
very enthusiastic, but principally because of the
market he was prepared to recommend it as a
station.[16] The Mission Council endorsed the idea
and the Foreign Missions Committee, whose financial
position had improved a bit in recent years, made a
grant of 2,000 towards buildings. Hitchcock moved
in before the buildings were up and stayed their
until he was transferred to Itu in 1918.[17] The
station then entered a dreary period until W. M.
Christie was appointed the District Missionary to
Okposi in 1921 and Harry Hastings took over the
hospital in 1922.[18]

Even then the district did not prosper.
Christie's meticulous diary is a long story of
schools opened with difficulty and closed for lack
of interest. He had so little to do that he taught
regularly in Okposi Central School. It was not
until the 1930s that permanent schools were
established in any number apart from Uburu itself
(1913) and Okposi Central (1928). Despite frequent
attempts, virtually no progress was made with the
Ezzas to the north or with the related clans, the
Izzi and Ikwo. In 1914, when a Christian
exploratory party visited a town called Okpoto, the
Ezzas raided it and another town; 2,000 people were
reported killed.[19] In 1922 Christie managed to get
a school opened, but the elders of the clan ordered
it closed. It was not until 1937 that a school was
finally started in Ikwo, and another two years

before the first permanent foothold was established in Ezza.

The North East Igbos, especially the three clans, Ezza, Izzi, and Ikwo, are notoriously conservative. As late as 1918 the Ikwos were still hopeful of getting rid of the British. A government report from 1930 described Ezza "as a clan which remained for many years the open enemy of Government which has retained almost completely its fundamental organization and which has absorbed a minimum of advantage from Government."[20]

The experience of both missions in the area, the Presbyterians and the Catholics--the latter moving in from the west--was the same. It was not until the late 1930s that signs of a change began to appear, and the Roman Catholics, with more staff at their disposal, opened European stations at Abakaliki (1939) and Afikpo (1942). From then on the Presbyterians had to face stiff competition, especially in Ezza and Afikpo. Neither church has found the going easy.

Part of the difficulty was geographical. The country is north of the forest belt, open, rolling, and dry. The people, in the apt Nigerian phrase, "live scattered," each family on its own farm rather than in compact villages after the fashion of Ohafia. But much more serious was the almost total disinclination of the Ezza-Izzi-Ikwo group to take the modernizing agents--the government and the missions--seriously.

A possible clue to the conservatism of these clans lies in what one district officer described as their single-minded devotion to the growing of yams. Religion and culture are not separated in

traditional Nigerian thought. Therefore, since the
British had no objection to yam-growing, and
because the Arochuku oracle continued to provide
its services in secret, these clans found they
could continue their traditional way of life with
only a few minimal adjustments. They cooperated
with the British in road-building, probably to keep
the government happy, and they either ignored or
resisted the missionaries.

The traditional society and the traditional
worldview could remain intact as long as no part of
it was threatened. But the people were forever
pioneering, extending the frontiers of their yam-
growing world into the property of their
neighbours, either driving them out by force or
absorbing them peacefully. The British discouraged
this sort of activity, and it could well be that
the closing of the agricultural frontier led to the
gradual change in attitude which appears in the
1940s and 1950s. Education began to appear as an
alternative form of livelihood. The first
Presbyterian openings were through schools operated
directly by the mission and through the posting of
Presbyterian teachers to the Native Authority--the
local government--schools.

Even so it was slow going. The Izzi were
virtually abandoned to the Roman Catholics. By
1939 there were only two schools in Ezza and one in
Ikwo. Ten years later the count was not much
better, two in Ezza and one in Ezzagu, an offshoot
of Ezza. Ikwo, however, had four schools. By 1966
Ezza and Ezzagu still had only a minimal
Presbyterian presence, but Ikwo, with fourteen
preaching points, had finally opened its doors,

albeit cautiously, to the Presbyterian church. In
1955 the situation was sufficiently hopeful for the
district to be declared a Home Mission Area.[21]

The idea of Home Mission areas dates from the
centennial of the mission in 1946. The first
location was in Ogoja, north of Abakaliki, but the
work never prospered and it was hard to keep it
staffed. When an American Lutheran group showed an
interest in the area, the Presbyterians were
willing to negotiate, handing the work over to the
Lutherans in 1958 and moving the evangelist, Mr.
Ulu Eme, down to Ikwo.

Ikwo had changed a great deal in the preceding
fifteen years. One of the early teachers described
the clan as a wild people and recounts how he only
escaped death on a path one day because he had a
bicycle and his attackers were on foot.[22] But in
the 1950s, Chief Nwancha Otuma appeared as the
leading layman whose influence opened the clan to
the church. It was he who encouraged the opening
of schools and lent a hand to Mr. Eme when he first
came to the district. He was a polygamist and
never a church member, but his support of the cause
was constant for the duration of his life.

Once established, Eme used the standard
evangelistic methods which had been employed forty
years earlier. With the assistance of interested
teachers he toured the district, holding open air
services and visiting homes. When sufficient
numbers had shown interest in further instruction,
he began holding classes in the school, or, if
there was no school, in a "shade," a kind of
marquee made of palm thatch and supported by poles
cut from the bush. He was not the first evangelist

in the area, a man had been in Ezza for several years before his arrival. However, the campaigns of the late 1950s and 1960s mark the point at which the church, as distinct from the school, was first established in Ikwo and, to a lesser extent, in Ezza. Certainly the mission could not report a mass movement, but the rate of adult baptisms was commendable, and in 1967 the church was ready to ordain three elders, two from Ikwo and one from Ezza.[23]

The Ikwo mission had yet another dimension. If the first entry had been through the schools and the second by the preaching campaigns, the third was through an agricultural scheme. Shortly after Eme's arrival at Ikwo, changes in the organization of the Rural Training Centre at Asaba meant that the Presbyterian member of the staff left the centre and moved to Ikwo. Charles Hutchison was as much an evangelist as he was a farmer, and oral tradition speaks repeatedly of his campaigns. It has been said that the church in Ikwo rests on two pillars: the connections of Chief Nwancha Otuma and Hutchison's farm settlements.[24] Hutchison's rural improvement program, as he called it, had two aspects: the settlement of young men on their own land, providing them with advice on proper rotation and the growing of both food and cash crops, especially rice and yams. The second aspect was directed especially at women and dealt with nutrition, health, and child welfare.

Related to, but independent of, the Rural Improvement Mission was NORCAP, the Norwegian Churches' Agricultural Project. NORCAP was a research centre operated by the Norwegians in cooperation with the Presbyterian Church, working on livestock, annual crops, and "economic" trees, and feeding their results into the Ikwo community as a whole.[25]

Agricultural missions were a new departure for the Presbyterians, and they attracted no government grants. NORCAP was financed from Norway, and the Rural Improvement Mission relied on the church itself for its evangelistic work; the agricultural missions drew their money from the World Council of Churches and other international charities. Although the work was new, the objectives were traditional. Like the schools and hospitals, the rural missions were both witness and service--the old kinds of Christian presence in a new guise.

Although the Ikwo work was the most dramatic manifestation of changes among the North East Igbo, it was not the only one. In 1939 the Uburu parish was little more than a Christian presence among a group of small, conservative Igbo clans. In 1951 there were only eight churches in the parish, but five years later there were nineteen.[26] In the ten years between 1956 and 1966, the number of communicant members rose from 322 to 500, a growth rate much higher than that of the church as a whole. In 1966, during the brief ministry of the late Nwosu Udo, the parish recorded no less than 359 adult baptisms. By the 1960s, the North East Igbos, if not exactly rushing into the church, were at least moving in that direction.

FROM COUNTRY TO CITY

When the Protestant missions first divided southeastern Nigeria between them, the traditional economic life of the region was still intact. People did not travel a great deal, and apart from the Aros, when they did travel they did not normally settle down away from home. But as the colonial government established itself, it set in motion profound changes in the living habits of the people it conquered. It offered a cash income within its own service, attracting people to live in government towns like Calabar and Enugu. It built a railway from Port Harcourt to the north and developed a road system which took no account of the traditional pattern of Aro trade. Consequently, market towns like Uburu and Bende withered away and their place was taken by the colonial cities of Port Harcourt, Aba, and Umuahia.

The comity arrangements were adjusted with difficulty to this new development. As early as 1925 there was talk of special arrangements for the towns, but the Scottish Mission held that opening the towns to all comers was asking for denominational strife. So strongly did the Scottish Mission insist on this point that when some Abiriba people living in Umuahia wanted to make a presentation to their old missionary Robert Collins as he was passing through town, he insisted that they bring their gifts to the railway station, lest he suggest any recognition of their worshipping community by going to the church.[27] Only after the Second World War was the principle of "open towns" accepted, and even then, Synod, the governing body of the church, regarded it with suspicion. The official view was that if Presbyterians left their own area, they should attend the churches they found in their new homes.[28]

The official view proved hard to maintain. Before long, pressure was building to take advantage of the principle that anyone could establish a church once a town had been declared open. Because the Presbyterian area contained no major urban centre other than Calabar, it was constantly losing some of its best people to Port Harcourt or to Enugu. As early as 1952, the Synod agreed to look seriously at the Presbyterian communities which had sprung up in Umuahia and Aba. The following year, they were recognized as outstations of Abiriba, and in 1956 Aba parish, including Umuahia as well as Aba, was made a separate pastoral charge.[29]

There matters stood until March 1959 when a group of Presbyterians in Kaduna, the capital of the then Northern Region, asked the Synod, representing the legal holding-body, to take out a lease for them on a piece of land on which they proposed to build a church. On the advice of the clerk, the court replied that they could only do so if the community became a recognized outstation of Duke Town Church in Calabar, of which many of them were members.[30]

The man behind the scenes was Etim Onuk, the minister at Duke Town, who for some time had been in touch with groups calling themselves the Calabar Evening Service in Kaduna, in Lagos, and to some extent, in Enugu. It was he who advised the Kaduna people on how to approach the Synod, and for the

next four years, he made many tedious journeys on
the train to get them organized. When he reported
on his work at the Synod of 1960 it was decided
that "any other similar group should make
application to Synod for recognition." At long
last, missionary resistance to Presbyterian
churches in the cities had given way to Nigerian
pressure.[31]

Once the decision to go ahead had been made,
things moved quickly. Onuk reported to the Synod
in 1961 that he was in touch with people in Lagos
and Enugu, and a committee of three was appointed
to get things organized in these towns and in Port
Harcourt as well. Finding Presbyterians who were
willing to go ahead was not difficult; the more
serious problem was finding ministers. The church
had none to spare, and few on the staff in 1960 had
the education and experience abroad that was
considered essential for ministers among people,
many of whom had studied or lived abroad for years
and often held very senior positions in the civil
service.

The church cast its net wide, with
considerable success. Nigeria was popular in
western countries during the euphoric days of early
independence, and men were willing to come forward
for a few years at least to get things started. In
all, six men were recruited between 1960 and 1966:
two from the United Presbyterian Church in the
U.S., three from the Presbyterian Church in Canada,
and one from the Church of Scotland. The
missionaries were divided among Lagos, Port
Harcourt, and Enugu, while the northern churches,
which had precipitated all this activity in the

first place, received a senior Nigerian minister who was with them until the work was closed following the disturbances of 1966.

The move to the cities was long overdue. The church had been losing the services of some of its most talented laymen for some years. But this was not, nor was it ever intended to be, a move towards people with no previous connection with the Presbyterian church. With the partial exception of the North East Igbos, the clans that accepted the church before 1920 have formed its consistency ever since.

REFLECTIONS ON CHURCH GROWTH

The most striking thing about the expansion of the church, whether it is measured in membership statistics or by the number of churches opened, is that it corresponds in time to pacification, the process of British conquest, and establishment of effective government. Before the Aro expedition, the church showed significant growth only in Calabar, which had been effectively occupied ten years earlier. But when Cruickshank returned to Ikorofiong after the expedition he found that things had changed: "Submitted letter (Ikorofiong March 14, 1902) from the Rev. A. Cruickshank in which he says that he has now returned to his station and that things have taken a wonderful turn during the last fortnight. The attendance at church and at the meetings has increased greatly."[32]

The British conquest had two immediate effects on the church. In the first place, it opened the country to missionary occupation. Most of the

major stations were established within ten years of
the Aro expeditions: Itu, Ikot Obong, Arochuku,
Ohafia, and Uburu.   Only Unwana of the northern
stations dates from before the conquest.   Of
greater significance, however, is the effect it had
on the people.   A missionary may be essential, but
if nobody is prepared to listen, a missionary's
work bears no fruit.   Ikorofiong did not become
significant until after 1901, despite its antiquity
and the fact that it was almost continuously manned
by missionaries of conspicuous ability.   The
question, therefore, must be why the British
conquest with the changes it precipitated in the
social life of the Cross River valley inclined so
many people to take the missionary message
seriously.

Ohafia and Abiriba may be taken as examples
because they illustrate so many of the factors at
work.   The opening of the Ohafia station was seen
as part of an agreement whereby the missionary
assisted in disposing of a tyrannical government
official, the court clerk, in return for the
opening of a station.   In Abiriba, Otisi argued
that if the clan did not have a school, it would be
at a disadvantage in any court case with Ohafia;
the turning point in his campaign seems to have
been the incident over the rest house repairs, when
those who cooperated with the government, who were
also those who supported the school, got better
treatment from the District Officer than those who
did not.   It would seem then, and some have argued,
that people became Christians in order to protect
themselves against the colonial government or, in
the Abiriba case, against their neighbours.   In

other words, people became Christian for purely
secular reasons.[33]

The difficulty with this argument is that
distinctions between sacred and secular are common
enough in Western countries, but rare in
traditional African thinking. John S. Mbiti, the
East African theologian, for example, has insisted
that it is almost impossible to separate the one
from the other.[34] His point is illustrated by the
Abiriba story again. Otisi, who argued for a
school on purely secular grounds, was also the man
who refused to walk out of the sermon, but
commented: "Go on with your message, I am
listening to you." If secular and sacred are not
separated in traditional African thought, then
secular actions have theological implications. The
decision for Christianity was a theological as well
as a secular one, for the Nigerians in question did
not separate the two. The conversion process
requires a theological explanation.

Such an explanation is offered in Robin
Horton's article on African conversion.[35] In his
view, traditional African theology is primarily
concerned with the microcosm, comprising the
village and the network of immediate face-to-face
relationships, and the relationships between
community and nature that make up village life.
Traditional Nigerian villagers had little to do
with the wider world, the macrocosm, and their
theology reflects their preoccupations. Most
Nigerian tribes have some motion of a supreme
being, but it is not a major factor in their
religious lives. Of greater importance are the
lesser spirits and the ancestors, beings whose

impact on their lives is immediate and real. If, however, a people with this kind of theology suddenly find themselves catapulted into the wider world, their theology undergoes a shift in emphasis. The supreme being becomes much more important in their thinking than before and the lesser deities fade away or become evil.

Although Horton's argument was advanced in another context, it has a definite bearing on the situation under discussion. The conversion process, he says, is the development of traditional theology to deal with changed circumstances. That the circumstances changed was obvious enough, and if the Christian message had not contained elements that were intelligible to Nigerian audiences, they would not have listened. People do not change theological ideas the way they change their shirts; if they became Christian it was because the missionary message made sense in terms of traditional theological thought. So far we may agree with Horton, but it is unlikely that his contention that the supreme being became more important as the world widened is valid for the Cross River valley. In the first place, it is by no means certain that the supreme being was a deity of only marginal importance in Igbo and Ibibio theology, and even if it were, the wider world was common currency in the Cross River before the conquest. The travels of the Calabar traders and the Aros we have already seen, and even the Ikom people traded not only on the Cross River but as far away as the Cameroons.[36] These people became Christian at the same time as the stay-at-home Ibibios. Whatever theological changes took place, it does not seem likely that they were in terms of Horton's microcosm and macrocosm.

Elizabeth Isichei has suggested that Igbo religion was fundamentally eclectic. One could try this or that cult until the desired results were obtained.[37]   Christianity could therefore be adopted in the same way as a variety within traditional religions, without any fundamental reorganization of traditional theology at all. Certainly it is true that even today when people come to their ministers to ask them to pray they are concerned, as traditional evangelicals in the West might be, not with guilt before God, but with very mundane things like sickness, prosperity, and the welfare of their children.[38] These are exactly the kinds of problems to which traditional religion addressed itself, and it is tempting to conclude that no significant theological change took place at all. Christianity was simply incorporated into traditional theology for the good and sufficient reason that the God of the Christians had conquered the gods of the country.[39] If this were the case, we would find ourselves with a situation not unlike Islam in West Africa. Wherever it has established itself as a mass religion and has not experienced a major reform movement, traditional religion and Islam have "mixed." People joined Islam as they might join a cooperative, not as the result of a conversion experience.

There is enough evidence of traditional African religious thought in the Presbyterian Church to suggest that something similar might have happened to the Christians. People will come to the minister to ask him to pray for them because

the minister is a "middle man," somewhat closer to
God than are ordinary mortals. It is an African
idea which has prevailed over the priesthood of all
believers. The number of such survivals can
obscure the fact that people did become Christians,
they did undergo pressure and sometimes persecution
from the village, and they did react violently to
the suggestion, for example, that African music be
used in church. Their reaction was entirely
natural, for the music had entirely the wrong
associations. In the same way, the Arochuku
Session was harder on those who took part in
traditional sacrifice than on those who committed
adultery. Adultery was a human weakness;
participation in sacrifice was a betrayal of
Christian profession.

It is clear, then, that conversion did mean
something. It is also reasonable to assume that it
meant different things to different people.
Slaves, mothers of twins, and other outcasts found
a community in the church which they did not find
in traditional society.[40] This much is easy to
grasp, but the Presbyterian church was built not on
slaves and mothers of twins, but on ordinary
members of the clan and often people of some
standing. The real question is why people like
Chief Onoyom, Agwu Otisi, or Eja Esaga became
Christians. When the leaders of the churches were
asked in the 1960s why the first generation became
Christian again and again, the reply came back in
some form of "They were tired of the old ways" or
"They wanted an education." In other words,
pacification shook traditional society to its
foundations, and because traditional society was

shaken, traditional theology was shaken. Christianity, the professed religion of the conquerer, provided an alternative answer. Christianity can be seen as the response of the clans to pacification.

Their response was not so much intellectual as instinctive. For Nigerians the basic problem was how to live successfully in a dangerous and often capricious world. Because the British seemed to have mastered that problem, people came looking for the secret of their power in the churches and schools which the missionaries were so willing to provide. They were not just looking for knowledge, technical skills, or managerial technique which would give them power. They were looking for that which enables a person to be more human, to live a richer and fuller life. It was fundamentally a quest for personal or spiritual power, and the quest moved at different levels. For some the literacy and arithmetic the schools provided was sufficient, but they were not just "learning book in order to make trade." Education in the nineteenth century was technique, but in the twentieth century it was part of a total response to a changed situation. Even more clear is the response of those who added the Christian profession to their learning, or who became Christians without going to school. Their response is more clearly religious, but because traditional thought did not separate the sacred from the secular, the apparently utilitarian response of those who went to school in order to "get on" can and should be seen as a theological response as well.

Response is the key factor. Mission policy and staff can be important, but the most carefully worked out strategy and the most gifted staff will not produce a church unless people are prepared to come. Conceivably, if the Presbyterian Church had had more money and more people at its disposal, it could have placed missionaries among the Ezzas in 1920 and left them there to do what they could, to establish a presence among the clan to which people could turn when they were ready. This is what happened at Ikorofiong. But no amount of staff and no amount of money can make a church if people are not willing to take it seriously.

Why some people declined to take the mission seriously is a much more difficult question. In any community, some people will come to church and some will not. But in the Cross River valley, whole clans resisted the blandishments of the missionaries while others accepted them with open arms. No solutions are offered here, but some progress can be made towards the clarification of the problem.

In the related clans of Edda, Unwana, Amaseri, and Afikpo, there is a secret society known as Egbele. Egbele is the name of the spirit or deity, a proper name, and membership in the society is compulsory for all males. The Presbyterians refused to regard membership in the society and membership in the church as compatible, except in a case where the person had been initiated before he was baptized. Christians and Muslims alike have identified this society as a main focus of traditional religion in Afikpo.[41] Secret societies are common enough in the Cross River valley, but in most places some kind of compromise was possible. In Ibiono, for example, it was possible to obtain the freedom of the town by paying the fees and taking no further part in the society. In Nkporo, a town not far from Edda, the town was sufficiently keen on Christian education to arrange a compromise,[42] but in Edda, Unwana, Afikpo, and Amaseri no compromise was possible. One belonged either to the society or the church and most people preferred Egbele. The District Missionary commented in 1945: "There must be few places in Southern Nigeria where to take one's stand for Jesus Christ shuts one more completely from the social and political life of the community than the Afikpo and Edda federation."[43]

But among the North East Igbo, the secret societies are not the problem. The mark of conversion in Ikwo was the destruction of the nte. Every compound had such a shrine, a stone buried in the ground and marked by a stick. Destruction of these shrines was a common feature of the campaigns of the 1950s and early 1960s, and they were not replaced, not even during the three-year vacancy which followed Eme's departure in 1964. In Uburu parish, the mark of conversion was the destruction of the ancestral shrine. Veneration of ancestors is common throughout Africa, but it has usually been possible to find some sort of compromise; however, among the Igbos of the northeast plain the destruction of the ritual objects connected with the cult is the sign of conversion, of departure from the traditional ways. Clearly, the practice is much more central in these peoples' lives than it is elsewhere.

If the centre of traditional religion is
different in Afikpo and Ikwo, the same is true of
most other aspects of their lives. The Ezzas
people cooperated with the government in the 1920s
and 1930s simply to keep the British happy;
otherwise they went about their affairs
undisturbed. The Afikpo group are not notoriously
conservative conservative in other ways. The
Ezzas, Izzis, and Ikwos are great yam growers, as
are the Afikpo, but Edda and Unwana are not noted
as agriculturalists.

In other words, no single explanation is
possible. All that can be said is that the
conquest did not affect these clans the way it
affected those to the south. It would be wrong,
however, to conclude that the church has had no
success at all. The work in Ikwo and Uburu has
already been described, and it should be added that
the church in Unwana has touched some member of
almost every family and has produced, despite its
small size, two ministers and Dr. Akanu Ibiam, for
many years a mission doctor and at one time
president of the World Council of Churches. These
clans are not without Presbyterians, and in Afikpo,
a rather larger number of Catholics, but they have
come to the church as individuals rather than as
part of a major movement within the clans.

A strong church, a church which is
sociologically significant, does not usually arise
merely out of a series of individual conversions.
This pattern of church growth normally means that
Christians are in some measure moving out of their
own society and into one centred on the
missionaries. Anderson's early congregation in

Duke Town was a church of this type. The British
conquest had created a major crisis in Nigerian
life, and a large number of people saw its solution
in the Christian church-school system. In the
space of thirty years, the Presbyterian Church was
transformed from a handful of small congregations
to an institution spread along both sides of the
Cross River from Calabar to Ikom. As the
institution matured it became more complex, and as
it became more complex, its government became more
problematical.

Chapter 2

AROCHUKU AND BEYOND

[1] F. I. Ekejiuba, "The Aro System of Trade in the Nineteenth Century," *Ikenga* 1, no. 1 (January 1972), 11-26.

[2] Notes on a conversation with the Rev. Mr. Isaac Uwakwenta, a native of Arochuku, 1966.

[3] A. F. Montanaro to the High Commissioner of Southern Nigeria, April 5, 1902, CSO 1/4/2.

[4] Elizabeth Isichei, *A History of the Igbo People*, 136-137.

[5] *Council*, November 11, 1903.

[6] W. P. Livingstone, *Mary Slessor of Calabar*, 206.

[7] *Council*, November 11, 1903.

[8] Stevenson to Wilkie, January 29, 1904.

[9] FMC, April 25, 1905.

[10] Much of the information in this section is drawn from questionnaires circulated through the church in 1965 and 1966.

[11] Ikorofiong Diary, November 23-25, 1908. Ekpe is a secret society; an *abiaidiong* is a diviner.

[12] FMC, March 26, 1907.

[13] Geoffrey Johnston, "Some Aspects of Early Church History In Ohafia," Bulletin of the Society for African Church History 2, no. 2 (1967).

[14] O. A. Otisi, ed., History of the Church in Abiriba, typescript, no date. This work is in the possession of the author and was supplemented by a further conversation with Mr. Otisi and other Abiriba elders in 1966. Mr. Otisi is the son of Agwu Otisi. A session is the governing body of a Presbyterian congregation; once a church has its own session, it is an autonomous unit.

[15] Notes on a conversation with Dr. S. I. Imoke and the elders of Itigidi church, 1966. Their account perhaps lays greater stress on Eja that I have here. For Ugep, notes on a conversation with Elder B. O. Otu, 1966.

[16] Hitchcock to Wilkie, May 7, 1902.

[17] For a romantic biography of Hitchcock, see W. P. Livingstone, Dr. Hitchcock of Uburu.

[18] Okposi is a few miles east of Uburu. It was chosen in the early 1920s as the district missionary's station while the hospital remained at Uburu.

[19] The Annals of Okposi, vol. 1, 1914.

[20] G. B. C. Chapman, Intelligence Report on the Ezza Clan, Abakaliki Division, 1930, CSE 1/85/4148.

[21] Questionnaires of 1966, supplemented by further information from the then minister of Abakaliki parish, the Rev. Mr. P. B. Onwuchekwa.

22 Ocha Mbila, "The Story of My Life," 15-16.

23 Synod, January 1967.

24 Notes on a conversation with the Rev. Mr. Akanu Otu, minister in Ikwo from 1967-1977.

25 Recommendations of the Rural Development Sub-Committee, 1966.

26 Notes on a conversation with the Rev. Mr. Nwachuku Eme, minister in Uburu, 1951-1956, 1977.

27 Notes on a conversation with Chief Emole, 1977. Chief Emole is an elder in St. Andrew's Church, Enugu, and a native of Abiriba. As a small boy, he carried part of the presentation to the train on his head.

28 Synod, June 1948.

29 Ibid., June 1952; June 1953; June 1956.

30 Ibid., March 1959.

31 Ibid., June 1960; and E. F. Roberts to E. H. Johnson, October 17, 1960.

32 FMC, April 29, 1902.

33 F. K. Ekechi, Missionary Enterprise and Rivalry in Igboland, 1857-1914, 147-155; and "Colonialism and Christianity in West Africa, the Igbo Case, 1900-1915," Journal of African History 12, no. 1 (1971), 103-107. E. A. Ayandele, The Missionary Impact on Modern Nigeria, 1842-1914, 157-158.

34 John S. Mbiti, _African Religions and Philosophy_, 1.

35 Robin Horton, "African Conversion," _Africa_ 41, no. 2 (April 1971), 101-107.

36 Rosemary Harris, "The History of Trade at Ikom, Eastern Nigeria," _Africa_ 42, no. 1 (1972), 122-139.

37 Elizabeth Isichei, "Seven Varieties of Ambiguity, Some Patterns of Igbo Response to Christian Missions," _Journal of Religion in Africa_ 3, no. 3 (1970), 209-227.

38 Notes on a conversation with a group of Presbyterian ministers, Trinity College, Umuahia, March 1977.

39 John C. Messenger, "Religious Acculturation among the Annang Ibibio," in W. R. Bascom and Melville J. Herskovits, eds., _Continuity and Change in African Cultures_, 290.

40 Conversation with the Rev. Mr. Agwu Oji, 1977. His mother was a twin mother and an early convert at Ohafia.

41 Conversations with the Rev. Mr. Nwachuku Eme, minister in Afikpo, 1961-1968; 1977; and Simon Ottenberg, _Leadership and Authority in an African Society_, 173, 279.

42 Conversation with district missionaries, 1977.

43 N. C. Bernard, cited in the Afikpo Division Annual Report, 1945, Ogprof (Ogoja Provine), 10/1/44.

Chapter 3

THE GOVERNMENT OF THE CHURCH

MELVILLE AND VENN

John Knox, the founding father of the Church
of Scotland, was too busy organizing a revolution
to worry much about the proper form of government
for an established church. It was the second
generation of reformers, particularly Andrew
Melville, who established Presbyterianism in
Scotland. Presbyterianism is a system of church
government comprising a series of courts in which
all ministers are equal and laymen participate at
every level. To this sixteenth-century system the
nineteenth century added a network of assembly
boards and committees, often with a permanent
staff, the head office, which reported annually to
the senior court. This was the pattern of
government with which the Presbyterian Church in
Nigeria began in 1858, and to which it returned in
1960, but for the first forty years of this century
it was not really a Presbyterian church at all, but
something modelled after the work of an Anglican
missionary statesman, Henry Venn.

Venn was the secretary of the Church
Missionary Society from 1842 to 1871. Between 1851
and 1868, he developed a theory of missionary
organization which became orthodox for the later
years of the nineteenth century and the early years
of the twentieth. Venn began with a distinction
between mission and church. A mission was sent to

preach the gospel, while a church was developed out of the preaching. The church was indigenous; the mission was foreign. The function of the church was pastoral care; that of the mission preaching the gospel. Therefore, as the church developed, the missionaries were phased out and went on to new country, leaving a self-governing, self-supporting, and self-propagating church behind them.

Melville worked in his own country; Venn organized missions overseas. Melville's contemporaries never thought of phasing themselves out, for they had nowhere to go. Melville's successors in Nigeria always regarded the mission's presence as temporary. Whatever distinctions Melville made in the church's life, he did not separate preaching the gospel from pastoral care. For Venn the distinction was crucial. Preaching and teaching were separate functions; missionary and pastor were separate offices. If missionary and pastor were fundamentally different, the mission had to be separate from the church. The Presbyterians in Nigeria followed Melville in the nineteenth century, adopted Venn in 1901, and returned to a Presbyterian system in 1960.

GOVERNMENT BY COMMITTEE

For the first eleven years of its life the mission followed neither of these alternatives, but managed its common life through an ad hoc committee of missionaries. From its first meeting in 1847 until its last in 1858 this committee handled everything that came its way. It managed the mission ship until it was sold in 1853, supervised the press, regulated the practice of buying and freeing slaves, settled questions of ecclesiastical policy, and undertook the training of the ministry. In other words, it functioned as a church court.

But it was a committee, not a court, and even worse its powers were not well defined. Samuel Edgerley, the printer, was a headstrong and somewhat tempestuous individual who fell out with the ordained men, in particular, with Hope Waddell, and took his case to Scotland. The Board's reply indicated that its first preference would be for a coordinating committee only, while each station dealt directly with Scotland. But the Board also recognized that Calabar was a long way off with a notoriously unhealthy climate, and that emergencies were bound to arise which could only be handled by a committee of missionaries. It was, therefore, prepared to delegate a measure of authority to the Old Calabar Committee, but it did not define the nature of that authority. In this ambiguous situation, the Committee could function only if the senior missionaries managed to hang together.[1]

But that is precisely what the missionaries failed to do. In 1855 and 1856 Anderson quarreled violently with both Edgerley and Hope Waddell, and there was little the Committee could do with him. In these circumstances Hope Waddell proposed that they ask the Mission Board for permission to form a presbytery, a court with well-defined disciplinary powers.[2] Andrew Somerville, the secretary of the Board agreed, but felt that he had to take the question to the Synod of the United Presbyterian Church of Scotland. Much to the missionaries' disgust, the Synod turned them down. They returned to the attack in 1858, this time without waiting for permission, and formed the Presbyterian Church of Biafra, named after that part of the Atlantic into which the Cross River emptied, the Bight of Biafra.

It was not a novel step. Two of the five ministers at the first presbytery meeting, Goldie and Anderson, had been in Jamaica, and the elder, Dr. Hewan, was a native of that island. The Jamaican church had been governed by a presbytery since 1837. The various seceders from the Church of Scotland had organized their separate lives in the same way. Furthermore, Andrew Somerville was totally unconvinced by the ideas being developed at the time by men like Henry Venn and Rufus Anderson. Missions are the extension of the home church, he argued, and if ministers are equal at home they must be equal abroad. Besides, how are the native ministers to learn the arts of self-government and self-propagation if they are relegated to a secondary status?[3] Both tradition and theory led to the government of the mission based on simple Presbyterian principles.

GOVERNMENT BY PRESBYTERY

The system fitted the situation. Presbyterianism works best when ministers are in charge of manageable congregations. The church in Calabar did not grow very quickly in the nineteenth century, and the missionaries were able to function very much like ministers in Scotland. Creek Town, under Hugh Goldie's gentle guidance, from 1858 to 1895 was the largest station and normally had a second minister superintending the outstations among the farms. In 1877, the farm communities

were sufficiently advanced to have their own
Session, and E. E. Ukpabio, the first teacher, the
first elder, and the first minister, was inducted
to the new charge known as Adiabo. Duke Town,
where Anderson was minister until 1891, was not as
large, but it usually included Old Town as well.
Ikorofiong had a series of ministers until 1885,
when Alexander Cruickshank became head of station.
He remained there until 1935. Ikunetu led a
chequered existence until 1880 when Asuquo Ekanem,
who had been a teacher there since 1862, was
settled as the minister.

In addition to the minister, the larger
stations, and at times Ikorofiong as well, might
have a European teacher and one or two women; but
the overall management of the church was in the
hands of the Presbytery which consisted of
ministers and elders without distinction of races.
The really serious division in the Presbytery was
not between black and white, but between Duke Town
and Creek Town. With the exception of Anderson,
all the major figures of the nineteenth century are
associated in one way or another with Creek Town:
Hugh Goldie, S. H. Edgerley, and Alexander Robb
among the missionaries; Ukpabio and Eyo VII among
the Nigerians; Anderson was odd man out. Duke Town
was a very different place from Creek Town. It
remained a commercial town and resisted Anderson's
message much more doggedly than Creek Town. The
congregation at Duke Town was for many years made
up of strangers and natives who had been raised in
the mission yard. It was not until the 1880s that
there was clear evidence that the church had
penetrated significantly into Duke Town society as

a whole. Anderson was not an easy man to live with. The history of the Calabar church is dotted with disputes between Anderson and his colleagues, only one of which may be noted here.

The dispute with Alexander Ross is the only one of Anderson's many disputes that led to a schism, and because in some ways it resembles the quarrel that broke out in the Church Missionary Society's Niger Mission ten years later, J. F. A. Ajayi has suggested that it marks the same kind of transition--the shift from the days of optimism about African churchmen to a pattern of more exclusive missionary control.[4] Such a transition did take place in the Calabar mission, but it was quite independent of the Anderson-Ross affair.

Ross came to Calabar in 1875. He reminds one of Anderson in his younger days--headstrong, tactless, and deeply concerned with righteousness. Anderson went on leave shortly after Ross' arrival, leaving the newcomer in sole charge of the station until his return in 1877. The two worked together for two years until Ross went on leave.

Late in 1879 the Foreign Mission Board received a petition from the Regent and eleven other Calabar chiefs asking that Ross not return to the country, because his attempts at social reform were high-handed and his command of Efik was imperfect. Ross, when asked to comment, described the signatories as "murderous tyrants and oppressors whom he used to denounce for their wickedness and who trembled before him when he reasoned of righteousness, temperance and judgement to come."[5] Early in 1880 more letters arrived, signed by James Eyamba and others, regretting the

action of their fellow chiefs and asking for Ross'
return. At the February meeting the Board tabled
another letter from Anderson, saying that the
letters from Eyamba and company should be ignored.
All documents were filed pending advice from the
Presbytery.[6]

The origins of this dispute are by no means
clear, but a reasonable reconstruction is that
after his return from leave, Anderson found Ross
very difficult to live with, and vice versa. But
Ross had by this time got his roots down in some
sections of the community, so that what started out
as a missionary argument came to involve the
community as well. Further, the quarrel between
Anderson and Ross coincided with the first
chieftaincy dispute to take place in years. Ross
backed James Eyamba, who was an elder in Duke Town
Church; Anderson was either neutral or favoured
Prince Duke, one of the candidates from the
Archibong ward who was not a church member. The
Eyambas naturally supported Ross, as did the
Henshaws, who had recently tried to defy the house
of Archibong and had been severely trounced for
their pains.[7] What had begun as an ordinary
missionary quarrel became mixed up in Calabar
politics.

The Board dithered for almost a year and
finally decided to send Ross back, but without
specifying his location. The Presbytery suggested
Akpabuyo, but Ross refused on the ground that the
Presbytery was not fully cognizant of the agreement
between himself and the Board. Presbytery referred
the matter back to Scotland, noting that Ross'
position was undefined.

Presbytery never said a truer word. In June 1881 Anderson called a Session meeting at which Ross insisted that his name be inscribed in the minutes as co-pastor. Anderson refused, and when the majority of the Session backed Ross he pronounced the benediction, picked up the lamp, and walked out. Without the moderator there could be no Session; Ross and the elders were left high and dry. When the laymen refused to back down, Anderson suspended them.[8]

By September Ross was hinting at secession; the Board appointed deputies to visit Calabar and told Ross to desist from his missionary duties pending the settlement of the case. The deputies were in Calabar in December and on the whole found against Ross, especially for his conduct during 1881, his use at times of dubious methods, and his defiance of the Board's ruling that he should suspend his missionary work.[9] Ross promptly resigned and took with him about half of the Duke Town congregation, mostly those connected with James Eyamba, and four teachers from the Presbytery staff. He died in 1884, but the church continued for many years with increasingly cordial relations with the Presbyterian Church until it finally disappeared.

About the only resemblance between this dispute and the quarrel in the Niger Mission is that in both cases we find a brash newcomer zealous for righteousness in conflict with the missionary establishment. But Ross went down to defeat; Anderson outlived him by eleven years and the Ross church failed to prosper. The quality of African leadership was not the issue it was on the Niger.

It was a simple missionary quarrel which was
significant only because of its connection with a
chieftaincy dispute. The Calabar Mission did
undergo a major change at the end of the nineteenth
century, but that development had nothing to do
with the quarrel between Anderson and Ross.

The process of change may be dated from 1881,
the year that James Buchanan became secretary of
the Mission Board. Unlike Somerville, Buchanan was
a man who both took initiatives and was also a
disciple of Henry Venn. He therefore set out to
separate the affairs of the church from the
mission, instructing the missionaries in 1884 to
set up a committee which would handle all the
secular affairs of the mission, including the
location of African and missionary staff, and
report to the Board. "The Presbytery will be
relieved of all the work and will be free to devote
itself, as a Presbytery, to the spiritual care of
the mission churches."[10]

This was the opening shot in a long argument.
The Calabarians, black and white, resisted this
pre-emptory instruction by picking on its most
obvious weakness. As long as the African staff
were being paid from Scotland, Buchanan argued,
their location was a matter for the mission, just
as was the posting of missionaries. The
Calabarians tactfully replied that locations would
seem to be Presbytery business, for it would be an
odd church that had no control over its own
preachers. Buchanan did not agree, but he did
concede that the three senior Africans, the two
ministers and King Eyo, might be added to the
committee.[11]

If a line between mission and church can be
drawn at all, Buchanan was drawing it in the wrong
place. The criterion was the source of money. If
a man was being paid from Scotland, then Scottish
personnel would have to decide on his location. If
he was being paid from local sources, even if he
were doing exactly the same work, his location was
a Presbytery matter. If this anomalous system
worked at all, it was because for the next ten
years or so the Committee and Presbytery consisted
largely of the same people. But potentially
Buchanan's policy was extremely divisive.

An example of the sort of thing that could
have happened but did not arose in 1896. When
Goldie died, E. E. Ukpabio moved from Adiabo to
become minister at Creek Town, and naturally
assumed that he had inherited Goldie's duties as
head of station as well as minister of Creek Town
Church. But by this time there was a hospital at
Creek Town, and Dr. Porter asked whether the native
minister or the senior missionary was head of
station. The Presbytery referred the matter to the
Board, and the Board answered with no answer,
saying simply that they couldn't understand why the
question was asked.[12]

The Board simply did not know what was
happening. Porter, a relatively young man, was
thinking in terms of Venn's distinction between
mission and church. Ukpabio, by this time the
senior minister, continued to think in terms of the
biracial Presbytery he had always known.
Fortunately the dispute was patched up, and before
long incidents of this type ceased to occur. When
Ukpabio retired, there was no African of comparable

status to replace him. The African staff in
Calabar was neither as numerous nor as formidable
as the Sierra Leone contingent among the Anglicans,
and in any case they passed away at the same time
as their missionary colleagues. If there was no
dispute among the Presbyterians comparable to that
which split the Anglican Church on the Niger and in
Lagos, it was because the possible protagonists
disappeared at the same time.

The decisive factor in the peaceful shift from
Presbyterian government to mission government was a
changeover in personnel. Edgerley died in 1883;
Anderson resigned in 1891; Eyo VII died in 1892;
Ekanem retired in 1893; Goldie died in 1895; and
Ukpabio retired in 1900. The missionaries who came
in the 1880s and 1890s were a kind of floating
population, many of them capable but none of them
permanent. On the other hand, between 1898 and
1905 a whole series of new faces appeared, the men
and women who were to dominate the affairs of the
church for the next thirty years: men like
Collins, Dean, Gardiner, Macgregor, Rankin,
Robertson, and Wilkie, and women like Mary Chalmers
and Martha Peacock. By the time the new generation
had found their feet, the old one had gone. Only
Cruickshank and Mary Slessor belong to both
periods. Mary Slessor had little to do with the
central affairs of the church, and Cruickshank,
though a loyal Presbyter, was primarily concerned
with Ikorofiong. Besides, he was something of an
anachronism of the twentieth century.[13]

Because of the relative weakness of the
African staff and the rapid turnover of
missionaries, the transition from Presbyterian to

mission government was accomplished with relatively
little difficulty. By the time Mission Council was
reconstituted in 1901, the Presbytery had been
relegated to a minor place in the affairs of the
church and a new generation of men and women
constitutionally secure in the new Council looked
forward to a long period of unchallenged control in
the affairs of the church.

THE YEARS OF MISSION COUNCIL, 1901-1935

The new Council consisted of the ordained and
medical men only; the women had their own
committee. A joint meeting was held at the
beginning of each session to discuss their
business. In 1917 the Foreign Mission Committee
became uneasy about this division of the sexes and
changed the rules to allow women with degrees or
two years at a recognized training college to be
members of Council. As more and more trained women
appeared, the Ladies' Committee died a natural
death. But this is a change in detail; the real
point is that the affairs of the church, apart from
those specifically reserved to the Presbytery, were
in the hands of the missionaries.

The second and equally important change of
this period followed from the rapid expansion of
the church. The head of station, who had
functioned rather like a minister of a
congregation, was transformed into the District
Missionary. He had to deal not only with a handful
of Christians in one or two places but also with a
growing network of churches and schools spread out
over the whole clan. The parish minister became a
bishop, an overseer of other men's work.

In its simplest form, a mission district
consisted of a missionary and his wife with a staff
of Nigerian teachers. At the central school near
the station, usually a full primary school with
government grants, were a number of trained
teachers, initially Efiks, responsible for the
management of the school and the supervision of
untrained teachers. Scattered throughout the
district were smaller schools, usually in the hands
of untrained teachers who were responsible for both
the conduct of the school and the conduct of public
worship. The clearest example of the model was
Ikorofiong; the others were complicated by
institutions and other extraneous factors. In
Ohafia, for example, the elders took a more
prominent part in the affairs of the church than
they did in Ibibio country. In Calabar District,
in addition to the primary schools, there were
three major institutions: the Hope Waddell
Training Institution, which was a law unto itself;
Edgerley Memorial School for Girls; and the Creek
Town Girls' School. Even Anderson's old school at
Duke Town was a major institution run by Jamaicans,
and during the long tenure of S. M. Hart, it was
one of the best primary schools in the country.
Also in Calabar District were the major churches,
Duke Town and Creek Town, which were in the hands
of Nigerian ministers and under the supervision of
the Presbytery rather than the Council. In Itu and
Uburu were the hospitals, which were related to the
normal church and school but administered quite
separately.

One district was unique in having a Nigerian
as a District Missionary throughout the Mission

Council period. In 1895 a young Ikorofiong teacher, Akpan Essien Uwa, was appointed to Ikot Ana. He remained there for the rest of his life. After his ordination in 1905 he became, in effect, the District Missionary. It was in his time that the outstations were started; his influence reached as far as Ohafia. Although he had little success in converting the Ikot Ana aristocracy, he won their affection, trust, and support. He was their brother, the posthumous son of Onebiene.[14] As a preacher, he was spellbinding,[15] and it seemed that the missionaries were quite happy to have this small out-of-the-way district taken off their hands. Technically, one could not have a Nigerian manager of schools, but the Council got round by having someone provide minimal supervision. Until his death in 1945, Uwa was District Missionary in all but name.

But despite many differences in detail, the districts had two things in common: the dominance of the District Missionaries and the complete dependence of the system on the village schoolmasters, all of whom were Nigerian and who had "ministerial" duties as preachers in addition to their work in the schools. The logical development of this system would not be Presbyterian government at all, but diocesan, and the teachers who were already preachers would become, through ordination, responsible for the sacraments as well.

Some thought was given to this possibility in the twenties, but the Council turned it down on the ground that the teachers had enough to do looking after the schools without worrying about

congregations as well.[16] Council policy was in an
entirely different direction, entailing the breakup
of the districts into smaller ecclesiastical units,
each with its own Nigerian minister. In 1929, the
Council asked the District Missionaries to draw up
maps showing how their districts might be divided.
Christie's alone has survived; he envisaged half a
dozen parishes within his district, divided roughly
along clan lines. It was probably typical, for as
Nigerian ministers became more plentiful, they were
normally settled as ministers of groups of churches
within an area sufficiently large to support them.

The institution which tied everything together
was the Mission Council. In the Council the
missionaries were responsible for everything but
the self-supporting churches; they looked after the
schools, the hospitals, the women's work, relations
with other churches, and the care of congregations
which did not have their own ministers. Those
missionaries who were ministers or elders sat in
the Presbytery, and after 1921 in the Synod, and by
their prestige and ability, they managed to
dominate that body as well. Only Hope Waddell
Training Institution stood apart from the Mission
Council, but relations between the school and the
Council were cordial after 1905, and the school's
anomalous position caused no difficulty.

It should not be assumed that the system was
static. In fact, no sooner was it established than
it began to come apart. The network of schools and
churches was not even reasonably complete until
1920, and before 1930 it began to show signs of
disintegration. On the one hand, the graduates of
the theological college who were settled in

self-supporting congregations became more numerous; and on the other hand, education became increasingly professional after the publication of the Phelps-Stokes Report. It is not surprising, then, that in the thirties signs of the new order begin to appear.

A logical consequence of the church's growth was the reorganization of the Presbytery into a synod with two subordinate presbyteries. The idea was mooted first in the 1890s, but it died and was not revived until 1913. At that time Cruickshank and Wilkie, who were supposed to carry the idea forward into the Presbytery, thought the proposal premature and refused to act. In 1920, the Arochuku Session asked specifically for an Igbo Presbytery; this time the scheme went through. The motion was laid on the table until 1921 and then taken up and passed. The Presbytery resolved itself into a synod with two presbyteries, northern and southern, and adopted a minimal constitution of the Presbyterian type, relying for details on the practices of the United Free Church insofar as they were applicable.

"New Synod" was but "old Presbytery" writ large. It still had little to do; its debates were mainly concerned with the training of the ministry and the perennial difficulty of congregations in debt to the Students' and Pastors' Fund. It was still dominated by the ordained missionaries who were not even full members of the court. Until the 1930s it was a largely ineffectual body. But it could not remain ineffectual forever, and certainly not after the systematic training of ministers got under way after 1918. By the mid-1930s there were

fourteen Nigerian ministers including Okon Efiong,
subsequently a member of the Legislative Council,
and A. A. U. Ana, an Ikot Ana man who had been to
Fourah Bay. The sheer numbers of these men raised
the question of the relation of the missionary to a
self-supporting congregation within his district.
The question was first referred to the presbyteries
and the replies came before the Synod of 1935. The
Northern Presbytery had no objection to the system
as it was then operating, whereby the missionary
was _ex officio_ a member of all sessions within his
district. The Southern Presbytery, which contained
both Ana and Efiong, suggested a return to the
nineteenth-century system "as before, when the
Mission came among us." The question went to a
committee which recommended not only that the
District Missionary should be _ex officio_ a member
of the Session, but that he should also be
treasurer and responsible for reporting to the
Presbytery whenever a congregation fell behind in
its annual subscription to the Synod funds.[17]

The debate lasted two hours and forty minutes.
Christie and Dean moved for the adoption of the
committee's report; Johnson Kanu and W. E. E.
Ukpabio replied with a motion that a missionary
could only be a member of the Session if duly
invited. Kanu's motion carried thirty-three to
seventeen, with two of the members of the committee
voting against its report.[18]

Though there were difficulties in the
application of this decision which generated a fair
amount of heat and took some time to clear up, the
principle was clear enough; missionaries could
participate in congregational life only by

invitation and not by right. Not only is the
principle significant, but of equal importance is
the fact that the decision was an early sign of
independence on the part of Nigerian churchmen. It
is the first case of a Nigerian motion prevailing
over a missionary one; but it is typical of this
church that such confrontations were rare. The
subsequent constitutional development of the Synod
follows the pattern first established by the
schools.

The issue all began because Samuel Hart was
unhappy about text books. From a Council committee
on text books it was a short step to a committee on
education in general, and in 1933 R. M. Macdonald
and J. K. Macgregor brought to the Council a long
proposal, the gist of which was that educational
business, including appointments from the Normal
School, should be handed over to the Education
Conference, consisting of Council members with a
small number of Jamaican and African teachers, on
the understanding that all decisions would have to
be ratified by the Council. On procedural grounds
alone it was a sensible idea, for educational
business was taking up an inordinate amount of
Council time. But the really significant
suggestion was the addition of Jamaican and African
teachers. The proposal met with considerable
opposition, particularly from the northern
districts, and was finally carried by a vote of
thirteen to four, with the minority, Beattie
(Arochuku), Hastings (Uburu), Christie (Okposi),
and Chapman (Unwana) recording their dissent.[19]
The conference began to function forthwith and the
Nigerians immediately applied pressure for more

local representation, but apart from adding the
Okon Efiong, the council was not ready for further
concessions.

The Synod debate of 1935 and the formation of
the Education Conference are the first signs of the
breakup of the Mission Council system. The
increasing professionalization of education and the
growing maturity of the church required some kind
of institutional change.

THE RETURN OF ANDREW MELVILLE

In 1935, at the beginning of the debate over
missionaries and congregations, the church--
apparently under Church of Scotland pressure--began
in a very halfhearted way to draft a constitution.
The missionaries were in no hurry: the argument
over missionaries and their place in sessions had
generated so much debate that they were unwilling
to raise questions over which the Foreign Missions
Committee and the Nigerians would disagree. But
Edinburgh persisted, and in 1937 a drafting
committee was set up. It moved at such a leisurely
pace that it took until 1940 to prepare the first
draft. Christie was instructed to have a finished
version ready by the Synod of 1941, but he was
neither optimistic nor probably enthusiastic. In
any case, no constitution was forthcoming.

It took a court case to get the project
moving. In 1943 some members of the church at
Ututu took their minister to court, demanding a
statement of account. The Synod acted on behalf of
the minister and lost, principally because their
case, which was valid enough in Scotland, had no
standing in Nigeria. The Presbyterian Church was

not a legal entity. Scotland promptly urged the
missionaries to get on with the constitution as
quickly as possible to ensure that it was valid in
Nigerian law and that it clearly stated the
autonomy of the church within civil society.[20]
Lawsuits have unexpected consequences. The draft
constitution went through the Synod in 1944 and was
finally adopted in 1945.

The constitution is a slim document declaring
the independence of the church and adopting, no
doubt with church union in mind, the Apostles and
Nicene Creeds as subordinate standards rather than
the Westminster Confession. Apart from a reference
to the handling of money, most of the actual
working details of the constitution are settled by
a simple reference to the Practice and Procedure of
the Church of Scotland, "except as it shall be
modified by Synod." Hence the new constitution
made little difference to the day-to-day life of
the church. It still operated according to the old
procedures; it was still dominated by missionaries
who were not even members of the court, but only
"assessors with full voting powers." Even more
seriously, wide areas of the church's life,
especially education and medicine, were outside the
Synod's authority altogether. Of greater
significance in the church's constitutional
development, therefore, was the formation of the
Education Authority.

The Education Conference had worked reasonably
well over the last ten years. Its decisions were
rarely questioned in the Council, but from time to
time a senior missionary like Christie could make
life difficult. In any case, the younger men,

Mincher, Macdonald, and Lewars, were convinced that
the time had come to "devolve" some of the
Council's responsibilities on the Nigerian
leadership.[21] The decision in principle was taken
in May 1944, and two years later the Education
Authority had replaced the Education Conference.
Overall management of the school system had been
extracted from the Council and placed in the hands
of an independent body, on which Nigerians formed a
majority.[22]

Devolution, the handing over of responsibility
to Nigerians, had been in the air for years, but it
was not a process for which the missionaries of the
colonial period showed much enthusiasm. As late as
1940, the Council was still of the opinion that
"devolution of either the educational or the
medical work on the indigenous church cannot at
present be contemplated."[23] But the Council
changed with the times. In 1945 it handed over the
schools to the Education Authority, and in the
course of the next ten years, it gradually passed
on to the Synod responsibility for women's work and
relations with other Nigerian churches. By the
mid-1950s the Council was responsible only for the
Bookshop, the hospitals, correspondence with
overseas churches, and the details of missionary
housekeeping.

But the Council did not shed its
responsibilities in the same direction. In the
1930s and 1940s the missionaries had managed things
directly in the Council or indirectly in the Synod,
but when devolution was complete, no less than four
autonomous agencies handled the affairs of the
Church of Scotland Mission, the Hope Waddell

Training   Institution,   which   was   directly
responsible to Edinburgh since the beginning of the
century, the Education Authority, the Synod, and
the Council itself. A once thoroughly integrated
system was breaking up into its component parts.

A. G. Somerville was the man primarily
responsible for putting the pieces back together
again. In May 1952 the Council instructed him to
prepare   a   paper   "provoking   thought   on   the
integration of all work done by the Church, Mission
and Education Authority" for discussion at the next
Council.[24] By May 1953 the Council was ready to
call a meeting of the four agencies: the Hope
Waddell Institution, the Council, the Synod, and
the Education Authority. When the joint committee
met the following October it took two fundamental
decisions: first, that the work of the various
agencies would be integrated under the Synod and
not under some additional body; and second, that
the Synod would be provided with an executive
called the standing committee. By June 1954 it was
agreed that business from such agencies as the
Education Authority would go first to the standing
committee; only matters of general interest and
policy would come before the Synod itself. The
following year, Scotland prudently pointed out that
since the budget of the Education Authority was
many times larger than that of the Synod, it would
be well to ensure that the church was not
responsible for the Education Authority's debts.[25]
It took some time to clear this point up, but in
the   meantime   Somerville   was   simultaneously
appointed Secretary of the Mission Council and
clerk of the Synod in order to have as much of the

business of the dispersed agencies as possible pass
through the same hands. In 1957 the question of
the Education Authority's debts was settled--the
Synod was not responsible. All that remained was
to work out the numerous constitutions and put them
through the appropriate bodies.

The long process was finally completed in June
1960, and when officially notified the Council met
for the last time. John Paterson, the senior
missionary, conducted worship with the austere
beauty of the Church of Scotland and the Council
placed on record: "its gratitude to God for His
unfailing goodness and guidance, its sense of
privilege in sharing the heritage of those who have
laboured in the past and its faith in the coming of
the Kingdom in this land."[26]

THE MARKS OF THE CHURCH

It was characteristic of the Presbyterians
that this momentous transformation went through
with relative ease. Undoubtedly the most
significant factor in this happy development was
the departure of the older generation in the 1940s
and 1950s. By the time Somerville started on the
road to integration, the key missionaries were
himself, R. M. Macdonald, Lewars, Mincher, and John
Beattie, who had, however, been out of the country
from 1939 to 1959. Christie, whose opposition to
developments like the Education Authority had been
articulate and consistent, had resigned in 1945;
the others had simply retired. Lewars, Mincher,
and Macdonald had all taken a leading part in the
formation of the Education Authority. These men
recognized that they were living in the twilight of

empire in Nigeria. While they might not have been
enthusiastic nationalists, the prospect of an
independent Nigeria was something with which they
were reasonably comfortable, and they had no
serious qualms about a similar independence in the
church. With them during the five or six years of
discussion that led to integration were ministers
like Efiong Utit and Isaac Uwakwenta and teachers
like E. E. Esien, the Otisi brothers, Usang Iso,
and Mrs. Inyang. These people were their
contemporaries or older: they had worked together
for years and shared a common concern for the
welfare of the Presbyterian Church in Nigeria.
Perhaps a classic example of smooth transition was
in the clerk's office. In 1960 Nwachuku Eme, one
of the foundation students at Trinity College,
became assistant clerk of the Synod, taking over as
clerk in 1963. Somerville, who had been clerk,
assumed office as assistant. Throughout the eight
years from 1960 to 1968, these men worked together
with remarkable ease, sharing ideas and
responsibility in genial harmony.[27]

It was just as well they got along, for the
Synod office in Afikpo was the place where all
roads met. The Synod clerk was also secretary of
the standing committee, and the standing committee
was the keystone of the church. The Presbyterian
Church of Nigeria in 1960 was a very complex body.
In addition to the normal ecclesiastical functions,
it operated a school system with some 60,000
students and over 2,000 teachers, four hospitals, a
bookshop, and the Hope Waddell Training
Institution, and it had part shares with other
churches in a variety of institutions of higher

learning and in Queen Elizabeth Hospital. The
Synod had its own network of committees which,
apart from the Women's Work Committee, were not
directly represented on the standing committee, but
all the other boards, the Hope Waddell Institution,
the Medical Board, the Bookshop, and the Education
Authority, were represented on the standing
committee, and the committee was in its turn
represented on the various boards. Normally these
boards functioned as autonomous agencies, but the
standing committee representatives could delay the
implementation of any of their decisions until a
joint meeting of the standing committee and the
board concerned could be held. But of more
importance in the daily life of the church was the
practice of discussing major questions, like the
Education Authority's debts, in the standing
committee. It was the place where all the threads
came together, the central coordinating agency of
the church where the senior members of the church
thrashed out its problems. The clerk in his turn,
as secretary of the standing committee, was the one
person who was in touch regularly with all the
church's varied activities. The centrality of the
standing committee and therefore of the clerk's
office was the outstanding characteristic, the
first mark of the church.

The second mark of the church was the
prominence of laymen. One of the first decisions
taken in the integration discussions was that the
first principles of Presbyterianism, especially
representation of the laity, should be scrupulously
observed. The Synod of 1962, for example,
consisted of ninety people: forty-two ministers

and forty-eight laypeople. Of the forty-eight, fourteen were representatives of the various boards and the standing committee rather than congregations, and they included some of the most gifted and articulate people in the church: among the doctors, Herman Middlekoop and Clyne Shepherd, and among the teachers, N. A. Otisi and B. E. Okon. Lay participation in the church was an inheritance from the days of the district missionaries. Because the missionaries functioned as bishops or overseers rather than as pastors and they relied so heavily on the village school masters for leadership at the congregational level, and because a corps of trained teachers developed earlier than the trained ministry, even in the colonial period, the tradition of lay leadership was well established. The prominence of laymen in the Synod's debates was so natural that perhaps only the newcomers, the missionaries of the 1960s, noticed it.

The diocesan structure of the parishes is the third mark of the church. Although the breakup of the old mission districts had continued steadily from the late 1920s, in 1963 there were still 427 individual churches divided among forty-nine parishes. The new city charges might have only one congregation, but at the other end of the scale were Abakaliki with twenty-two, Uburu with twenty-three, and Ohafia with twenty-four. The diocesan structure of the mission-dominated church had not disappeared; it had simply been altered. The dioceses might be smaller, but the ministers, unlike the missionaries, travelled by bicycle. Although cars were possible, they were expensive

and only began to appear for regular ministerial
use in the 1960s.

The fourth mark of the church was an almost
complete lack of theological reflection. Theology
is developed in controversy, and the great
controversies of modern Protestantism caused no
stir in the Cross River valley. There were no
modernists or fundamentalists, Barthians or
Bultmanites in the Presbyterian Church, but only
Presbyterians, and Presbyterian meant not so much a
way of thinking as a way of doing. The pioneers,
with one or two exceptions, were not men of
scholarly habits. Their principal field of
intellectual activity was translation. The
district missionaries were much the same. The
first generation, men like Collins and Cruickshank,
often had little or no formal theological
education, and the second generation found
themselves too busy to spend much time reflecting:
"You were up to your ears and submerged; you were
shaped by events all the time. I had no grand
plans of what I was doing. From year to year I was
struggling to keep above the tide. I can't claim
to have had great ideas of what we should be doing.
You always had the feeling that you had more to do
than you could cope with. . . ."[28]

A. K. Mincher put the same point more
whimsically: "For the first few days I wandered
around the house wondering what I was supposed to
do, how I was supposed to be a missionary. The
rest of the time I spent catching up on arrears."
These men were the church's main contact with the
world of theological ideas, and if they were not
given to reflection, it is not surprising that the

church over which they presided was not noted for theological discussion.

It would be unfair to accuse the District Missionaries of not thinking at all. Their thinking normally began not with the problems of European theology but with the problems of being a Christian in Africa. Sermons tended to be written on Saturday night after the Session meetings.[29] Certain practices were established and followed but rarely discussed. It is not suggested that the church would have profited by what Europeans would call a regular theological debate, for the controversies of the North Atlantic are not necessarily important in the Bight of Biafra. But it is suggested that the discussions which should have developed over traditional religion, secret societies, and more recently, with the prophet healing or independent churches simply did not happen because the church's leadership thought more in terms of concrete solutions than in terms of the first principles of theological analysis.

This lack of theological reflection is part of a general quality which is hard to define, the ethos of the church. Despite the presence of a half-dozen senior Scots and despite the formal Presbyterian structure and liturgy of the church, it was unmistakably Nigerian. The faith of the leadership, the way they conducted debates, and the way they developed the church in the busy years between 1960 and 1967 were indigenous to the soil. There were no striking new initiatives in those days, but there was a great deal of development along traditional lines because that was what the church wanted. Not all the missionary staff and

certainly not all the younger men were happy with
what was happening,[30] but there was little they
could do about it because Nigerian opinion
controlled the church. Compared to the independent
churches, the Presbyterians might have seemed a
carbon copy of the Church of Scotland, but no one
who lived and worked with the church in those days
could have any doubt that it had taken root in the
soil of the Cross River valley.

Chapter 3

THE GOVERNMENT OF THE CHURCH

[1] UPMB, July 4, 1848. Cf. list of abbreviations.

[2] Old Calabar Mission Committee, Appendix to December 12, 1856.

[3] Andrew Somerville, 227.

[4] J. F. A. Ajayi, Christian Missions in Nigeria, 1841-1891, 264-266.

[5] UPMB, November 25, 1879.

[6] Ibid., January 27, 1880; February 24, 1880.

[7] A. J. H. Latham, Old Calabar 1600-1891, 129-131.

[8] Appeal by Prince James Eyamba, Peter King Cameroons, Obong Ene, A. Ross co-appellant, September 15, 1881; see Anderson Ross file.

[9] Ibid., Findings of the Deputies, December 24, 1881.

[10] Buchanan to Goldie, October 17, 1884.

[11] Presbytery, December 17, 1884, UPMB, February 24, 1885.

[12] UPMB, December 30, 1896.

13 Ikorofiong was the only station to continue
the mission yard into the twentieth century, and it
was always in Cruickshank's hands. Secondly, R. M.
Macdonald once remarked that Cruickshank would
always take the African side in any dispute between
the Africans and the missionaries. It rather looks
as if Cruickshank never lost the habits of thought
he acquired in the twenty years between 1881 and
1901.

14 U. A. Ana, "Ikot Ana Record," 25-26. In
1966 this manuscript was in the hands of the
author, who is now dead. Onebiene was the founder
of Ikot Ana.

15 R. M. Macdonald, in conversation with the
district missionaries, 1977.

16 FMC Policy Committee Report, 1924; and
Council, May 1925.

17 Synod, 1935.

18 Ibid. Both Ana and Efiong were members of
the committee.

19 Council, May 1933.

20 FMC, April 20, 1943; and Appendix I.

21 Conversation with A. K. Mincher, May 1977.

22 Report of the Deputies, FMC, April 15,
1947, Appendix I, 407.

23 Council, May 1940.

24 Ibid., May 1952.

[25] Ibid., May 1955.

[26] Ibid., June 1960.

[27] Conversation with Nwachuku Eme, 1977.

[28] A. G. Somerville, in conversation with the district missionaries, 1977.

[29] John Beattie, in conversation with the district missionaries, 1977.

[30] Conversation with R. G. Browne, 1977.

Chapter 4

A LEARNED AND GODLY MINISTRY

EDUCATION BY PRESBYTERY

One of the marks of the church in Scotland has been an insistence on a high standard of academic achievement for its ministers. On the whole, the policy has been reasonably successful at home, but it was not necessarily for export to Nigeria. Not until after 1880 did the normal recruit for the Calabar Mission hold degrees in arts and theology. Between 1846 and 1881 there were fourteen ordained appointments, of which five had taken regular university work, four had special courses in Britain, two were ordained after study under the Presbytery of Biafra, and two or three received their training in Jamaica before there was a formal theological college. By contrast the last twenty years of the century saw eleven ordained appointments. All nine Scots had taken a regular university course, followed by study at the United Presbyterian Hall, and the two Jamaicans had been to their church's academy in Kingston. This improvement in the educational standards of the missionaries did not result in any noticeable pressure for improvement in the standards of the African ministry. Though the situation improved after 1918, it was not until the 1960s that the Nigerian ministry began to receive university-trained men.

When theological education began in 1852, it followed the same pattern as in Jamaica. In that year the Scottish missionary teacher, W. C. Thomson, asked to be taken on as a candidate for the ministry. After some hesitation because they were a committee and not a presbytery, the ordained men agreed and sent him lessons in Greek and church history. For sixty-five years this was the pattern of ministerial training: one or two men, under the care of the Presbytery, which would assign and examine exercises until they were satisfied the men were ready for ordination.

In Jamaica the system of men studying under the Presbytery had developed in the 1850s into a one-man theological college, and the Board wanted to see the same procedure adopted in Nigeria. In 1856 they called a promising young missionary, Alexander Robb, from Jamaica and appointed him to Calabar, partly for translation and partly for the training of the ministry, in order that "in the matter of agents [the mission might be] not merely self-supporting but self-propagating."[1] For the next ten years Robb's time was taken up mastering Efik and translating the Old Testament, and the pattern of training continued to be according to that established in Thomson's case. When the Old Testament was finished, both the Board and the Presbytery prodded Robb to start a preachers' class, and although he took one, his heart does not seem to have been in it. He was unwell after 1870 and finally left Calabar in 1875.

By default, therefore, the training of preachers fell into the hands of the Creek Town missionaries. In 1859 Ukpabio was taken on as a

teacher and set to work on the Shorter Catechism.
In 1864 a group of teachers was formed into a
class which met once a year for four years, and in
1871 the class became an annual four-to-six-weeks
event. The first students, those who studied in
the 1860s, began with the Shorter Catechism and
moved on to biblical exegesis and Old Testament
biography. By the 1870s Edgerley had sixteen
students working on scripture exposition, natural
philosophy, geography, history, anatomy, physio-
logy, and "common things."[2]

The course was designed for all the Nigerian
staff, not just those who were thinking of the
ministry. But it is clear that Edgerley was not
training men to be teachers in any system of public
education. His course was modelled on the standard
of education of a minister in Scotland, a training
in both secular and theological subjects. As long
as there was no colonial government to regulate the
training of teachers, the mission could organize
things the way it wanted. For those who were
planning to go forward to the ministry, assignments
were added to the teachers' class and examined by
the Presbytery. In 1865 Ukpabio spoke on
"Justification" and was assigned the topic "The
Place of Faith and Good Works in the Plan of
Redemption." Not surprisingly, he misunderstood the
intent of the second assignment and spoke on "What
is Faith?" They made him do it again. In 1866 he
delivered a paper on "The Holy Spirit and His
Work." In 1871 his examination for license,
usually decisive for ordination, included a lecture
on II Corinthians 5-18 and following, a sermon on
Psalm 25:1, a thesis on the subject "What should be

followed, the religion of Jesus Christ or the superstitions of the country, and why?" and an examination on the Epistles of Timothy.

Ukpabio went from Adiabo, the congregation in the Creek Town farms, to Creek Town itself before he retired in 1900. Ekanem was settled in Ikunetu. The two men who succeeded them, William George and Itam Okpo Itam, followed similar careers. Itam was in Ikunetu from 1893 to 1903 when he was suspended following a dispute with the Presbytery over his conduct at his mother's funeral.[3] William George gave distinguished service both to Duke Town Church and the Presbytery until his death in 1919. He had been a slave, but was redeemed by George Waddell, Hope Waddell's houseboy. His ordination was the last of those trained under the Presbytery.

Without the papers it is impossible to know or even guess at the standard expected of Ukpabio and his successor. It is significant, however, that when a question of relating to the customs of the country arose in the Presbytery, Ukpabio was sometimes asked to prepare a paper on the subject for the guidance of the court. Ekanem, for his part, was a keen student and a reasonably successful translator. It would seem that these men achieved a higher degree of theological sophistication and had more opportunity to use it than their successors, certainly those of the early twentieth century.

The Victorian missionaries probably achieved more than they intended. In their view, there was nothing of the noble savage in Africa. Robb was one of the more dramatic:

In estimating the vile, sunk and wretched
moral condition of the heathen, it matters not
whether we look to China, Japan, Burmah or
Hindustan, lands in which a barbaric
civilization has existed alongside of the most
childish superstitions, or to Africa whose
Negro tribes have, since the days of their
father Ham, kept on sinking from age to age
unaided, until now a dreary and bloody
fetishism has swallowed up all, and made them
the lowest of beings that are called men.[4]

Could these bones live? Of course the answer
is yes, but the treatment would have to be drastic.
In September 1861, Robb published in the Record a
proposal to establish a boarding school for the
training of "eloquent preachers." He was a voice
crying in the wilderness; neither the Board nor the
Presbytery took up the idea. It may be that Robb's
disagreement with his colleagues on this subject
was one of the reasons for his reluctance to take
up the theological training for which he had been
appointed. Robb took Africans seriously. In 1869
he pointed out that it was eight years since a
fully trained young man had been sent to Calabar,
even though such a man would in all respects be the
most efficient agent.[5] Not all his colleagues
agreed; the opposite and probably more typical
opinion appeared early in 1870: "In intelligence
and attainment the ministry ought not only to keep
pace with, but be in advance of, the mass of the
people. Granted: and in so far as this point is
concerned the humblest city missionary in Britain
would be a thousand times farther in advance of
regions such as that in which these lines are
penned, than are the most learned divines in
reference to average congregations in cities such
as Edinburgh and Glasgow."[6]

The majority missionary assumption seems to have been that Africans were a simple, unlettered people, and therefore learning was not of much use to a missionary. Robb, who spent ten years struggling through the Old Testament, was a good deal more cautious, but he seems to have been odd man out. Edgerley, for example, did not expect to produce a class of educated African gentlemen in his six-weeks-per-annum course, nor did he think it necessary. One did not need the same educational standards as in Scotland and, therefore, as long as staff training was in the hands of the missionaries, almost any missionary, it would seem there was nothing to worry about.[7] Because of this tendency in missionary thinking the mission was very vulnerable to shifts in European opinion which, by the beginning of the century, brought the mission to a point far removed from where it began.

The Calabar mission grew out of the Jamaica mission and the Jamaica mission out of the anti-slavery campaign. One of the difficulties with which the abolitionists had to contend was the evidence, which they did not deny, of moral laxity among the slaves. The reason for this laxity, they contended, was not racial, not inherent in the nature of black people, but sociological. They had known only the old barbarism of Africa and the new barbarism of slavery. Emancipation and missions would provide the cure. It was natural for men in this tradition to go on to assume that evidence of moral and spiritual advance would appear fairly quickly; indeed, Venn's experiment on the Niger set out to prove this assumption.

The Anglican Church in Nigeria began with freed slaves from Sierra Leone who found their way back to Yoruba country north of Lagos and invited both Anglican and Methodist missionaries to follow them. Among the missionaries was a young Yoruba named Samuel Crowther, who attracted Venn's attention and support. Venn placed enormous confidence in Crowther. He appointed him to manage the Niger Mission, which was to be entirely African in staff, and engineered his consecration as the first non-European bishop of the Anglican communion. The experiment was only a partial success. The Niger Mission produced a number of outstanding men, including Crowther himself, his son Dandeson, and James Johnson, but the relatively small Creole community in Sierra Leone could not go on producing first-rate men forever. By the 1890s the Anglicans were scraping the bottom of the barrel. The experiment was dismantled and handed over to the European missionaries.

But it produced a schism in the process. Some people left the Anglican Church altogether to found the first of the independent African churches, while those in the Delta achieved a measure of independence within the Anglican communion through the Niger Delta Pastorate. The division in the Anglican Church was precipitated by a new generation of zealous young men whose behaviour was interpreted by the African leadership as an attack not on specific instances of African incompetence or immorality but on Africans as such, as people not to be trusted with any serious measure of responsibility. The men of the 1890s were a different generation from the men of the 1850s and

1860s. The fathers had high hopes for Africa, the sons were more pessimistic.

Part of the difficulty lay in the failure to distinguish clearly between race, a biological category, and culture, which is sociological. As Darwinism thinking penetrated into the conscious-ness of the average British churchgoer, therefore, it became relatively easy to confuse the two and attribute the "backwardness" of Africans to racial rather than to cultural causes, or at the very least to hold that since evolution is a slow process African development would take a long time. The Scottish missionaries did not talk about these subjects very much, and it is hard to assess the influence of this change of opinion on their thinking. But this much can be said: the teachers' class died a natural death when it was replaced by the Normal School, but theological training simply withered away. The last reference in the Presbytery minutes to the training of the ministry is a note of July 1903 saying that Ekpe Nko should continue his studies under Mr. Weir. Since Weir had no theological training himself, this is not very encouraging. The development of a senior African staff continued to be discussed privately, but nothing was done about it until the rapid growth of the church forced their hands.

J. T. DEAN AND THE REFORMS OF 1918

At first a Nigerian ministry did not seem a pressing question. There were enough teachers to get by; the three Calabar churches all had their own ministers, and by stripping the southern stations, the Council was able to staff the new

positions which were opening up further north. It
was not until the middle of the First World War
that the missionaries realized they had too much to
do and took two immediate steps: the resumption of
serious thought about theological training and the
ordination of six men out of hand. They chose six
veteran assistants and presented them to the
Presbytery for ordination. In one sense they chose
well, for all six men seem to have been good men;
unfortunately, three died within a year and a
fourth, Ejemot Ecoma, died in 1920. The other two,
Nwafor Oguma and Efiong Utit, were spared for many
years of useful ministry. Nwafor Oguma was one of
the six chiefs of Arochuku and worked there until
his death in 1935. Efiong Utit was an Ibiono who
lived until the 1960s and died an old and honoured
man.

Including these men, there were thirteen
ordinations between 1900 and 1925. Only two,
William George, the last of the men trained under
the Presbytery, and Osonye Ikpeme, the first
graduate of the new course at Arochuku, received
any kind of serious training. The fall in academic
standards required of Nigerians is comparable to
that among the missionaries. Seven university men
were appointed between 1900 and 1925, but only
three were District Missionaries. One lasted two
years, leaving only Christie and Rankin as
university-trained men in the upriver stations.
Cruickshank had had a special course, four others
were Bible School graduates, and three had no
theological training at all. Learning was clearly
not a prerequisite for a career as a Calabar
missionary.

Nevertheless, some kind of training for Nigerians was considered essential; the ordinations of 1918 were a special case. The matter came up in the Council in 1916, where it was decided that "the most immediate duty . . . [was] . . . to make arrangements for the educating of native agents to do all that can properly be committed to their care." Macgregor and Wilkie were instructed to discuss the matter with Mr. Dean and bring forward a scheme for the training of "catechists and evangelists."[8] Clearly they were not fired with enthusiasm for an African ministry; their primary concern was with trained assistants for the District Missionaries.

John Taylor Dean appears in the story for the first time. He had been a missionary in the 1890s but had retired for medical reasons. In the meantime, he had revised the Efik New Testament and made something of a name for himself as a theologian. At one stage, he was suggested for Creek Town, but it was a staff crisis at Hope Waddell that brought him back to the country for a short time.

Compared to the minutes of 1916, Dean's proposals to the Council in May 1917 represent a significant advance. He accepted the Council's concern for training evangelists, who he did not think required much further education: "Men of capacity, who can awaken and sustain interest" were what the mission needed. He then went on to propose a more serious program for ministers, a course that would not only impart information but would also develop studious habits, the "desire to seek opportunities of study through books etc. in

later years." But he would not go beyond these
initial observations. The program could not be
imported ready-made from outside; it had to be
developed in Nigeria for Nigeria. The important
thing was to get the right man and give him his
head.[9] The right man, said the Council, was J. T.
Dean. He was appointed in 1918.

Dean's initial proposals contained two key
ideas: education for the ministry should encourage
studious habits, and it should be developed in
Nigeria for Nigeria. Judged by these standards,
his actual achievement leaves something to be
desired. In the first place, his teaching method
was hardly designed to stimulate independent
thought. He lectured on the move, pacing up and
down as he spoke, but at the end of the class,
notes were provided on the blackboard for copying
in the students' hard-covered exercise books.[10] It
was a method that might impart information, but
that was not likely to develop studious habits.

Theological reflection was not Dean's main
interest; the most striking aspect of his course
was a concern for practical work. He was the only
tutor, and when he went on leave the students were
sent out to the districts to learn the techniques
of congregational leadership. When he was in the
country, the classes broke up early on Friday so
that the students could be out on fieldwork on
Saturdays and Sunday mornings, returning in the
afternoon to have their journals checked, and in a
fashion more reminiscent of Scotland than Nigeria,
to sing hymns around the organ in Dean's parlour.[11]

Even the location of the college reflected
Dean's concern with the techniques of ministry

rather than with the first principles of theological analysis. Traditionally ministerial training had been in Creek Town, and the Council decided it should stay there. But when Dean heard of this idea he threatened to resign. Training in Creek Town, he argued, would be one-sided and academic, a disaster to the mission. Unless the college was in a place like Arochuku, he would have nothing to do with it.[12] Arochuku in 1918 was on the frontier of the church, and it was convenient to both Ibibio- and Igbo-speaking congregations. Dean got his way, the college was moved to Arochuku, and appropriately named after Hugh Goldie. Despite his earlier remarks about studious habits, therefore, Dean's course was designed to produce, not a generation of theologians, but competent working ministers.

For its time, it was not a bad system. In the first place, it was easy to run, depending as it did on only one man who did not need to be relieved when he went on furlough. In the second place, both the church and education were very new outside of Calabar. In view of the circumstances of the church as a whole between the world wars, not much more could be expected. But Calabar was a different matter, and in Calabar opposition to the program developed early in its life.

In 1921 two Efik students suggested that the college in Arochuku be affiliated to one of the Scottish colleges. The missionary establishment declined, arguing that the course had been designed for Nigerian conditions and that affiliation would be both undesirable and impractical. Ashcroft, the secretary of the Foreign Missions Committee,

agreed, insisting that since everything needed for
the study of the Bible was available in English,
the study of Greek and Hebrew--as the students were
suggesting--would be a waste of time. Affiliation
didn't stand a chance against both the missionary
establishment and the secretary of the Foreign
Missions Committee.   The Calabar churches then
refused to pay into the Students' and Pastors'
Fund.

In Dean's opinion, the root of the trouble was
the presence in Calabar of a number of Sierra
Leonians. These men were quick to point out that
the Presbyterian course could hardly compare with
that offered by the Anglicans in Sierra Leone,
where Fourah Bay was affiliated with Durham
University.   The demand for affiliation was a
demand for a more academic training for the
ministry, one comparable to that provided for
theological students in Britain. When they didn't
get a more academic course, the Calabar churches
refused to pay for the one at Hugh Goldie, and the
ministers outside Calabar were soon complaining
that their churches wouldn't contribute if the
richer congregations in Calabar did not.
Consequently, the income of the Students' and
Pastors' Fund in 1924 was only £124 when it should
have been £1500.   Instead of paying for what they
regarded as a mediocre course, Duke Town Church
proposed to send a man to Britain on a regular
theological program at the church's expense.   The
Synod tabled the idea until the church had paid its
debts.[13]

This was probably a mistake. Duke Town Church
was not simply complaining about Dean's course, it

was suggesting an alternative and offering to pay the bill. The Synod could have called the bluff, if it was a bluff, and possibly got a fully qualified minister. Certainly one was needed. The Presbyterian Church was running a large educational system, but hardly any of its graduates turned up in the ministry. Only two representatives of the new class of well-educated Nigerians entered the ministry: A. A. U. Ana and Okon Efiong. Ana got himself to Fourah Bay and was a Methodist minister in Lagos before Duke Town called him, and Efiong was ordained without any formal theological training. This failure to attract to its ministry a significant number of the ablest young men going through the schools is the most serious charge to be laid against the mission-dominated church.

THE LIMITATIONS OF MISSION TRAINING

The root of the problem was the missionary estimate of what was good for Africa. In the course of the argument over Hugh Goldie, J. K. Macgregor insisted "that the mission was in deep sympathy with the aspirations of the people."[14] No doubt he meant what he said, but the mission consisted of a group of institutionally minded men and women who were profoundly convinced that they and they alone knew what those aspirations ought to be. Their system was what Africa needed. Thus, when in 1918 a proposal came from a woman in Jamaica offering £159 a year to a Hope Waddell graduate studying medicine, the Council turned it down as "inexpedient." Four years later, a young Calabar man showed up in Edinburgh determined to study medicine and return to Nigeria, but his

sponsor had died, leaving him stranded. Ashcroft
asked for advice in this case and Mary Chalmers,
the principal of Edgerley Memorial School in
Calabar, replied that she knew little about the
"boy" in question, but since he was a trained
teacher, he should return to Calabar and teach.
The mission needed teachers badly, and since the
man's only reason for studying medicine was to
increase his income, the mission should not help
him in any way.[15]

One can sympathize with an institution which
does not have money to burn for declining to
educate a man who did not intend to enter its
service, but in this case the woman in Jamaica
would pay. The only thing the mission was asked
for was a recommendation; however, even this was
unacceptable since the man, although qualified,
declined to teach in the mission system. Mary
Chalmers did not ask whether Calabar needed
doctors. She did not ask whether the man's motives
were commercial or humanitarian. She simply
dismissed him because he did not fit the system.
To some extent, this was a normal reaction from
people who were responsible for an institution
which was just getting under way and who were
concerned lest somebody "rock the boat." It was
quite typical. In 1924 the Foreign Missions
Committee gently prodded the Council to speed up
progress towards ecclesiastical independence. The
Council replied that the District Missionary was
the best judge of a person's qualifications to be
an evangelist and suggested that the same should
apply to candidates for the ministry. To justify
maintaining missionary control, the Council members

argued that the granting of independence to ministers in congregations had not been followed by an outburst of apostolic zeal. Supervision, they argued, was essential for some time to come. When Scotland pointed to South Africa, the Council replied that the Bantu Synod could not be compared with Calabar.[16]

One can have some sympathy for the missionaries. In 1924-1925 the church outside Calabar was very young indeed; however, this kind of reasoning can lead to a self-fulfilling prophecy. Because the mission insisted on supervision, it tended to get solid, reliable men who would bear the heat and burden of the day, but who either could not or would not undertake the leadership of the church as a whole. The mission may have been operating with fairly clear ideas about the difference between mission and church, but to the average Nigerian the Presbyterian system was a single unit. In missionary thinking, because of the transitory nature of the District Missionary's job, there could be no question of training men to be missionaries, but only to be missionaries' assistants, or at one remove, pastors. But in Nigerian eyes to be a pastor or an evangelist was to hold a second class job, a job only part way up the hierarchy.

At the same time, Dean's insistence on a special type of education for Africa was suspect. Consciously or otherwise, Nigerians believed that European-style education was the key to power. To deny Nigerians education was to deny them power. The debate over Dean's curriculum is a classic instance of people who will never agree because

they are arguing from different premises. The
missionaries were trying to do what they felt was
best for Africa; the Nigerians believed that what
was good for Scotland was good for them. When they
didn't get it at the hands of the mission, they
went out, like Ana, and got it for themselves or,
like Efiong, entered the ministry through the back
door. Sometimes they went into teaching or took
secular employment outside the mission.

It is not suggested that if mission policy had
been any different certified teachers would have
poured into the ministry. The demands of the
extended family on the income of an educated man
were, and still are, considerable, and the ministry
was not a well-paid job. Nor is it suggested that
training for the ministry in the Third World is an
easy matter. But it is suggested that the
atmosphere of the mission between the two world
wars, in the childhood of the church, was not
conducive to the encouragement of bright and
probably brash young men who might think of the
ministry as a vocation. With key jobs reserved for
Scots, with the social life of the church often
separating Nigerians from missionaries, and
particularly in light of the cautious Scottish
approach, which was at variance with the instinctive concerns of the small class of articulate
Nigerians, it is certainly not surprising that the
mission council period cannot claim a sophisticated
ministry as one of its more outstanding achievements. Only when the third generation of
missionaries rose to the top in the 1940s do signs
of a new era appear.

EDUCATION FOR A NEW NIGERIA

When Dean retired in 1936, his last comment on his work was that it should be revised. The task fell to J. M. Lewars, the supervisor of schools, who had been associated with the Theological Students' Committee almost from the time of his arrival in 1926 and who was, by this time, its chairman. In the late 1930s, Lewars' committee put forward two proposals: the stiffening of qualifications for entry into the ministry, and the recommendations that a joint college with the Anglicans and Methodists be founded.[17]

The Council had long believed that ministers should have some training as teachers, and some of Dean's students actually did, but the Committee now proposed that the Higher Elementary Certificate be regarded as the norm for entry; only in exceptional cases should evangelists or uncertified teachers be accepted. It was a rule more honoured in the breach than in the observance, but at least they were trying.[18] The second initiative was more fruitful, leading eventually to the founding of Trinity College.

Approaching the other churches was duly authorized by the council; however, there were complications. It appeared that the Anglicans were contemplating a college at Yaba, near Lagos, with a view to a possible connection with a centre of higher learning. Yaba was too far away for the Presbyterians to take seriously; in any case, the project seemed to envisage a higher standard than the Presbyterians were contemplating at the time. Union negotiations with the Anglicans and Methodists east of the Niger seemed on the point of

bearing fruit; it was obviously more sensible to
press for a joint college in the eastern provinces,
where the tradition of cooperation was well
established.[19]

The joint college thus became settled
Presbyterian policy, but nothing could be done
until the Anglicans had made up their minds. In
the meantime, J. B. Cameron, a relatively new
missionary, went ahead with a new class, along the
old lines at Arochuku. By 1944, when the class was
finished, the joint college was settled in
principle, but it didn't even have a site let alone
buildings.[20] It was too late to start a new class
on the old lines and too early to begin on the new.
Four years were to pass before the college became a
reality, albeit in temporary quarters, and it was
not until 1950 that it was settled on its permanent
site outside Umuahia and named, with singular lack
of inspiration, Trinity College.

For its first ten years, Trinity College lived
a rather hand-to-mouth existence. Staff changes
were rapid, and there were four principals before
the Anglican tutor P. J. Ross took over the office
in 1959. A degree of stability, at least in the
principal's office, set in. Ross was a veteran
missionary--no scholar, but a first-rate schoolmaster with a real concern for the needs of the
ministry in all three supporting churches. His
meticulous annual reports detailed the
qualifications of the students year by year,
prodding the churches to recruit and send in men
with secondary school or equivalent qualifications.
During his tenure he had the satisfaction, not
necessarily entirely because of his efforts, of

seeing the average age of the students fall and their qualifications rise. In 1964 the college began preparing a few men for the London Diploma of Theology and the performance of the first class, while not impressive, was at least encouraging. In the first twenty years of its life the college expanded twice, first in 1959 and again in 1966, to a total enrollment of fifty-four students. The staff increased dramatically, from three to six, and Ross began talking of serious professional training for lecturers.[21] Normally the staff were expatriates, but from the late 1950s it included usually one and sometimes two Nigerians. If theological education fell short of what most people, both Nigerians and missionaries, would have wanted, it had come a long way from the days when the college was first suggested.

The Presbyterian share in this development went from dreadful to reasonable. Six students had entered during the foundation year, but from their departure well into the 1960s the Presbyterian candidates trickled through one, sometimes two, at a time. In the twelve years between 1950 and 1962 there were eight candidates, while in the next four years there were eleven, all but two of whom finished. The quality of the men, as measured in academic achievement before entering the college, certainly did not decline with the rising numbers; if anything, it improved.[22]

The reasons for the long drought in Presbyterian recruitment are by no means clear. The church was inclined to compare itself unfavourably with the Anglicans and Methodists, but the comparison was unfair on two counts. In the

first place any one of the three participating
Anglican dioceses was as large or larger than the
Presbyterian Church, and in the second place the
majority of the Anglican candidates, and except for
1965 the majority of the students in the college,
were evangelists or catechists. The Anglicans were
simply upgrading men already in full-time service.
Because the Presbyterians had had to abandon the
training of evangelists for lack of staff
throughout most of the first twenty years of
Trinity's life, they did not have this pool on
which to draw. They were getting their recruits
from the very areas which Ross encouraged: from
teaching and from secular employment. Neither the
Presbyterians, nor anyone else, had much success
among students in secondary schools. In comparison
with the other churches, the Presbyterian
performance in the 1960s was not as bad as the
church sometimes thought.

It should be mentioned that there were other
ways to enter the Presbyterian ministry. In 1957,
in the middle of the recruitment drought, the Synod
decided to create a category known as ordained
assistant. A few of the holders of this position,
such as Ulu Eme, had been evangelists, but most
were teachers, men with long and often
distinguished careers in both church and school.
Chima Oji, the principal of Macgregor Teacher
Training College, was among the first group to be
ordained. The original thought was that these men
would receive short courses and continue to work as
teachers, with some regular but limited ministerial
duties on the side. However, the pressures of
parish work and the fear that they would find

themselves in an anomalous position in a united church meant that there was a steady shift from part-time to full-time status. The Synod of 1967 contained eleven men in full-time parish work and three men in teaching who had entered the ministry in this way. Their training tended to be either sporadic or non-existent until 1965, when some of the later recruits were trained, along with a group of evangelists at Ohafia.

In the late 1950s the church was finally able to make progress in an area where it had lagged behind the other churches. Both the Anglicans and Methodists had graduate ministers by the 1950s, but it was not until 1957 that the first candidate with university prospects, Inya Ude, entered Trinity College. E. H. Johnson, the secretary of the Canadian Board of Missions, promptly began talking about bringing Ude to Canada for a degree.[23] Somerville was dubious; in light of his experience in other churches, he doubted whether Ude could stay with the church if he were not in a school where he could attract a government grant. But he agreed that the offer would have to be accepted.[24] Ude went to Canada in 1960, returning with both a B.A. and a B.D. He was the first of a series. In the next few years four men started on university courses; the Presbyterian Church in Canada paid for two, one in Canada and the other at the University of Nigeria, Nsukka; a third man had a scholarship at Edinburgh from the American Presbyterians, and the fourth went to Nsukka at the expense of the Nigerian Church.

Training ministers abroad had been in the air as far back as 1944, when the Synod, embarrassed at

the prospect of union with churches which had a
"stronger ministry," raised the question with
Mission Council, asking for "financial and other
assistance." Some Council members were sceptical,
doubting that the church could pay British-trained
ministers even if it had them, but Lewars and
Mincher saved part of the proposal, with the
suggestion that "in view of the cost and the
difficulty of providing adequate support on return
. . . a short refresher course [was more to the
point]."[25] The Foreign Missions Committee added
the further proviso that "a short refresher course"
meant not more than one year, and other matters
rested for a decade. In 1955 the missionaries
found enough money in the Hope Waddell accounts to
send a man to Scotland for a year. The Synod
accepted the offer, stipulating that the emphasis
should be "on practical training rather than a
course of lectures at New College."[26] Etim Onuk
was the first man to go; his experience was so
successful that four more men were offered a
similar opportunity. Nwachuku Eme went to Canada
in 1958 and three others went to Scotland in the
early 1960s.

Nwachuku Eme commented that his time in Canada
gave him an opportunity to read that he had never
had, not even in college, and his research paper on
the Long Juju is one of the few examples of
theological reflection from a Nigerian churchman of
the period. But perhaps even more important, the
chance to see how another church worked and the
experience of living abroad gave the men a
confidence and a social standing they could not
have obtained otherwise.

On the other hand, the program illustrates the failings of the church's theological training. It began in the 1940s as an initiative from the Synod to train, by implication, graduate ministers. The Council watered it down to a refresher course and nothing happened for ten years. A serious criticism was that the church could not afford a graduate ministry. Graduates in Nigeria, even in teaching, were very well paid; graduate ministers would have to receive something comparable. In 1959, when the question could no longer be avoided, the synod undertook a salary revision which gave graduate ministers, if not as much as teachers, at least a great deal more than other ministers. But in a sense, this was locking the door after the horse had been stolen.

The Mission Council's approach to the development of a trained ministry was hardly inspired. This is a problem without easy solutions. Degrees are expensive and neither the Scottish nor the Nigerian church had money to spare. Handing out scholarships can be wasteful if a significant number of the recipients are never seen again. Even those who do come back often find that they can only meet their family responsibilities by taking other work. However, the Council regarded these difficulties as a reason for inaction rather than as a challenge to the imagination. Dean was anxious to experiment, even though his results were rather orthodox; the missionaries of the 1940s and 1950s had been reluctant even to experiment until political realities forced their hands. As Somerville noted,

they had to offer Ude a chance at a degree if it
were at all possible.

If, as Presbyterians agree, a theologically
sophisticated leadership is essential to a church's
health, then developing it must be a priority.
Trinity College was a step in the right direction,
but it was not enough. The Presbyterian Church did
not respond adequately to the challenges of the
country's development until the 1960s. Just as in
the 1920s and 1930s so in the 1940s and 1950s,
theological education was not one of the more
outstanding achievements of the Presbyterian
Church.[27]

Chapter 4

A LEARNED AND GODLY MINISTRY

[1] Somerville to Robb, January 20, 1858.

[2] UPMB, November 25, 1879.

[3] _Presbytery_, August 1902; and March 10, 1903.

[4] Alexander Robb, _The Heathen World and the Duty of the Church_, 1.

[5] _The Record_, July 1869.

[6] Ibid., January 1869.

[7] UPMB, November 25, 1879.

[8] _Council_, December 6, 1916.

[9] Ibid., May 4, 1917.

[10] Conversations with the Rev. Mr. A. O. Anicho and the Rev. Mr. P. B. Onwuchekwa, 1977.

[11] Ibid.

[12] Dean to Ashcroft, June 28, 1922.

[13] _Synod_, October 1925.

[14] Ibid., October 1924.

15 Chalmers to MacLaren, December 19, 1922.

16 Council, April 1924, replies to the Policy Committee; May 1925, reply to the Policy Committee.

17 Synod, 1939.

18 Minutes of the Theological Students' Committee, October 23, 1936.

19 Council, May 1938; and Synod, 1939.

20 Synod, 1944.

21 The missionary staff tended to come and go and were often men who were available rather than those with particular qualifications for theological education. Ross was thinking primarily of further training for the Nigerian staff.

22 Of the seven students entering the college in 1963 and 1964, four were trained teachers: one was an uncertified teacher, one was an older man, and two had been in outside employment.

23 E. H. Johnson to John Watt (FMC), April 1956; and Johnson to Somerville, July 3, 1957.

24 Somerville to Johnson, August 27, 1957.

25 Synod, 1944; and Council, October 1944.

26 Synod, 1955.

27 Except for the Canadians it might have been worse. Theological education was one of the areas in which the Presbyterian church in Canada pressed

for improvement and provided a large part of the
necessary money. For an account of the Canadian
contribution, and especially that of E. H. Johnson,
see Geoffrey Johnston, "The Canadians in Nigeria,
1954-1967."

Chapter 5

NEIGHBOURS IN THE GOSPEL

> It is not our wish to disturb any other body
> of Christians who may be engaged in similar
> labours. We would rather cooperate with them;
> and for that end, would respect their
> arrangements for the benefit of the natives
> and avoid disturbing their operations, even as
> we would expect the same consideration from
> them in respect to ours.[1]

The principle that has governed Presbyterian
relations with other churches was stated before the
mission founded and has not changed since. The
first test came on the day the mission began.
Before leaving Britain, Hope Waddell learned that
the Baptists had objected to the proposed mission
in Calabar. They had been established in Fernando
Po, but were under a year's notice to leave by the
Spanish government and were looking for a location
on the mainland. Calabar was an obvious possibility, but the London office was not sure how far
their missionary, Mr. Clarke, had committed them.
The Presbyterians replied that since everything was
so vague, they had better send Hope Waddell to
Africa to find out what was happening. Hope
Waddell called on the Baptists in London and
assured them that if he found their man in Calabar,
he would go elsewhere.[2]

On arrival in Calabar, Hope Waddell found that
Clarke had given up the idea of going to Calabar
but that his colleague, Sturgeon, had not. The
arrival of the Presbyterians seems to have stirred

the Baptist into action, for he went up to Calabar
on the same ship, proposing to take Creek Town and
leave Duke Town to the Presbyterians. Hope Waddell
suggested referring the matter to Eyo Honesty.
What the king said was not disclosed, but Sturgeon
soon abandoned Calabar and everyone remained
friends.   The   Baptists   eventually   settled   in
Victoria in the Eastern Cameroons.

So ended the last serious brush with another
Christian body for many years. In the nineteenth
century, missions along the West African coast were
few and far between. The Presbyterians used to
take their holidays with missions in Fernando Po
and Gabon, and for a time there was a body known as
the Evangelical Alliance which met twice to discuss
matters of common concern. In the 1880s and 1890s,
other missions explored the possibility of opening
in Calabar, and while the Presbyterians declined to
place any obstacles in their way, they regretted
that anyone should come to Calabar when there was
so much country with no Christian presence at all.
It was not until the last years of the century that
another mission was established close enough to
Calabar to make some kind of working agreement
advisable.

COMITY AGREEMENTS, 1905-1927

In 1893 the Methodists moved out of Fernando
Po and opened a station at Archibong, a fishing
village southeast of Calabar on the borders of
Akpabuyo. Three years later, they opened a station
at Jamestown near the mouth of the Cross River on
the invitation of a man who had been a student in
Calabar. In both cases their line of advance was

in the direction of places with Calabar connections, and when the more promising opening at
Jamestown was opened, they asked the Presbytery if
it had any objections. It had none and wished them
well. When Buchanan heard of it, he suggested to
the Methodist office in London that if they planned
any further expansion it would be helpful if they
communicated with the Presbyterians first.[3] The
Methodists found this suggestion quite acceptable.
When they proposed to move out of Jamestown four
years later they notified the Mission Council,
asking for a conference, in which the Methodists
waived any claim to Akpabuyo in return for
considerable latitude around Jamestown.[4] It was a
good beginning which did not entirely work out, but
the petty frictions around Calabar were soon
overshadowed by the more serious question of Ikot
Ekpene.

Ikot Ekpene is a town in Ibibio country
towards which both the Qua Ibo Mission and the
Presbyterians had been working, but to the surprise
and chagrin of both the older churches, the
Methodists secured land and proposed to open a
station before either of them could get around to
it. At the same time the Methodists suggested a
conference to settle the problem of Ikot Ekpene and
the other smaller disputes which they had with
their neighbours.[5]

It was an aggressive move, perhaps not quite
within the proprieties of friendly missionary
societies; but in fairness to the Methodists, it
must be said first that they initiated the
conference and second that they had been dogged
with bad luck. They had started in Fernando Po,

only to be turned out by the Spanish government.
Archibong was a blind alley, so they moved to
Jamestown. But as soon as they began expanding
from their new station, they found themselves
hemmed in by the Qua Ibo Mission on the one hand
and the Presbyterians on the other. The occupation
of Ikot Ekpene was a bold but necessary attempt to
give themselves some elbow room.

The conference was held in April 1909,
principally about Ikot Ekpene. The debate was full
and frank, but rather tense, because everyone knew
that a major question was at stake. Towards the
end of the meeting the chairman called for a short
break, presumably because the tea was ready, and
after the break the Methodists made their final
offer: if they were allowed Ikot Ekpene, they
would compromise on the minor issues; if not, they
would do what they liked. Since the Methodists had
already established a foothold in Ikot Ekpene,
there was not much the others could do. An
inspection of the ground was arranged before any
final decisions were made,[6] and when they met again
in June the Methodists, in return for concessions
elsewhere, got a corridor running north from Ikot
Ekpene to Bende.

They had won hands down. From being in
serious danger of being hemmed in against the sea,
they had won a corridor running as far north as
they could reasonably expect to go, through which
the government subsequently built a railway.
Further, by gaining this corridor they accidentally
took over from the Presbyterians the advantages of
occupying Arochuku. The Aros carried Christianity
with them as they carried everything else, and

since their main trade connections ran west and
northwest, the churches they started were outside
the Presbyterian area.[7] When the Methodists posted
F. W. Dodds in Bende a few years later, the
churches fell into his lap. By 1913 his mission
had extended far beyond the horizons of the 1909
conference and he was in correspondence with the
Calabar Mission Council asking for another meeting.
Council replied that they were ready to negotiate.[8]
As it turned out, they didn't have to bother, for
Collins, the missionary in Ohafia, and Dodds found
they could work out a boundary as they went along.[9]
Settling the northern boundary was a little more
difficult.

In 1917 a boundary conference was called for
Aba, which the Presbyterians, through an
administrative error, did not attend. In their
absence, the brethren decided that the Methodists
should move north along a front forty to fifty
miles wide with the railway as their western
boundary while the Presbyterians should advance
northeast from Uburu, east of a line drawn from
Uburu to Abakaliki.[10] Uburu is less than forty
miles east of the railway, so if the Presbyterians
were to act in accordance with the second decision,
they would be inside the Methodist territory
defined by the first decision. But the Council
ignored this anomaly and concentrated on other
points. In the first place, the decision put
Unwana, a station they had occupied for almost
thirty years, inside Methodist country; in the
second place, a boundary which started at a station
and left no room for working all around the station
was impossible; in the third place, the proposed

line cut through Ezza, a tribe more homogeneous, or
so the Council believed, than any they had ever
met.[11] The Council refused to recommend the
decision to the Foreign Missions Committee and
matters rested there for another ten years. Since
neither mission was making much headway with the
northeast Igbos and their neighbours, there was no
particular urgency. In 1927 the Methodists
proposed to open a station in a place called Iyono,
which Christie believed was within his district.
He referred the case to the Council asking that the
matter be raised at the next meeting of the
Evangelical Union, the precursor of the Christian
Council, and suggesting that the boundary of Ogoja
Province was as good as any. They didn't get all
they wanted, but settled for Ezza and Abakaliki,
handing over a portion of northwest Ogoja to the
Methodists.

These decisions settled the western and most
difficult boundary. On the east was a range of
mountains and the Cameroons border, on the south
the sea, and on the north, theoretically at least,
Presbyterian country up to the boundary of the
northern provinces. But, as we have seen, the
Presbyterians were unable to occupy effectively
these sparsely settled hills, and eventually
reached an agreement with the Lutherans.

On the whole, the Presbyterians worked out
satisfactory boundary arrangements. Their nearest
neighbours on the east were on the other side of an
extensive forest, and on the west, workable
arrangements with the Methodists, once the Ikot
Ekpene question was settled, were established
without much difficulty. Their contacts with the

Anglicans were minimal, and the one potential conflict, Arochuku, was settled in exchange for an Anglican chaplaincy in Calabar. The Methodist experience on their eastern and southern boundaries was not nearly as satisfactory. The problems they had with the Anglicans were serious but proved open to amicable solution, especially when Bishop Howells took over the Niger Delta Pastorate in 1920. On the other hand, their arguments with the Qua Ibo Mission were frequent and bitter. It is significant that the three churches which settled their boundary problems with the least difficulty were the same three that took up serious discussion of church union. Boundary agreements are at once a test of the willingness of churches to cooperate and the foundation of further association.

But the boundary agreements cannot be regarded as being written in stone. In this particular case, the decisions were made when the nature of the country was very imperfectly understood; constant adjustments were necessary as everyone became better informed. Dodds felt that the best boundary was a natural one, a river or a range of hills, but failing that it should follow clan lines. If neither were possible, two missionaries, such as himself and Collins, could create a boundary. But even under ideal conditions, boundary agreements work only as long as people stay at home. As the country developed and changed its trade patterns under the colonial regime, people began to cross the boundaries almost as fast as they were drawn, moving from the villages where their fathers had lived and died to seek their

fortunes in the raucous and vibrant environment of
the colonial towns.

THE PROBLEM OF THE TOWNS

In 1905 the Presbyterians accepted an Anglican
church in Calabar in return for undisputed
possession of Arochuku, but it was four years
before the Anglicans actually did anything. In
1909 a section of Duke Town Church, composed mainly
of immigrants, took exception to Arthur Wilkie's
evidence before the Liquor Commission and seceded,
taking as their minister a Wesleyan from Sierra
Leone. This gentleman, however, was under
suspension in his own church and, since most of the
congregation seems to have originally been
Anglicans, Bishop Tugwell and James Johnson came to
Calabar and set up an Anglican congregation called
Trinity. The church was soon prospering and
cordial relations with the Presbyterians developed
without difficulty.

In 1913 a further secession took place, led by
a man who had fallen out with the minister over a
question of discipline. This group applied for
recognition to the Wesleyan Methodists in Lagos,
and, according to Ekpe Nko, started services in
Creek Town, drawing mainly on the fringes of his
congregation. Wilkie had a low opinion of this
group and pressed the Methodist superintendent in
Lagos to disown them. Unfortunately for the
superintendent, the schismatics were connected to
some influential Methodists in Lagos; he dithered
for a number of years and finally suggested that
the congregation be recognized as Methodist, but
placed under the supervision of the Scottish

Mission Council. The Council agreed reluctantly,
but within a year the experiment had broken down.
With no other options remaining, the Council agreed
to a Methodist chaplaincy. The Methodists
understood chaplaincy to include freedom "to
exercise all the functions of a complete Christian
church, both pastoral and evangelistic," but the
council replied that, in its opinion, the word
"chaplaincy" excluded "active evangelistic work in
the Calabar region."[12] The Wesleyans accepted this
interpretation with regret and the matter rested
for ten years, at the end of which they washed
their hands of the problem by handing it over to
the Primitive Methodists.

Without a doubt, the Methodists had a point.
The Presbyterians interpretation of chaplaincy
amounted to denying the Methodist Church in Calabar
the rights and duties of a Christian church. But,
on the other hand, in this imperfect world, its
evangelistic work would undoubtedly be most
successful among those who were on the fringes of
the Presbyterian Church, or who were, for good
reasons or bad, at odds with their minister.

In the middle of this unfortunate affair, in
1925, Mr. Banham of the Methodists proposed to the
Evangelical Union that "certain towns on the
railway, Port Harcourt, Aba, Umuahia, Enugu, be
considered open towns for missions." At this stage
he did not win the support of his Methodist
colleagues, and the motion failed six to one, with
Banham abstaining.[13] The Council's reaction was
immediate and unequivocal: open towns would tend
to "denominational rivalry and strife."[14]
Gradually, however, opinion in the other churches

began to go the other way. In 1930 an interchurch
committee to study the question was set up by a
vote of four to three. The close vote seems to
have engendered caution, for nothing more on the
question appears until 1948, when the Eastern
Regional Committee of the Christian Council, the
successor to the Evangelical Union, approved with
caution the idea in principle. The Presbyterians
agreed:

> Synod agreed with the judgement of E.R.C.
> which held that strangers should normally
> attend the church of the area but in some
> cases it might be expedient to organize a
> separate group with their own leader and funds
> under the supervision of the church of the
> area. Only in exceptional circumstances
> should E.R.C. sanction an organized
> congregation, only in the very large towns and
> provided that they can pay [their minister]
> and he does not proselytize.[15]

It was not exactly an enthusiastic endorsement
of a potentially exciting development, even if it
were consistent with Hope Waddell's principle. But
looked at in the context of the time, the Synod's
position was reasonable. It could be argued in
1948 that urbanization had not reached the point
where Presbyterian expansion into towns
undisputably outside their area could be justified.
Five years later the census showed that Aba had
just under 58,000 people, Enugu, 62,764, and Port
Harcourt, 71,634. Umuahia had less than 13,000. A
case could conceivably be made for saying that
these towns were simply not big enough to support a
Presbyterian church without creating friction
between the newcomers and the established church of
the area. However, in the next ten years these
circumstances changed completely; Umuahia, for

example, by no means a major town, more than
doubled its population in the next decade.

    To insist on the founder's principle was to
insist on an argument which had lost its validity
in a new, urban society. It cut the Presbyterian
off from any share in the witness of the church in
the barbarous conditions of Nigerian cities, and it
denied the church the talents of some of its most
gifted people. At least since the end of the
Second World War these towns drained off from the
Presbyterian area some of its most talented
converts, and the church made no effort to retain
their services. But it was typical of Presbyterian
leadership, particularly the expatriates, that they
thought in terms of the Protestant community rather
than of the Presbyterian Church. Scottish
reluctance to move into the towns was in part
inspired by the fear of "creating denominational
rivalry and strife" that would harm the chances for
church union. Nigerian leadership was probably
less moved by that concern and more by a real
feeling for the sons abroad who retained an
emotional connection with the Presbyterian Church
but were given no opportunity to put it into
practice. By the time the Nigerian leadership was
strong enough to force the issue, the Scots,
particularly R. M. Macdonald, had come round to the
same view, or at least to arguing that a
Presbyterian presence in the major towns would do
church union more good than harm.[16] Macdonald may
have been the most consistent exponent of the view
that the church should think in terms, not of
itself, but of Protestantism as a whole. His

argument struck a responsive chord in a church
which had for years been committed to church union.

THE APPROACH TO UNION

Cooperation in other fields dates from the
same period as the boundary conferences. In May
1911 the first of a series of meetings was held in
Calabar at the instigation of the Calabar Mission
Council, which was devoted to a number of practical
problems the missions had in common. The meeting
was so successful that Arthur Wilkie made a
stirring speech at the end in which he urged that
the missionary community not stop at discussion but
press on towards union.[17] At that point, the
missions themselves were too pressed by the
response to their message to think about union, or
even about more conferences, but when things had
settled down a bit in the twenties, the series of
consultations resumed. In 1923 the Evangelical
Union, an institutional framework for consultation
and cooperation, appeared, and in 1930 it was
replaced by the ERC, the Eastern Regional Committee
of the Christian Council of Nigeria. It continued
to talk about the problems of running churches, but
it also picked up a dormant idea from the
conference of 1911, a conference of African
churchmen called the Senior African Agents'
Conference. A number of these teams were held; the
one that met in Ovim in 1930 revived Wilkie's call
for a union of cooperating churches.[18] By this
time people were ready to go ahead, and J. T. Dean
sketched out an idea for a federation of missions
under the aegis of an expanded Eastern Regional
Committee.[19]

However, general opinion seemed to favour
something more thoroughgoing. In the next few
years the Council put some thought on an initial
negotiating position, a statement of first
principles for the guidance of its representatives,
some of which seems a little odd in light of what
actually happened:

1. That the basis of union which we are
    endeavoring to frame is for the church in
    Africa.

2. That there should be admitted into it no
    ambiguous phrase which may be interpreted
    in different ways by the different people
    concerned.

3. That in the basis of union no reference be
    made to past and present controversies
    which may have had, or may still have
    meaning for churches in Europe, but which
    can only bewilder the church in Africa.

4. That nothing which has proved valuable in
    the life of the various missions be omitted
    from the life of the United Church.

The Council then went on to affirm a series of
items on which no disagreement was probable and
added that it would like "the members of the Joint
Committee to understand that an administrative
episcopacy is not inconsistent with Presbyterianism, and that the Church of Scotland Mission
would not be averse from it."[20]

By this time 1929 draft of the Church of South
India scheme was available, and once the
Presbyterians had admitted the possibility of some
kind of episcopacy, events took a predictable
course: the reworking of the Indian scheme.
Progress was not without difficulties; in 1938 the
Council reproved the Anglicans for backing from
their earlier openness on the subject of bishops
and "tending to insist on a retention of the full

Anglican episcopate," but the most serious setback was the Anglican decision in the late 1930s that they could not go into union with the eastern diocese alone, but would have to wait until the Anglicans in the west were ready. The Council discharged its union committee and handed the now moribund negotiations over to the Synod.21

Five years passed before anything further developed, but in the meantime some interest in the project had been aroused in the west by the advocacy of the Bishop of Lagos. Discussion resumed in 1944, but only in 1947 was a major conference held, this time including Methodists and Anglicans from the west. Even so it was necessary, both for educational and propaganda purposes, to bring a bishop from South India before any real progress was made. At last, in 1957, a revised draft appeared.

In the meantime the Anglicans had been coming under pressure from other members of their communion who had doubts about the suitability of the South India scheme. The bone of contention was the Indians' acceptance without question of each other's ministries, at least for the first thirty years of the church's life. The Presbyterians were committed to the South India procedure and would only consider alternatives if serious progress was possible. The concession was not necessary; the 1957 scheme accepted all ministries without qualification, a decision which the Council noted with gratification.22 But church unions are a case of "love me, love my relatives." In 1958 the Lambeth Conference of the Anglican communion recommended the Ceylon scheme of union, which does

have a liturgy of the unification of the ministry.
The Nigerian Anglicans, understandably concerned
with retaining their contacts with the rest of
their church, brought the alternative schemes of
union, those of North India and Ceylon, to the
negotiations. At first the Presbyterians insisted
on South India, but after consultation with
Scottish missionaries in India, they decided that
they could live with a service of the North India
type, a type which took place after the
inauguration of the union and was, therefore, an
act of the united church and not the uniting
denominations, and which involved everyone laying
hands on everyone else.[23]

In 1963 the Synod started the Scheme of Union
through the courts, a long process which involved
acceptance by sessions, presbyteries, and the Synod
itself for two years in succession. The process
was completed in January 1965. In the meantime
work had been begun on matters of immediate and
practical importance, hitherto left untouched--
questions of finance and administration, relations
with overseas churches, theological education,
women's work, and the like. During 1965
provisional committees were formed in each of the
new dioceses, invitations were despatched to
ecclesiastical dignitaries to attend the
inauguration in December 1965, and the orders of
service were sent off to the printers. Then in
November, only weeks before the great ceremonies
were to begin, the whole thing was called off.

The immediate cause of this debacle was a
split in the Methodist Church, but behind that
division lay the tradition of western Methodism and

the pattern of interchurch relations in Yorubaland,
where the habits of cooperation taken for granted
in the east had never developed. Behind these
ecclesiastical divisions were the deep divisions in
Yoruba society itself. The last years of church
union negotiations were not happy ones in western
Nigeria. Division in the state was rife, and could
have affected opinion in the church as well.[24] The
Methodists decided that, rather than split their
church, they had better withdraw from the whole
scheme for the time being, and the others, after
discussing briefly a Presbyterian-Anglican merger,
abandoned it as well. In the meantime the coup of
January 1966 had taken place, followed in a few
months by the riots in the north. The country
began to slide towards secession; any discussion of
a nationwide church soon became inconceivable.
Church union was a dead issue.

Disappointed though they were, there was
nothing the Presbyterians could do. Church union
had foundered on a dispute among Yoruba Methodists.
Any attempt at intervention would have been
fruitless. Their disappointment was real, for
union was something they had worked on, albeit in a
desultory fashion, for over thirty years, and the
Nigerian leadership had been involved from the
early days. The question had come regularly to the
Synod since the early 1950s, and between 1963 and
1965 it was presented twice at the congregational
and Presbytery level. In those years the proposal
to unite had had an easy passage; nowhere in the
Presbyterian Church was there any evidence of the
kind of opposition which developed among the
western Methodists.

This is not to say there were no misgivings;
rather they never developed into coherent
opposition. Some of the misgivings were peculiar
to missionaries, especially the Canadians.[25]
Others, and the more serious varieties, developed
among the Nigerians and concerned, not the
theological questions which had taken up so much
time in the church union negotiations, but the
practical working out of the scheme in the daily
life of the church. Such misgivings appeared
naturally and obviously at Trinity College, where
the students of the three uniting churches lived,
worked, and argued together. The reaction of the
Presbyterian students tended to be that of a
minority rather than anything arising out of the
Reformed tradition. Only in one case, which was
serious enough to precipitate a special meeting of
the Synod, did a Nigerian minister take issue with
his colleagues on the negotiating committee, but he
failed to find significant support within the
court.[26] There can be no reasonable doubt that the
Presbyterian Church was firmly, if not absolutely
wholeheartedly, behind church union.

It remains then to ask whether, in the scheme
of union, the Presbyterians achieved what they set
out to do. If one looks to the first principles of
Presbyterian government, the equality of ministers,
government by standing committees, and the
participation of the laity at all levels, their
record is reasonable. Acceptance of the episcopate
was a necessary concession, but the office was left
studiously undefined. The united church was to be
governed by the boards and committees which would
include both laymen and ministers. They did,

however, by some oversight fail to introduce the eldership into the scheme, and when the mistake was caught, it was too late to make any changes. It was decided to press the point early in the life of the united church.[27] If the scheme was not a model of Presbyterian government, it was at least acceptable, and nothing better could be expected from church union negotiations.

But if one turns to the first principles with which the Presbyterians started out, it is clear that something went seriously wrong. The united church was to omit nothing that was valuable in the life of the participants; it was to avoid all reference to European controversies; it was to be unambiguous; and it was to be for "the church in Africa." On the first point no comment can be made, for in the first instance congregational life was to continue as usual and only time would tell whether anything valuable would disappear. Avoiding European controversies was a total failure, for the whole debate, especially after 1958, turned on episcopal ordination. Consequently they failed to avoid the ambiguous. The word "bishop" has different meanings for different people, and the service of the unification of the ministry was a drama in ambiguity. But, worst of all, they lost track entirely of the first principle they had enunciated: that this union was to be for the church in Africa.

In a sense, the Presbyterians went wrong from the moment they accepted the Church of South India scheme as a basis. If the new church was to be for Africa, they should have started with Africa, not with India, and worked their way forward from what

they had. But the diversion to India was probably
inevitable; importing a scheme was too powerful a
temptation for men who were uniting churches in
their spare time. Even more serious, the
Anglicans' concern for retaining their connection
with the rest of their communion led the debate to
concentrate on an issue which was primarily of
European concern and away from the broader and more
serious questions of what the church ought to be
doing in Nigeria. The church union discussions
were almost exclusively structural. The Nigerians
were as open to this failing as the missionaries.
The Senior African Agents' Conference, after a bow
in the direction of Christ's prayer "that all may
be one," went on to deplore division as a source of
weakness. If division is a source of weakness,
then the obvious answer is to unite, and the
contemporary popularity of church union schemes led
everyone astray. But at the same time the church
union debate was pursuing its leisurely course, the
churches were almost automatically strengthening
their work in a series of joint projects in
education, theological training, and medicine. And
at the same time, a more radical solution to the
weakness of the church in Nigeria was being
proposed by the independent churches, a solution
which the Presbyterians, almost to the last, chose
studiously to ignore.

THE INDEPENDENT CHURCHES

African independency developed in the wake of
the Niger Mission crisis of the 1890s, a reaction
against the high-handed way the Europeans took over
a project which had been almost entirely African.

The first churches were orthodox in liturgy and doctrine (except for their toleration of polygamy), but entirely under African management. At first they tended to concentrate in Yoruba country. A policy toward them was not necessary until a branch of the African church was opened in Calabar. William George, the minister at Duke Town, raised the question in the Presbytery, expressing grave doubts about the new organization, and the Presbytery agreed that the African church was in reality no church at all, a decision from which the church does not seem to have officially departed.[28]

It was not until the late 1920s that indigenous African Christianity posed a serious problem to the Presbyterians. In 1927 a religious revival known as the Spirit Age broke out among the Ibibios, keeping the missionaries extremely busy for a time and precipitating the only conversation with the local Roman Catholic priest that Cruickshank recorded in his diary. It was a fairly typical revival with shouting, shaking, singing, an intense consciousness of sin and the destruction of the cult objects of traditional religion. The concern for sin led it astray, for confessing sins led to hunting for them, especially for witches. By November, joint bands of Christians and non-Christians were on a witch hunt, and between November 23 and December 3, five people died and three additional deaths were attributed indirectly to the movement. The government intervened, and by the end of the year the revival was past its peak.[29]

Missionaries divided on the Spirit Age. Some of the Qua Ibo staff regarded it as a genuine

movement of the Spirit which only needed to be
protected from excess. The Presbyterians and Roman
Catholics were more sceptical.[30] The immediate
result was a sharp increase in the catachumen
classes, so large that the inadequate staff at the
disposal of the Ibibio missionaries could not
handle it and a good deal of the momentum generated
by the revival was lost. But R. M. Macdonald, who
worked nearly forty years in Ibibio country after
1930, felt that the movement, especially the
experience of leading one's own church, was the
beginning of the enormous proliferation of
independent churches in Ibibio country following
the Second World War.[31]

"Independent" is probably the best word for
these churches. Some had an international
connection, some did not, some went through several
connections looking for the one which could deliver
schools and hospitals most efficiently, with a calm
disregard of the theological questions that are of
such concern in western circles. Some were small,
some were quite substantial, but they all shared a
total reliance on local leadership and support. If
they looked for an international connection, it was
to assist a work which was firmly and unques-
tionably in local hands. This reliance on local
leadership was both the strength and the weakness
of the movement, for while it was undoubtedly
indigenous, its leadership was often of limited
intellectual and sometimes ethical attainments.

In the face of this movement which was taking
place on their doorstep, and sometimes at their
expense, the Presbyterians maintained, at least
officially, a profound silence. Until 1960 not a

single reference to the indigenous churches appears
in the Synod minutes, but in that year, Macdonald
presented to the court an American Mennonite
couple, the Reverend and Mrs. Edwin Weaver, who had
come to work among the independents in Uyo
Division.

The Americans had been invited to Nigeria by a
group of some fifty independent churches which
claimed to be Mennonite. Weaver was in the county
on a visitor's visa in the hope that a permanent
work could be developed. He soon realized that
something could and should be done with the
independents, and also that he was far from sure
what it was. The traffic sign "Go slow through
Uyo" became a kind of watchword. Initial contacts
with the missionary community were not encouraging
until somebody recommended Macdonald, who was
managing Itu Leper Colony and acting as secretary
of the ERC at the time. Macdonald was prepared to
be helpful. He took the matter to the ERC, but
official church opinion still held that a
missionary would be of more use in Northern
Nigeria, where missions were few and opportunities
great, than in Uyo, where some form of Christianity
was common currency. Macdonald turned to his own
church and things began to happen. After his
presentation in the Synod, Weaver was visited by an
impressive delegation of Presbyterian leadership
with a straightforward proposition. The Presbyterians needed secondary school teachers and, above
all, staff to reopen Abiriba hospital. If the
Mennonites could undertake these responsibilities,
the Presbyterians would sponsor them before the
immigration department and make their permanent

residence possible. By this time, Weaver's permit
to stay in the country was running out. He
invested £10 in a telephone call and was authorized
to accept the proposition.

Important though this bargain was for
specifically Presbyterian work, its real
significance lay in the fact that it constituted a
breakthrough in relations with independent
churches. These churches were clearly not about to
go away, nor would they be reabsorbed in the
churches from which they originated. The wise
course of action, therefore, was some kind of
constructive relationship, and particularly some
assistance in improving the leadership the movement
had produced. Macdonald eventually got the other
churches to support the Mennonites, and in the
years before the war, Weaver built up among the
independents a program which tried to retain their
strength and reduce their weakness.[32]

Presbyterian interest in Weaver's work
remained genuine. The Presbyterians supplied an
evangelist, sponsored a Mennonite student at
Trinity College, and participated in the Inter-
Church Study Group. But once the project had
become ecumenical they simply shared in it, as they
shared in so many others. Their real contribution
came at the beginning, when they were instrumental
in keeping the Mennonites in the country and
persuading the other churches to support the
project once it was launched.

The Uyo project was a new departure, significantly widening the range of cooperation and
introducing a new form. Traditionally Presbyterians had cooperated with other Protestants,

particularly the Anglicans and the Methodists, but
the Uyo project was a breakthrough into a new group
of churches. It pioneered a new form of
cooperation, providing legal sponsorship and
sharing in a common study rather than a common
institution. The new departure was possible
because, by 1960, the earlier rigid attitude
towards the independent churches was softening. In
university circles, independent churches were
positively fashionable, and academic interest was
reflected to some extent in the church. On the
other hand, cooperation with the Catholics, the
other major Christian presence in the Presbyterian
area, was conspicuous by its absence, except for in
marginal activities like the Seminar on Religion,
Worship, and the Arts at the University of
Nigeria.[33] The new look in Roman Catholic
ecumenical relations designed at the Second Vatican
Council did not become fashionable in Nigeria until
some years later.

The forms of cooperation have varied over the
years. They began in the nineteenth century with
conversations on common problems and moved on in
the twentieth century to comity agreements, joint
projects, and the abortive search for union. In
the 1960s, the range of cooperation widened from
neighbouring Protestants to a promising beginning
with the Independents and a few tentative ventures
with the Catholics. But the policy as stated by
Hope Waddell did not change. Its roots are in the
Reformed tradition, which has always been
relatively open on this question, but it has been
nourished by a consistently happy experience. The
church has never had to regret its comity

agreements or its participation in joint projects
like Trinity College. The Presbyterian Church is
small and, other things being equal, a small body
finds the argument for cooperation more convincing
than a large one. But whatever the reasons, the
Presbyterian record of cooperation is one of the
more commendable aspects of the church's life.

Chapter 5

NEIGHBOURS IN THE GOSPEL

[1] Hope Waddell to John Beecroft, quoted in Twenty-Nine Years in the West Indies and Central Africa, 229.

[2] USMB, November 25, 1845; and Twenty-Nine Years, 229.

[3] Presbytery, September 29, 1896; and Buchanan to Dean, October 9, 1896.

[4] Old Calabar Mission Committee, Minutes, November 19, 1900.

[5] The Qua Ibo Mission was and is an inter-denominational society based principally in Ulster. Its Nigerian work was begun in 1887 by S. A. Bill, an exstudent of Grattan Guiness College in London.

[6] Minutes of a conference of missionaries from the United Free Church, Qua Ibo, and Primitive Methodist Missions, Calabar, April 15, 1909.

[7] Notes on a conversation with Isaac Uwaezuoke. Mr. Uwaezuoke's father was a pioneer missionary in the Aro settlements.

[8] Council, October 23, 1913.

[9] F. W. Dodds, "Boundaries," dated 9/2/39.

[10] Minutes of the Aba Conference, 1917.

11 Council, May 4, 1917.

12 FMC, April 20, 1920, and January 18, 1921, citing Council, November 10, 1920.

13 Minutes of the Evangelical Union, Aba, March 4, 1925.

14 Council, May 1925.

15 Synod, 1948.

16 E. F. Roberts to E. H. Johnson, October 17, 1960.

17 Minutes of the conference of 1911.

18 Resolution of the Conference of Senior African Agents, Ovim, 1930.

19 Council, May 1931.

20 Council, March 1933, First Report of the Committee on Union.

21 Council, May 1939.

22 Council, May 1957.

23 G. Johnston to R. M. Ransom, April 2, 1965, and Annual Field Report for 1964, prepared for the Canadian Board.

24 Conversation with R. G. Browne, 1977. The most complete discussion of this question is in

O. U. Kalu, <u>Divided People of God, Church Union Movement in Nigeria, 1867-1966</u>.

[25] G. Johnston to R. M. Ransom, April 2, 1965; and Annual Field Report, Nigeria, 1964, prepared for the Canadian Board.

[26] <u>Synod</u>, August 1965.

[27] <u>Synod</u>, January 1964.

[28] <u>Presbytery</u>, October 20, 1915.

[29] Annual Report, Enyong Division, 1927, Calprof, 5/18/60.

[30] Ibid.

[31] R. M. Macdonald, in conversation with the district missionaries, 1977.

[32] Edwin and Irene Weaver, <u>The Uyo Story</u>.

[33] The author, as Presbyterian tutor at Trinity College, and Murray Ross, the Presbyterian architect, were regular attenders of this seminar. Cooperation with the Catholics was almost exclusively at the university level in this period. Ross was subsequently asked to design for the Enugu campus of the University of Nigeria something that looked sufficiently like a table to satisfy the Protestants and sufficiently like an altar to satisfy the Catholics!

Chapter 6

RELIGION AND LITERATURE

THE NINETEENTH CENTURY

Hope Waddell once rather facetiously described
his lifework as teaching the ABC's of religion to
the children of Ethiopia.[1] For 120 years the
school, whether it was a simple mud-and-thatch
shelter or an elaborate complex, like the Hope
Waddell Training Institution, was the characteristic mark of the Presbyterian Church. It was a
natural emphasis for a Scottish mission, but not
peculiar to them. If a great deal of the expansion
of Christianity in southern Nigeria rested on
schools, it was not necessarily because
missionaries wanted it that way, but because of the
Nigerian thirst for education. The difficulty was
that missionaries offered schools for one reason
and Nigerians accepted them for another.

For the missionaries, the schools were a means
of working into the community. The children were
the hope of the future; if they could be brought
round to Christian principles the community as a
whole could be reformed. Thus Somerville wrote to
Hugh Goldie: "The young are the hope of Old
Calabar, and it is by getting their minds imbued
with religious truth and right principles that you
will succeed in overturning the vast system of
cruel and deadly superstition which Satan has there
raised."[2]

Hope Waddell's curriculum started with
reading, writing, and arithmetic and moved on to

some social science with the older children, but
his main emphasis was religion. In addition to
prayers and religious instruction, the Bible and
catechism material formed the basis of his reading
program. It is probable that his colleagues and
successors followed the same pattern. Certainly
Edgerley's syllabus for his teachers' course
suggests that he had this type of school in mind.[3]

     That Calabar people had a different view of
education is indicated by Edgerley's difficulties
in building up a solid corps of trained teachers.
Children, he complained, were too fond of trade and
too irregular in attendance.[4] In other words, the
demands of traditional Calabar life took precedence
over schooling. If the children were needed on the
land, they went off to the farms; once they had
learned enough reading and arithmetic to start
work, they were drafted into the commercial
activities of the house. For the missionaries,
education was fundamental; it was the means of
altering the foundations of Calabar life. For the
Efiks, the school was supplementary, a means of
improving their performance in the palm-oil
business. As usually happens, the African view
prevailed. While there were a number of
distinguished exceptions, the church in Calabar was
not noted for the development of a native elite.

THE HOPE WADDELL TRAINING INSTITUTION

     For thirty years the church managed with a
system which, while it might have done something in
the way of Christian instruction, was not notably
successful by the standards of public education.
But after 1878, missionary thinking began to move

towards something more serious. On the one hand, there were men like Asuquo Ekanem and some of the younger missionaries, who were pressing for a general improvement of standards; and on the other, there was the growing interest in industrial or technical education.

Edgerley had suggested the introduction of technical education as early as 1878, indicating possibilities in carpentry, brickmaking, and bricklaying.[5] The Presbytery endorsed the idea, but the Board hesitated at the prospect of heavy costs. At this point, the deputation sent out to settle the Anderson-Ross dispute expressed some alarm at the state of the mission real estate and suggested the appointment of carpenters to the mission staff to maintain the buildings and also do something in the way of training apprentices. The Board preferred this cheaper solution and, if anything at all came of Edgerley's idea, it came through the apprentices trained in the 1880s by the mission carpenters, who became more numerous by the end of the decade.

During the 1880s, pressure for educational reform came from the men who wanted a better literary education, and little was heard of technical training until James Luke and Mary Slessor raised the question again in 1891-1892. Buchanan was interested, asking for more details, but no action was taken until Claude Macdonald, the High Commissioner, offered £200 a year for industrial education. With some prospect of sound financing, the Board decided to go ahead.

Two separate lines of reasoning, therefore, went into the founding of the Hope Waddell Training

Institution, and both were reflected in Buchanan's justification of the new venture before the church. One argument held that the ordinary day schools of the mission were inadequately staffed and, therefore, teacher training was essential. The other argument claimed that unemployment was a major problem in Calabar; young men were sitting about because the palm-oil business and farming could not absorb them all, while at the same time skilled workers had to be imported from the outside. It is significant that the second argument appeared particularly convincing in the years right after the protectorate was established and created a demand for tradesmen with European skills.[6] The Hope Waddell Training Institution did not spring directly from missionary policy. It was a creative response to a new situation.

Buchanan therefore proposed that students should go to the new institution after three years in school, first for a period of three years for training in both literary and industrial skills, at the end of which they would be divided into technical and teaching streams.[7] It was logical and orderly, typically Buchanan, but nothing ever works out as planned. Hope Waddell began to get underway in 1894, a year before the buildings were formally occupied. Three industrial departments were started at once: printing, carpentry, and engineering, to which were soon added bricklaying and tailoring. The women of the staff ran a small but successful bakery course on the side. By 1899 the institution had 136 pupils of various sorts, starting with a day school of 75 or 80 boys getting a general education, from which they would advance

either into a field like teacher training or into
one of the trades. For a pioneer venture, starting
from scratch in 1893, it was not a bad effort.

In another sense, Hope Waddell was Buchanan's
biggest mistake in Calabar. He poured men and
money into it; and while W. R. Thomson, the Jamaica
missionary he had called in as superintendent, was
able to use them, it was at considerable cost. Of
the twenty appointments in the first ten years of
the school's life, half resigned within a few years
over conditions of service. Calabar is a hot and
humid place, and it may be, as Buchanan's
predecessor remarked, that the connection between
temper and temperature is not simply etymological.
Nor does Thomson seem to have been the easiest man
in the world to work with. The trials of living in
a pioneer institution were not helped by the trials
of living with a difficult superintendent.

To make matters worse, Thomson was a new man
in charge of a new institution which was growing by
leaps and bounds, while the district staff was
actually shrinking. Naturally the field
missionaries regarded these developments with some
alarm and used a number of constitutional
obscurities in the institution's position to engage
in something like a running battle with this brash
newcomer. In 1901 the difficulties came to a head
in a major row after which the superintendent
resigned ostensibly for medical reasons. The
Foreign Missions Committee was now in the clear,
for despite his undoubted services, Thomson had
been an irritant. Drastic reforms of some kind
were urgent, for Sir Ralph Moor was threatening to
cut off the subsidy if the school were not put on

its feet. James Luke was recalled from Jamaica and
the superintendent, as Moor had suggested, was made
directly responsible to Edinburgh. With Luke's
arrival and the new arrangements the Foreign
Missions Committee and Moor made in 1902, the
fortunes of Hope Waddell took a turn for the
better.[8]

Luke lasted only five years until blackwater
fever drove him back to Jamaica. He was succeeded
by J. K. Macgregor, one of the most outstanding of
the twentieth century missionaries. Macgregor
joined the staff in 1905 and was principal from
1907 until his death in 1943. In his care, the
institution grew from a promising, comprehensive
school into one of the best examples of its class
in Nigeria. In 1907 he had 170 pupils; in the
1920s, including the satellite schools, it was
around 1,000. Even though it suffered somewhat
during the depression, the roll was back to 911 in
1939.

In these years the industrial training
departments did not grow a great deal. Most of
their work was connected with the church: the
apprentice carpenters learned their trade making
houses and furniture for the mission and for the
churches; the engineering department was primarily
concerned with maintaining the mission's river
craft and could not expand, despite the increasing
number of motor cars, for lack of money. The
printing department probably had a somewhat wider
clientele, but even then, as Macgregor remarked in
the 1930s all profits tended downward and, at best,
were very low.[9] The most significant developments
in the Hope Waddell Training Institution during

Macgregor's long tenure were in teacher training
and in secondary school teaching.

Teacher training had been an element in the
church's thinking about Hope Waddell since the
1880s, but apparently not in the government's. In
the negotiations of 1901-1902 the government was
interested in the primary, secondary, and
industrial training departments, while the Foreign
Missions Committee added that it wanted the school
to train "teachers, pastors and evangelists," a
concern with which the government expressed "entire
acquiescence."[10]   But things took a long time to
happen. In 1906 Luke was still warning that unless
post-primary classes were developed, "our senior
boys will pass into other hands." In 1907 some
boys were being taken on as pupil teachers, but not
until 1910 did the first class of fully certified
teachers graduate. By 1913 locating the graduates
was one of the Council's regular chores, and by
1924 Hope Waddell was graduating more than the
Council could use. It was not, said Macgregor,
because the country didn't need them, but because
of government parsimony. The way the grant system
worked, villages hesitated before taking the major
step into the more sophisticated, but more
expensive, category which would entitle them to a
certified teacher and, paradoxically, government
assistance.[11]   But a new day was about to dawn.
The next few years saw a major reform in African
education, with more government money, and at the
beginning of the depression, Macgregor found
himself calling for more staff and more buildings
to meet the new requirements.

Part of the new expansion was in the secondary department. As long as Standard Six, the last class in primary school, was a guarantee of a job, pressure for higher academic classes was not great. Nevertheless, a few were interested, and the secondary school grew gradually with the growth of demand. In 1923 the first candidate sat for and passed the Cambridge School Certificate, which was entirely in arts subjects. Science was introduced with the arrival of the first science graduate in 1930, and a few years later, the Secondary Department got is own building.[12]

The teaching staff between the world wars consisted of any number up to thirty. In the industrial training departments, there were three or four carpenters, an engineer, a printer, and, until 1916, a tailor. The Normal College and the schools, both primary and secondary, had a varying number of Nigerians, two or three Jamaicans, and three or four Europeans, including the principal. In the 1930s the addition of science teaching meant an additional European. The backbone of the staff consisted of Macgregor, E. B. Jones, and the Jamaicans. Jamaicans had served in the nineteenth century at various times and in various ways, but their contribution in the twentieth century was confined to teaching. Europeans might come and go, but both N. A. Sinclair and F. A. Foster served for over thirty years, and Manderson Jones served for more than twenty years. The only Europeans with tenure comparable to these men were Macgregor and E. B. Jones.

The Hope Waddell Training Institution had been intended as a school where the most promising boys from the districts would be given a more sophisticated education than was available at home and return as teachers, ministers, or evangelists. At the same time, it was expected to produce a generation of Christian artisans. Because of Dean's work, theological training was never taken up, but by and large the other objectives were achieved. At first, of course, the district school system hardly existed; most of the students were those enlisted by the government. But as the church developed, an increasing number of the students came from the Presbyterian schools, and the last of the government wards left in 1945.

A great many boys who went through the institution were never seen again, for the pressures on the income of an educated man in Nigeria are considerable and many could not resist the temptation of higher salaries in government or other employment. But the two generations of students who went through Hope Waddell in Macgregor's time and down to the late 1960s were the backbone of the church in teaching and, in some cases, in the ministry. These were the men who had learned to be Christian teachers or, at the very least, to be Christians at Hope Waddell--the men who could sit by the hour and tell stories of their principal in a way that showed their affection and respect. Few men have done more to make Christian Africans than J. K. Macgregor.

THE REVOLUTION IN THE PRIMARY SCHOOLS

Just as government initiatives were of decisive importance in the early history of Hope Waddell, the Presbyterian decision to cooperate with government policy led to a revolution in the primary schools. As already noted, the schools run in Calabar during the nineteenth century could hardly be considered as units in a system of public education; they were ancillary to the church-- agencies of Christian instruction. A government report in 1900 made this point quite clear. The government, it said, wanted schools to make useful citizens, while the churches wanted them to make converts. The result of mission endeavour in this area was that after fifty years of education in Calabar and thirty in Bonny, the government still had to import clerks from Sierra Leone. The inference was obvious: radical changes were necessary if the church wanted to retain any share in education.[13] Edinburgh, with encouragement from men like W. R. Thomson, agreed to go ahead; education henceforth was to bear some resemblance to recognized standards.

One approach, albeit a little belated, was the formation of the Normal School at the Hope Waddell Institution. A second was the improvement of the schools in Calabar, Duke Town, and Creek Town. At first the mission used Europeans, but after 1904 they began recruiting Jamaicans. There were Jamaicans at Creek Town from 1904 to 1929 and at Duke Town from Hart's appointment in 1905 until the departure of F. E. Jones in 1952. Of these men, Samuel Mordecai Hart was undoubtedly the most important. Duke Town had the makings of a good school when Hart went there, and in his care it went ahead by leaps and bounds. Even before the end of the First World War, he was thinking of adding a secondary department. It was actually

begun a few years later. In 1927 Sir Hugh
Clifford, the governor of Nigeria, was quoted in
the annual report as saying that Duke Town School
was the finest institution of it kind in the
country. Missionary literature is inclined from
time to time to be disparaging about the Jamaicans
and Sierra Leonians who served in West Africa. No
doubt there were failures; the Presbyterian
experience was not entirely happy, just as the
occasional missionary was far from what one might
want. But the church has no reason to regret its
Jamaican connection, and every reason to be
thankful for men like S. M. Hart.

Calabar was some ten years ahead of most of
the church. In the other districts, the church-
school system did not begin to develop until after
the Arochuku Expedition, and one could not
reasonably expect a full-grown educational system
to appear overnight out of the bush. The ground
was not staked out until 1920, and shortly
afterwards signs of professional teaching begin to
appear. In 1923, for example, Mr. O. Mkpanam, a
new graduate from the Hope Waddell Training
Institution, was posted to Ididep, a village in
Ibiono not far from Itu. Mkpanam's work was to
bring some sort of order into the vernacular
schools. In his view, they were only apologies for
schools, and in the fashion that later became
orthodox, he centralized the system around one
town, leaving a bit of vernacular teaching where
necessary, but only as a feeder to the main
school.[14] Such reforms were common wherever
graduate teachers were posted. But 1926 fifteen
Hope Waddell graduates had gone to Ohafia and

another twenty, to Unwana district. The system was
a long way from satisfactory, but at least it was
improving.

Improvement was essential. The British
penetration of Africa had brought the largest area
of tribal culture in the world into close contact
with the urban and industrial West. The major
agency of positive cultural contact between the two
was the school, and schools in Africa were almost
exclusively a missionary preserve. In 1923 the
Conference of Missionary Societies in Great Britain
and Ireland pressed the British government for a
statement of policy on African education and, after
considerable discussion at a senior level, were
given the Memorandum on Educational Policy in
British Tropical Africa of 1925, outlining
government policy in terms with which the
Presbyterians could have no serious objection.[15]

The first fruit of the reform was the doubling
of the course for teachers; the second was the
appointment of the first education supervisor. The
Council was interested in such an appointment from
the beginning, for such a man could go a long way
towards relieving the chronic staff shortage in
Ibibio country. The Council initially asked for
six, four on the field and two as relief, but had
to settle for one, J. M. Lewars, a young minister
with teaching qualifications who had first come to
the country in 1926. In 1928 he was appointed
supervisor of schools in Ibibio country,
responsible only for the improvement of classroom
standards. Cruickshank remained manager, handling
the financial and clerical work, hiring and firing
staff. In a few years Lewars extended his services

to Ohafia and Unwana, but Uburu and Calabar
districts, under more conservative missionaries,
resisted his offers. Lewars's appointment was
undoubtedly a good one; until 1960 he was the major
figure in Presbyterian education, presiding over
its fortunes in the hectic days in the 1950s,
remaining, until the eve of the civil war, one of
the most knowledgeable and formidable figures in
education in the old Eastern Region.

The 1920s, then, were an important period in
Presbyterian education. The pioneer period was
over and the time for consolidation and improvement
had begun. Improvement inevitably meant
professionalization and the gradual separation of
the school from the church, the two agencies which
in the pioneer days had been inseparable. (At the
same time the church was growing and congregational
life, at least in some places, was taking on a
character of its own.) Similarly, the economic and
social conditions under which the schools had been
founded were passing away, and although Nigerian
development was slowed down by the Depression,
after the Second World War it went ahead at a rate
that brought significant changes to both the Hope
Waddell Training Institution and the country school
system.

EDUCATION FOR A NEW NIGERIA

Hope Waddell Training Institution: The war
years were hard on the institution. Macgregor died
in 1943, E. B. Jones left in 1944, and Manderson
Jones, the last of the veteran Jamaicans, in 1946.
Two Europeans were lost at sea and the headmaster
died in Lagos in 1945. Nigerians with more than

the regular Normal School training were hard to
find and harder to keep on the staff, and the
others were not encouraged by a definite reluctance
to give them more than classroom responsibility.
Jones succeeded Macgregor briefly as principal, and
when he left the responsibility for the institution
fell on N. C. Macrae, a new missionary whose
principal qualification for the job was that he had
attended a boarding school in England.[16] Macrae
promptly went off to take a course in education in
London and returned to start a new era with the
assistance of a novelty in the institution's
history, a board of governors.

Although Macrae's tenure at Hope Waddell was
not an altogether happy one, his few years as
principal saw a series of far-reaching changes.
When he came the school was much as it had been in
1923, apart from the introduction of science
teaching in the 1930s. It was still a training
institution, from Infant I to School Certificate,
plus the industrial training departments and
teacher training. When he left teaching training
had been moved to a separate institution in another
location and the primary school had been phased
out. On the other hand, the first serious attempts
had been made to teach Higher School, the standard
required for university entrance.

These developments were in response to two
separate changes. On the one hand, the growth of
primary schools in Calabar and elsewhere in the
Presbyterian area made a special school at Hope
Waddell redundant. It was dropped by cutting off
the intake in the lower classes until the last
students left in 1951. The Normal College, on the

other hand, had come under some rather severe criticism for being divorced from conditions in the country schools. As early as 1945, a rural location for the Teacher Training College was under discussion, and in 1951 the whole department moved to Afikpo to begin a new phase in its life as Macgregor College, under the enterprising leadership of Chima Oji, the first Nigerian graduate teacher.

Behind the phasing out of the primary school was the rising demand for secondary education and the pressure of competition from the Roman Catholics. In 1949 the decision was made to start a Higher School course the following year, but only in arts subjects and with no guarantee that it would be offered in the second year of the normal two-year course. The problem, of course, was staff. The mission cast its net widely, but without much success, and the board told the Foreign Missions Committee that it was "essential that Protestant students in Eastern Nigeria have facilities for such a course in 1951 and that it would seriously affect the institution if the course could not be continued that year."[17] The course could not be carried on, though an effort was made at coaching for the Ibadan University entrance exam. Three years elapsed before the Higher School course in both the arts and sciences became a standard feature of the Hope Waddell curriculum.

The Higher School depended on staff, and staff was a chronic problem. Missionary personnel did not vary a great deal in the 1950s, with between five and seven officially on staff. The number

fell to two in the early 1960s, when the senior men
were drafted to start new secondary schools. The
demand for graduate teachers was met in part
through missionary wives, in part through the use
of expatriate volunteers, and in part through the
appearance of the first Nigerian graduates after
1954. The new Board began discussing the
possibility of a scholarship scheme at its first
meeting in 1946. It made the first award in 1948.
In the years between 1946 and 1954 seven men were
under active consideration: one entered the
ministry and the other six were given either full
scholarships or, more usually, supplements to
government awards for a short course or a degree.
Of these six men one failed, one went to Macgregor,
and the remaining four came back to staff. One of
them, B. E. Okon, became the principal following
Dr. Akanu Ibiam.[18] After the formation of the
Advanced Training Fund in 1958, which handled
scholarships for higher and technical education for
the whole church, a separate Hope Waddell scheme
was no longer necessary. The institution continued
to receive graduates, with the same mixed results.
People usually came, but they didn't always stay.
Calabar was a declining town in the 1950s and
1960s, and the grass, as always, was greener across
the river.

While the secondary school was going ahead,
the technical departments were in decline.
Printing and bookbinding continued to do reasonably
well, but the other departments found themselves in
increasingly serious difficulty. Brocket, who was
in charge of carpentry from 1922 to 1932, had
responded to changing tastes by starting furniture-

making, and developing the craft until it became a
mainstay of the department. But in the late 1950s
one could buy standard household furnishings more
cheaply in the market. The real expansion of this
department was in the area of building, for as
money from public sources became more available in
the 1950s, the church's institutions were expanding
and new ones were going up. A great deal of this
work was outside Calabar altogether, and the
training of apprentices became increasingly
difficult. The engineering department had become
little more than a maintenance department for the
Diamond, the mission's riverboat, and the
missionary cars. If it were to give a real
training, it would need heavy capital investment,
which was not likely to be forthcoming, and in any
case, other agencies were already in or were
entering the field. As long as the Diamond was
running and the upriver stations depended on Hope
Waddell for automobile servicing, the maintenance
of the department made sense. But in 1958 it
transpired that the Diamond needed extensive
repairs, and the Council decided that, with the
development of road transport, the riverboat was no
longer needed. At the same time, it was becoming
easier to get the mission cars serviced in Aba or
Enugu than in Calabar. The engineering department,
like carpentry, had served its purpose. The
engineer moved up to Itu at the beginning of 1963
to take over the extensive plant at Itu Leper
Colony, and the two builders transferred to the
church to undertake some of the numerous
construction jobs that were being planned.

Hope Waddell in the 1960s was a very different place from the distracted institution Macrae had taken over fourteen years earlier. In 1946 it was a training institution of a standard Scottish missionary type. In 1963 it had become a straightforward boys' residential secondary school. In 1951 it was dominated by the European staff. In 1961 B. E. Okon became the second Nigerian principal. Okon inherited from Ibiam a strong staff, both Nigerian and expatriate—a staff that could work together, ending the personal tensions which had plagued the institution as late as 1959. The 1960s were happy years for Hope Waddell: extracurricular performance was creditable, examination results were good, and the physical plant was well on the way to thorough overhaul.[19] For over fifty years Hope Waddell had been central institution in the church's life; if the 1960s were to be its last years, they were good ones.

The Halycon Years: The process of specialization in primary education, which began with the appointment of the education supervisor, bore further fruit during the Education Conference. The conference also marked the first entry of the Nigerian teachers into the general management of the system. The more articulate teachers pressed steadily for more representation, and in 1944 they finally got a response in the first steps taken towards the formation of the Education Authority.[20]

The crucial vote in May 1944 was a close one. Harry Hastings, the doctor at Uburu, wanted to hand over the primary schools to the local council when the time came. R. M. Macdonald moved that an

education authority for the church be formed
forthwith. Macdonald's motion carried four to
three with two abstentions, but the division
followed none of the traditional north-south or
old-young patterns. The Council then referred the
constitution of the new body back to committee,
stipulating that its membership should include the
managers of schools, principals of institutions,
and strong representation from the Synod and the
teachers. The huge increase in Nigerian
representation was a major advance, as was the
decision, at the suggestion of the Foreign Missions
Committee, to make the Education Authority the
proprietor of schools--the legal managing body.
The final organization of the Education Authority
in 1946 meant that the school system was both
formally and potentially in Nigerian hands:
formally, because in 1949 thirty-six out of fifty-
four members were Nigerian, and potentially because
almost all the key people--secretary, treasurer,
seven out of eight managers and three out of four
principals--were missionaries.[21]

Nevertheless it was a significant step, and
typically it came as a missionary response to
Nigerian conditions: "It was mainly a matter of
principle. Although the Mission Council rarely
exercised this controlling authority [over the
Education Conference] this controlling authority
was quite evidently incompatible with a developing
country and with people developing in ability and
responsibility."[22]

It was not quite as simple as that. Nigerian
teachers had been pressing for more representation
in the running of the school system for many years,

and in 1946 the nationalist movement was underway. The missionary community accepted what was both desirable in principle--their own principles--and inevitable in practice--the devolution of its responsibilities upon the Nigerian church.

The Education Authority was the framework within which the changes of the postwar years took place. African education again became a subject for discussion in the 1940s and the new interest was soon reflected in more and more government intervention. At the same time, the development of the country fostered both the rapid growth of educational institutions and the nationalist movement. Over the next twenty years the Education Authority's work grew by leaps and bounds and, at the same time, passed almost entirely into Nigerian hands.

Increased government interest meant more rules, and the District Missionaries, who were above all else managers of schools, soon found that the job was getting out of hand. Paper work piled up in all directions and constant supervision was essential to avoid costly mistakes.[23] But the staff of District Missionaries remained constant at nine or ten. At one time a man could manage a second district when a colleague went on leave, but by the end of the 1940s if a man had two districts, or if a district fell to an inexperienced missionary, the results could be disastrous. In 1949 the Foreign Missions Committee sent out Neil Bernard, an old Calabar hand, as a special commissioner, and his recommendations set in motion the Nigerianization of management in rural schools. Since the District Missionary's main job was

managing schools, the office disappeared entirely.
In 1950 E. E. Esien was made the first supervising
teacher, a euphemism for manager, east of the Cross
River, and the following year, two of the major
districts were in Nigerian hands, one of the new
men being Usang Iso. By 1954 all the districts
except Abakaliki had been transferred and that
followed, albeit belatedly, in 1963.

In the same years and for much the same
reasons, the major institutions passed into
Nigerian hands. The vocational school at Ididep
had a Nigerian principal in 1949. Edgerley
Memorial School went to Mrs. N. E. Inyang in 1951,
the same year as Chima Oji started Macgregor
College. Duke Town Secondary School had a Nigerian
principal from the time it was detached from the
primary school, and the rash of teacher training
colleges that appeared in the 1950s were all led by
senior Nigerian teachers. The last bastions of
missionary control were the Hope Waddell Training
Institution and Slessor Memorial School in
Arochuku. The first went to Akanu Ibiam in 1957
and the second to Bassey Itam in 1961. In 1960
Usang Iso succeeded Jack Lewars as secretary of the
Education Authority. In the last years of the
period, the only senior positions still held by
missionaries were the general managership, the
treasurer's office, and the principalships of two
of the new secondary schools. The two principals
were appointed because they were senior graduates
and also because, as Iso said, they could make
bricks without straw. By the mid-1960s missionary
authority, if not influence, was a thing of the
past.

Parallel to the indigenization of the system was a belated but reasonably successful attempt to raise the academic qualifications of the staff. The program began in 1943 with Chima Oji and continued in a small way for fifteen years, with heavy reliance on the ability of the candidate to get a government award. In 1958 after some prodding from Akanu Ibiam, the Synod adopted a comprehensive scheme called the Advanced Training Fund, financed by a voluntary salary contribution of two pence per pound. It called for applications in 1959 and awarded scholarships of all sorts and sizes until it ran out of money in 1965. By that time, seventeen people had finished and returned to service, while twenty-five more were still studying. Just under half were financed by overseas funds or government awards. The rest were the sole responsibility of the church. Not all, of course, but the majority of these people were from the educational system.

The 1950s also saw an enormous expansion of the facilities for teacher training. The subject had been under discussion in the 1940s, but wars and staff shortages held up progress. Some action was obviously needed; in 1947 only about half the teachers outside of Calabar were trained people, and the only sources of new trained teachers were the Normal College at Hope Waddell and the Presbyterian share of places at the Women's Training College at Umuahia. The first step was the founding of Macgregor College. Chima Oji was not a man to let the grass grow under his feet. He started with one class of about thirty men in a two-year course, and in 1965 he had a graduating

class of eighty from a four-year course. In the
same period a series of new colleges were started
with money from the government, and by the end of
the period there were four higher elementary
colleges giving a four-year course: Macgregor,
Creek Town, Ididep, and Arochuku. In 1952 the
maximum number of graduating teachers would have
been thirty from Macgregor, whoever was at the
Women's Training College, and perhaps a few others.
In 1965 the Presbyterian institutions alone
expected to graduate 146, with 36 more finishing at
other colleges.

At the same time as teacher training colleges
were appearing, patient and protracted negotiations
for the founding of secondary schools were
underway. Government money was more readily
available for teaching training than for secondary
schools, and the Presbyterians, both as a matter of
principle and because their funds were short,
insisted that they would undertake no new secondary
schools without substantial local support. In the
1950s many places were considered, but in the end
only three materialized: Itam, Afikpo, and
Abakaliki. Even when they were finally started
they were not easy to manage, for no government
grants were forthcoming for the first five years.
A good deal of the credit for these schools must go
to men like Iso, whose patient committee work
brought them into being.

With all this growth the Presbyterian Church,
a community of less than 20,000 people, was
managing, at the outbreak of the civil war, five
secondary schools, four teacher training colleges,
three boarding schools, and over two hundred

primary schools. Additionally, it had a share in
the secondary school for girls at Ibiaku and the
Women's Training College at Umuahia. The annual
budget ran to more than £250,000 a year, most of
which was paid in cash. Okon Effiong, the chief
clerk, used to travel the Cross River valley with
thousands of pounds in single notes under the seat
of a Land Rover. The risk of loss through theft
was considerable, and while there were a few
significant embezzlements, the most serious dangers
were a mistake in calculating grants so that a
teacher was paid for a year and given no grant, or
no the full grant, or a kindly manager failing to
close a school until it was hopelessly in debt.

The schools were financed from two sources:
government grants and local contributions, which
could be school free, a community subvention, or
both. Only careful handling of the two sources
could keep a school going. The central
administration, the managers, and the general
manager's office, with its battery of bookkeepers,
was badly underfinanced. The Education Authority
never had money to spare, but in 1962 a combination
of inflation and restrictions in government grants
made the situation almost impossible. At that
point, the Forward Movement was founded.

The Forward Movement was intended to be a call
to the church to advance. It had two aspects: the
deepening of the church's spiritual life, and a
levy on all employees' salaries of a shilling per
pound. Members not on the church's salary lists
were expected to contribute at the same rate.
While its work in establishing prayer groups proved
to be the more permanent feature of the movement's

program, the immediate result was an almost 400
percent increase in the church's budget, a large
slice of which went into education.[24]

In the three years of its existence, the
Forward Movement was a real boon to the Synod. For
the first and probably only time in its history,
the church's finances were on a sound footing. But
for the Education Authority, the new money was not
enough. Things continued to get worse, and in
February 1964 the standing committee seriously
debated closing down the primary schools. But, as
usual, the crisis was averted. The government
eased its restrictions and communities began to pay
their arrears. But the trouble, shared by all the
churches, does seem to have precipitated the
government's decision to take over the schools.

The government was not anti-church. The
permanent secretary in the Ministry of Education
was N. U. Akpan, an elder in St. Andrews Enugu and,
from 1965, chairman of the Synod's budget
committee. Nor was the church, in principle,
averse to the change. The Foreign Missions
Committee sometimes talked as if a government
takeover of the schools was both necessary and
desirable, but Lewars insisted that a premature
handover would mean, not a secular system, but a
Roman Catholic one. Unless the government was
ready with a comprehensive program for operating
the school system, the Catholics would simply move
into the vacuum. A Roman Catholic intrusion into
schools previously operated by the Presbyterians
would be a disaster.[25] As the schools went, so
went the church. No school, no church--it was as
simple as that.

It all had a familiar ring. Just as in 1900, in 1960 church and school could not be separated. The church had entered village after village because it could offer schools--schools which were not clearly distinguished from the church. But from the day the Presbyterians decided to accept government grants, a gradual distinction between church and school became inevitable. J. K. Macgregor, one of the few missionaries who put his educational ideas on paper, saw clearly that the acceptance of government grants opened the door to secularization, but he thought it was worth the risk. The inspectors did mean better work, and, in any case, the basic dynamic in missionary education was "Christian character-formed acting on Christian character-forming."[26] This kind of face-to-face intimacy between teacher and student and between missionary and teacher might have been possible in 1911, or even as late as 1937, but in the tumultuous years after 1950 it was not.

The dominant feature of the 1950s and 1960s was crisis. The church seemed to stumble from one emergency to another--emergencies usually brought on by rapid growth. The Presbyterians were running at full speed to keep up with the country's expansion in the face of stiff Roman Catholic competition. If they did not provide schools, the Catholics would. For many of the younger missionaries, the process seemed more than a little strange. The Synod was putting £10,000 a year into the Education Authority, which was opening secondary schools from Abakaliki to Itu. In the meantime, city churches were left unbuilt for lack of money.[27] Nor could it really be argued that the

schools were an effective form of evangelism.
Their only apparent justification was as a public
service. Surely the tail had come to wag the dog.

But the senior men, whether Scottish or
Nigerian, thought otherwise. When Usang Iso took
over the leadership of the Education Authority in
1960, he followed much the same policy as Lewars,
though with more enthusiasm. Where Lewars had
fostered teacher training colleges, Iso encouraged
secondary schools. The country was growing up and
its school system had to grow with it. In Nigerian
eyes, however, the problem was only partly one of
ecclesiastical competition. More fundamentally,
the school justified the church. The school
provided the means of social mobility, of "getting
on." Though it was put in apparently materialistic
terms, such motives are never entirely secular--
certainly not in Africa. The schools were not just
a means to making money; they were the means by
which people could realize their full potential as
human beings. They were, therefore, one of the
major reasons for the church's existence. The
young missionaries might shake their heads and
wonder, but the church would discharge its
responsibilities.[28]

In 1964, when the church seemed in such
parlous straits, one of the young missionaries
romantically described it as a "servant church."
It would be easy to get carried away with the
church's dogged determination to maintain and
expand its schools. Motives are always mixed.
Combined with a real concern for education was a
great deal of pride and an unthinking acceptance of
the inheritance received. But regardless of

motivation, the Presbyterians taught school for
seventy years, and as the Nigerian leadership
became more prominent, they taught at higher
levels. In those seventy years they made a major
contribution to the transformation of life in the
Cross River valley, for it was the schools that
enabled thousands of young people to respond
creatively to the new world which the British
conquest had thrust upon them.

Chapter 6

RELIGION AND LITERATURE

[1] H. M. Waddell, _Twenty-Nine Years in the West Indies and Central Africa_, 1.

[2] Somerville to Goldie, February 2, 1948; Waddell, _Twenty-Nine Years_, 348; _The Record_, June 1849, June 1852.

[3] UPMB, November 25, 1879.

[4] Ibid.

[5] Ibid., November 4, 1878; _Presbytery_, May 21, 1879; UPMB, August 4, 1879.

[6] _The Record_, January 1892; May 1893. The 1892 article is simply signed "One of the Zenana Staff." Its attribution to Mary Slessor appears to derive from J. T. Dean's revision of Goldie's _Calabar and its Mission_.

[7] _The Record_, May 1893.

[8] This is the origin of the special status of the Hope Waddell Training Institution. It was not finally reintegrated into the church's structure until the 1960s. For the relation between government and Hope Waddell in this period, see A. E. Afigbo, "The Background to the Southern Nigerian Education Code of 1903," _Journal of the Historical Society of Nigeria_ 4, no. 2 (June 1968).

[9] _Council_, 1933, Report of the Devolution Committee.

10 FMC, October 22, 1901.

11   FMC,   Report   to   General   Assembly,
Proceedings of the General Assembly of the Church
of Scotland, 1925.

12 N. C. Macrae, The Book of the First Sixty
Years, 41, 45.

13 UPMB, September 25, 1900. It is typical of
the period that nobody questioned the inspector's
analysis. The basic reason for the shortage of
clerks in Calabar was not the weakness of mission
policy, but the entirely rational Efik response to
missionary schooling. The Efiks took out of it
what they could use for their own purposes, and
obviously training to be a clerk in a government
office which did not exist was not high on their
priorities.

14 Notes on a conversation with Mr. Mkpanam,
1965.

15 J. H. Oldham, "Educational Policy of the
British Government in Africa," International Review
of Missions 14 (1923), 421-427.

16 S. Holbourn, Chief Inspector of Education,
Eastern Provinces, Inspection Report, October 1945;
and conversation with N. C. Macrae, 1977.

17 HWTI, December 6, 1949.

18 Dr. Akanu (Sir Francis) Ibiam was one of
the first Igbo doctors. He had founded Abiriba
Hospital, worked at both Itu and Uburu, spent some
time in early nationalist politics, and become
involved in many worthy activities before he was
appointed principal of Hope Waddell in 1957. He
was there until his appointment as governor of
Eastern Nigeria in 1960.

[19] Conversation with R. G. Browne, 1977.

[20] Council, October 1943.

[21] Education Authority, Minutes, October 1949.

[22] Conversation with A. K. Mincher, 1977.

[23]   Conversation   with   the   district
missionaries, 1977.

[24] Synod, January 1962. Financing by levies
or assessments had been practised since the early
days of the Students' and Pastors' Fund. It had
been adopted when the Synod Central Fund for the
payment of ministers was started in 1946 as the
means of raising funds for Advanced Training, and
was common practice among clan associations in the
Presbyterian area.

[25] Council, October 1959.

[26] Conference of Missions, Minutes, 1911, 29.

[27] E. F. Roberts, Annual Report, 1964; and
W. F. McLean to E. H. Johnson, March 26, 1963.

[28] See discussion in chapter 2, p. 63.

Chapter 7

TO HEAL THE SICK

HEWAN AND ROBERTSON

Medical work in the Calabar mission originated as a device to keep the missionaries alive. The Niger Expedition of 1841 lost a third of its European membership in a single season, and while the Calabar people never suffered to that degree, sickness was a constant fact of life. The idea of a doctor on the staff was first suggested in 1848, but it was not until 1854 that an acceptable candidate, Archibald Hewan, a young Jamaican who had just earned his diploma from the Royal College of Surgeons, was hired.

The Mission Board's instructions to Hewan stated clearly that his first responsibility was to the missionaries, and that only as he had the opportunity was he to "attend to the natives" in the hope that his successful ministrations would tend to "dispose them to listen with more favour to the instructions of the missionaries."[1] Although the Board was not altogether consistent on this point, it is safe to say that concern for missionary health was the major factor in the appointment of both Dr. Hewan and Dr. J. Robertson.

Between them, the two men were on the field from 1855 to 1873, during most of which time the medical station was at Old Town. We know next to nothing of their work. While their first responsibility was to the missionaries, they did some work among the sailors, and Hewan, at least, had ample time to build up a practice in Calabar. By 1861 he had a small mud hospital and was busy walking about the farms trying to attract business. In 1863 he prescribed for between 1,400 and 1,500 out-patients,[2] but since he did not always use the same system of recording his patients, it is impossible to say whether that was a good year or not. At the very least, he was on his way to building up a solid practice. Unfortunately, he had to leave on medical grounds in 1865. Robertson followed him in 1868, but in 1871 a staff crisis forced his transfer to Ikunetu, a place he regarded as useless as a medical station. He resigned when his tour of duty was over.

For the next seventeen years, the missionaries had to rely on the medical people serving the European traders, and on their own skill. Some of them, notably S. H. Edgerley, developed quite a reasonable competence, and they seem to have been lucky. During the tenures of Hewan and Robertson in Calabar, there were eleven deaths among a staff that averaged thirteen. Between 1873 and 1890, the staff averaged around fifteen and only three died, but after the doctors came back, between 1890 and 1900, there were seventeen deaths among a staff that averaged around thirty. Such figures prove nothing about the competence of the nineteenth-century doctors. They may well have been working with a higher rate of disease generally than had been the case in the 1880s. But the death rate does indicate that the provision of doctors was at best a partial solution to the problem of keeping

Victorian missionaries alive. A doctor's
effectiveness depends on the resources the
profession has put at his disposal, and in the
nineteenth century, those resources were by modern
standards very limited. The fortunes of the
medical work in the twentieth century varied
directly with the development of medical science.

THE FOUNDING OF THE HOSPITALS

The deputies sent out to settle the Anderson-
Ross dispute reported that the missionaries were
anxious to see the medical work reinstated. They
had not found the European doctors altogether
satisfactory; they were inclined to be expensive,
did not always respond readily to calls out of
town, and would not treat the African staff. If
the mission had its own doctor, doctors' bills
could be avoided, and with capable management a
dispensary might even become self-supporting. In
addition, the deputies added, a doctor could be a
good influence on the general population.[3] It was
easier said than done. They managed to find a
dispenser in 1885 but no doctors until 1890. At
this time there were stations up as far as Unwana,
but a recent war between Calabar and Enyong had
shown how tenuous communications could become. The
mission needed not one doctor but two, and in 1891
the Missionary Society of the United Presbyterian
College undertook the equipping of a medical
station at Unwana.

The Unwana hospital does not seem to have been
significantly different from Hewan's establishment
in Old Town, except that it was frequently vacant.
Peter Rattray served there from 1898 until 1906,

apart from the two years he spent relieving at the
Hope Waddell Institution and incidentally serving
on the Arochuku Expedition. His hospital was a
simple mud building and he had little if any
trained assistance. Despite these shortcomings, he
reported over 9,000 outpatients in 1903 and 11,000
in 1904, the largest number any hospital reported
before 1926. These were his peak years. In his
last two years at Unwana his volume dropped to
around 5,000. His patients were usually women and
the complaint was mainly some kind of ulcer.[4] The
station clearly had possibilities, but when Rattray
left in 1906 he was not replaced; medical work in
the north was to be centred in Uburu.

The Calabar station was a little more
complicated. William Rae opened a hospital in
1890, but three years later the government opened
one of their own. The mission then had to decide
whether or not to keep a medical station in Calabar
at all, and after some debate, it decided to
operate a hospital in Creek Town, at least until
the government establishment had proved itself.[5]
The Creek Town hospital, however, was short-lived.
By 1901 the doctor, David Robertson, had so little
business that he could seriously propose dividing
the building up to provide extra living quarters.
Under normal circumstances the Creek Town hospital
would have soon closed down, but the years after
the Arochuku Expedition were not normal. In 1903,
in an attempt to salvage half their medical work
and at the same time post a missionary in Ibibio
country, the Council proposed--and the Foreign
Missions Committee eventually agreed--to moving the
hospital to Itu. In the course of 1905 Robertson

moved himself and his building up the river to
begin a new phase in the church's medical work.

With the transfer of the Calabar hospital in
1905 and the closing of the Unwana medical station
in 1906, the church was left with a single hospital
at Itu. In 1911 the Foreign Missions Committee
persuaded a young English doctor, J. W. Hitchcock,
to try Calabar instead of Manchuria and sent him
out to relieve Robertson. When that job was
finished, Hitchcock was instructed to travel north
and advise on a location for a medical station in
Igbo country. Largely because of the market,
Hitchcock recommended Uburu and settled there in
1912. His house and hospital followed within two
years, and with Uburu permanently established, the
framework of Presbyterian medical work was
complete.

These were the boom years in the church. The
medical work grew, but not nearly to the same
extent. It is true that there were now two
hospitals where previously there had been either
one or none, but the establishments were small and
simple. One man, frequently not relieved, had to
handle all the work involved in medicine and in his
spare time supervise the churches in the districts.
Both hospitals were probably larger than Hewan's.
Itu claimed thirteen beds and Uburu forty, but
otherwise they were essentially the same kind of
operation. The major difference is that all
reference to the care of missionaries had
disappeared. The hospitals had become a service to
the African community.

With Robertson's departure in 1916 and
Hitchcock's death in 1919, this period comes to an

end. There was a short interregnum when Uburu was
closed, but in the early 1920s the two major
figures in Presbyterian medical work, Harry
Hastings and A. B. Macdonald, appeared, and a new
chapter began.

HASTINGS AND MACDONALD

The careers of Hastings and Macdonald began
quietly enough. Macdonald went first to Uburu and
then settled in Mary Slessor Hospital at Itu.
Hastings spent all his life at Uburu. Business was
quiet in the 1920s but growing enough to warrant
the addition of nurses to the Itu establishment.
Then came the campaigns against yaws. Most
children in Nigeria had yaws, and the sores
frequently became infected, often leading to anemia
and debility or, in more extreme cases, to chronic
arthritis. But the 1920s saw the development of an
arsenic compound usually called N.A.B. (novo-
arsenobenzyl), which was effective against both
yaws and syphillis. It was almost a miracle cure:
after one injection, or at the most two, the
children could go home and watch their skin clear
up.

The effect on the hospitals was equally
dramatic. Itu's out-patients jumped from 4,698 in
1925 to 30,061 in 1928; Uburu's went from 4,963 in
1924 to 60,401 in 1928. Over a single weekend in
Abiriba, Hastings gave 6,000 injections. On one
tour Macdonald was giving a thousand a day and
could have given more if his thumb had not given
out. Macdonald charged three shillings and
sixpence for an adult injection, a profit of

sixpence over the cost of the drug. Out of the proceeds, he built a new hospital.

The new hospital was almost incidental. The principal consequence of the yaws campaign was an enormous and permanent expansion of medical practice in the Presbyterian hospitals. No figures are available for Itu, but at Uburu, William Christie, the meticulous District Missionary, carefully recorded the volume of business done year by year at the hospital. In-patient activity was up slightly after the yaws campaign, but the number of out-patients, after falling off when the campaign was over, began to creep up again during the 1930s until, in 1936, it was not far short of the 1928 number.

The contrast with the influenza epidemic in 1918 is instructive. Itu's business increased sharply while the crisis was on but then fell back to a level somewhat above the 1918 rate. While between 1911 and 1917, out-patients averaged about 2,800 a year, between 1923 and 1925 they averaged 4,600 a year, a significant improvement, but partly attributable to an improvement in the staff situation, which allowed the doctor more time to devote to the hospital. But the yaws campaign meant an increase in Uburu's out-patient business by a factor of at least ten.

The campaign was a massive demonstration of the mastery of Western medicine over a disease which had baffled traditional methods. The European doctors were in direct competition with traditional practitioners. They had to show the superiority of their methods before people would patronize the hospital. It didn't happen all at once. Surgery was quickly recognized as a European specialty, and the women of Unwana soon found that Rattray could handle ulcers. The yaws campaign, however, was such a massive success that it carried the prestige of Western medicine into other areas. Just how far success against yaws carried acceptance of Western medicine is impossible to state without detailed hospital statistics, but certainly yaws injections continued to be a major attraction and therefore a major money-maker in the hospitals throughout the 1930s.[6] The enormous increase in business, plus the almost magical aura that came to surround injections, are certainly suggestive of a major breakthrough. And as it turned out, the yaws campaign came at almost the same time as the first significant progress against leprosy.

J. M. Lewars once told of the District Officer in Itu who found on his table one morning an excellent piece of fish. He instructed his steward to convey his compliments to the cook and inquire as to where this delicacy had been found. The lad replied that they had bought it from "dem lepers for de sandbank." The presence of such people was news to the District Officer and news calculated to spoil his breakfast, for it was April and the river was rising.

The report was all too true. There was a rapidly increasing colony of lepers on a rapidly diminishing sandbank in the Cross River waiting for treatment at Mary Slessor Hospital, where Macdonald had begun to use a drug which gave some hope of a cure for a disease widespread and much feared in southern Nigeria. Macdonald had read about it in the British Medical Journal, and when a leper came asking for treatment, he decided to order a supply of hydnocarpous oil, as the drug was called, and try it out. Six months after he began the first treatment, he had 400 lepers on his list. Those who did not live in the district were camped out on the sandbank.

The first problem was land. The lepers had to be moved off the sandbank before they were washed off it. After some difficulty a piece of forest next to the hospital was secured and the colony established, the lepers quickly putting up the usual mud-and-thatch houses. The first crisis was past, but the mission then plunged into a long argument over the suitability of the new site. The argument was not settled, nor was the site finally accepted for almost two years. By this time Macdonald had nearly 1,000 patients, some of whom required almost daily care, but many of whom could be treated with hydnocarpous oil and other drugs twice a week. The less serious cases could almost be treated as out-patients, except that Itu was a pioneer venture and lepers who heard of the place came knocking on the door, even if they lived miles away. Some kind of a colony was essential, and in any case, Macdonald had decided early on what might be called total therapy.

To contract leprosy was a shattering experience, psychologically as well as physically.[7] It was considered to be a social as well as a biological disease. Macdonald therefore tried to heal both body and spirit, the body by twice weekly injections and the spirit by forming a community in which everyone was busy doing something. The

organization of the community fell to the rest of
the European staff, but in the early years
especially to John Paterson, the missionary who had
built the hospital and who was appointed master of
works at the colony in 1930. Under Paterson's
direction the patients cleared the land, sawed up
the trees, and supplied the colony with timber. In
place of what they cut they planted food for
themselves and for those who could not work. Any
palm-oil trees growing wild were declared colony
property, the fruit harvested and the oil sold.
But Paterson also planted new trees, and when they
came into production, the processing and sale of
palm oil became one of the staples of colony
income. Although Paterson had started as a
builder, he rapidly became an agriculturalist as
well, reading all he could find and going to the
government agricultural officers for specialist
advice. Thus in the course of developing the
colony water supply, he also started fish ponds.
In the swamps down by the river he started rice
growing. After reading an article in the Reader's
Digest, of all places, he managed to get soya beans
growing in a country where they do not grow
naturally.[8] Paterson made Macdonald's total
therapy viable because he was able to utilize the
land and the patients to produce a good deal of the
colony's food supply and a cash crop for export.

Paterson, unfortunately, fell out with the
Macdonalds and left the colony in 1942, but he left
behind a functioning system which his successors
continued until the colony's last days. However,
life is not all economics, and certainly not in a
Christian leper colony. The same intensive use of

the patients' skills was applied in every aspect of colony life. Those who were teachers taught in the school. The older children were trained as temperature clerks, while other patients were drawn into administration and the junior ranks of the medical services. In the centre of it all was the massive mud-and-thatch church, capable of seating 3,000, and packed out twice on Sundays and full on Wednesdays. Macdonald's leper colony was an elaborate and expensive solution, but for the thousands who lived there during the forty years of its history, the judgement of Daniel Umo, himself a patient and teacher in the colony school, is undoubtedly valid:

> I had though that I was entering a place of death, but it was not long before I realized how wrong I was. Contrary to my expectations, I found an atmosphere of activity and joy and hope. Everywhere there was laughter. The teachers and pupils enjoyed their work and play. . . . The teachers were given a free portion for their private farms. As gardening was my favourite hobby, I began to be at peace. . . .[9]

Itu Leper Colony was a dramatic response to the possibilities of hydnocarpous oil, but it was not the only one. Hastings could read the British Medical Journal as well and, in 1928 he asked the council for permission to secure land for a leper camp at Uburu. He started with 70 patients, and by 1933 he had 200. In that year he began work on a second clinic at a place called Osu and three years later was in touch with 532 lepers, 197 of whom were in the camp.

Hastings' neighbours were already in the habit of isolating their lepers in separate communities. His approach was to use as far as possible what already existed, leaving the Uburu site only for patients in the neighbourhood and for those who required special treatment in the hospital. Though the system lacked some of the advantages of total therapy, it was cheaper and easier to manage. By 1939 Hastings had about a quarter as many lepers as Macdonald, but he had asked the Council for neither money nor staff. The appearance of the arsenic compound for yaws and hydnocarpous oil for treating leprosy meant an enormous expansion of medical activities, but Hastings handled it with a combination of ingenuity and a junior staff.

The system had its limitations. Hastings opened the Uburu camp in 1928 and Osu in January 1934, but nothing further happened until 1943, when he opened a third centre at Owerri Edda. When this place had been under discussion in 1939, Hastings refused to take it up, arguing that he already had all the work he could handle.[10] But in 1940 the Catholics began to take an active interest in Ogoja leprosy work, and this new dimension in ecclesiastical competition seems to have stirred Hastings into action. Over the next three years the government and the Catholics were in serious correspondence. When Hastings finally heard of it in 1943, he assured the government of his interest, opening three new clinics the next year and bringing the question to the Council in May 1944.[11]

The council's reply was positive but cautious. It had no objection to "wayside clinics" in principle, but it was very unhappy about the way they were administered by the public medical services. If the mission doctors were free to operate them the way they saw fit, the Council was prepared to recommend cooperation with the government's plan to the Foreign Missions Committee. Then followed the usual negotiations leading to the appointment in December 1946 of J. C. P. Logan to leprosy work in Ogoja Province.

Logan was by this time a veteran doctor, with experience both at Uburu and in Methodist leprosy work at Uzuakoli. For two years he toured southern Ogoja persuading villages to grant land for a centre and thus superintending the building. He worked hard to get a Presbyterian base at Ikom, but despite its long connection with the Presbyterians, it was really too far away. The final result was a division of leprosy services in the province between the Catholics and the Presbyterians, with the Presbyterians in the south. Logan left at the end of 1949, but his work had been worthwhile. He bequeathed to the next generation of doctors the framework of the Southern Ogoja Leprosy Service.

One further development must be noted before leaving the period dominated by Hastings and Macdonald. In 1928 the enterprising citizens of Abiriba offered 3,000 for a hospital if the church would provide a doctor. Robert Collins, the missionary responsible for Abiriba, didn't think the offer needed to be taken seriously and the question lapsed until 1934. In that year the Council had before it a letter from Akanu Ibiam asking for an appointment as a missionary doctor. The Council offered him a three-year term, and when Ibiam questioned such a short appointment, the Council replied that this was an experiment and that it was not prepared to commit itself any

further. He agreed and, after a short time at Itu,
went off to found the hospital at Abiriba.

Abiriba was the first choice of a number of
possibilities. Ibiam could have gone to Unwana,
his home, or to Ohafia. Going to Unwana would look
like favouritism, while Ohafia was too scattered
and too full of village rivalries. Abiriba, a
compact town with plenty of traders who were likely
to have money, was a better choice.[12] Ibiam
started with £1,000 for buildings, which he paid
back in three years. Everything had to be done
from scratch: the first essential buildings; out-
patients; a ward and an operating theatre built
with concrete; his own house, a big one with two
offices and several bedrooms made of mud blocks
with a thatched roof. The roof was done by men of
his own age grade who walked down from Unwana,
finished the roof, and walked back the next day--an
epic performance, as he put it.

Like the other doctors, Ibiam had to do
everything himself, even to devising a sterilizer
out of a kerosene stove and recycled containers
from the market. But his special interest was
obstetrics. Abiriba people were convinced of three
things: that the first child always died; that
educated women did not have children; and that no
pregnant woman needed a doctor. But the community
gave Ibiam a clinic in the town, and he spent three
afternoons a week promoting maternity care and
arguing that the bad deliveries he had performed
could have usually been avoided if the people had
come to him in time.

Related to Ibiam's concern for obstetrics was
his interest in the development of a female staff.

He didn't like male nurses, partly because he suspected them of being open to bribery and partly because he didn't like them caring for women. Like Hastings, he trained his own staff, at first two boys and later three girls, one of whom he was able, with the assistance of a British doctor, to send off to Britain for study. She was probably the first person to go abroad for study from within the Presbyterian system. When he left Abiriba in 1945 the hospital was closed down for many years, but he had taken the first step, and of equal importance, he had pioneered in obstetrics, an experience which he and his wife put to good use in Uburu in the 1950s.

Ibiam's main problems were not his practice but his colleagues. Though personal relations with the missionaries, especially his contemporaries, were good, the mission as a whole did not know what to make of him. To begin with, he was made responsible not, as were the other doctors, directly to the Council, but in medical matters to the doctor at Itu and in financial matters to the missionary in Ohafia. By the end of the first three years, the Council was ready to call the experiment a success and offered him a new six-year contract which removed him from the tutelage of the missionaries in routine matters. But the new agreement came after a strange interview in which three senior men, Christie, Hastings, and A. B. Macdonald, came to ask him his intentions. Did he want to take over the hospital, or did he think it should be closed? Ibiam was baffled. In the first place, Abiriba was the only hospital between Uburu and Itu, and in the second place, "If I had wanted

my own hospital I wouldn't have come to you.
Gentlemen, I don't understand you!"[13] In fairness
to the senior missionaries, Ibiam was probably hard
to understand as well, for in a country where
talented people headed for the comforts and the
incomes of the cities, a doctor who was prepared to
work in the country was more than a little strange.
But the interview indicates the underlying
uneasiness of the mission before an educated
Nigerian. Ibiam was tough enough to stick it out,
but it is significant that he was the only fully
qualified Nigerian on the staff, that his training
owed nothing to the mission, and that it was he who
pushed and prodded his church into taking the
training of its people seriously.

The colonial period in medical work closes
around 1950. Hastings went home sick in 1949 and
Macdonald finally retired in 1954. These two men
had dominated the medical work since the 1920s and
presided over its first significant advance. They
left behind them a framework of institutions: two
hospitals, two leper colonies, and a tradition of
reliance on locally trained junior staff. They
were succeeded by a generation of young men,
trained in different techniques, working in a
different environment, who both developed the
heritage they had received and came to recognize
its shortcomings.

THE NEW YOUNG MEN

In the early 1950s, the era of Hastings and
Macdonald gave way to one dominated by a series of
men who came to Nigeria fairly soon after finishing
medical school and had therefore been trained

during and after a major breakthrough in medical technology, a breakthrough which one of them called a chemotherapeutic revolution.

The best known of the new developments is antibiotics. Penicillin came on the market just after the Second World War, followed by a series of other drugs that made possible the successful treatment of a series of diseases which had hitherto responded only uncertainly to the therapies available. Pneumonia, once a traumatic illness, became almost a minor ailment. Along with antibiotics came major advances in vaccinations, and of more immediate significance, the appearance of the sulphones in the treatment of leprosy. At the same time, blood transfusions and especially the rise of intravenous therapy greatly increased the success rate of operations which had been technically possible but very dangerous. Before intravenous therapy, it was all too often true that the operation was a success, but the patient died.

At the same time as the range of treatments was widening, the government was finally beginning to take its responsibilities in medicine seriously. More money was available for capital expenditure and more pressure was applied for a better trained staff. The era of the one-doctor hospital with a staff he trained himself was almost over.

As so often happened, Akanu Ibiam was the man who started the process of staff training, in this case, nurses. European sisters had been common at Itu until 1936, when a dispute sent the last one off on transfer to the Anglicans. Uburu had never had nurses, other than Mrs. Hastings, who was a good practical nurse, but not formally qualified.

Dr. and Mrs. Hastings relied on their own staff,
with very considerable success. The doctors who
succeeded Hastings and worked with the four or five
men they had trained spoke in the highest terms of
their competence.[14] But Dr. Hastings was probably
unusual, and in any case, mastering a technique is
a different thing from mastering even the rudiments
of the theory on which the technique rests. The
traditional Western solution to the problem of
patient care has been the nurse, a person with a
basic scientific education and a thorough training
in the art of caring for the sick.

Like the other doctors, Ibiam trained his own
staff, but of more significance, he pushed the
Council into asking for nursing sisters, and
finally one arrived at Itu in 1943. With a sister
on the staff, training could begin. It started in
1950 and continued until the last nurse graduated
in 1967. Training nurses at Itu was always
something of a scramble. It was a small hospital
with only one sister-tutor, and if she went on
leave or resigned, the program could collapse. It
almost did when Miss Wight, the first sister, left;
it was saved only by the temporary appointment of a
woman whose husband taught at Hope Waddell. She
was relieved after two years, though she remained
on the staff, and the program settled down to a
relatively stable existence until it was driven out
of business by rising standards.

In November 1963, the sister-tutor reported
that the Nursing Council wanted to raise both the
standards required of training hospitals and the
educational level of admissions. No Presbyterian
hospital could meet these standards, and since the

Council would not be moved, there was nothing to do
but phase the school out. Any new women wanting to
train within the Presbyterian system would have to
go to Abiriba or Queen Elizabeth.

When the lease on the Abiriba hospital ran out
the mission did not renew it, but handed over the
unused buildings to the town. In 1960 agitation to
reopen the hospital built up within Abiriba, even
if this meant inviting the Catholics, an invitation
which would have seriously divided the community.
Some hard-talking by Abiriba Presbyterians kept the
question open until the Mennonites agreed to supply
staff. The hospital reopened in 1961 as a joint
venture of the government, the Abiriba Improvement
Union, and the church. In 1963 the hospital began
a Grade II midwifery course, an eighteen-month
program which would enable a woman to handle
routine care and deliveries and to report
abnormalities. On the eve of the civil war, the
hospital was anticipating receiving permission to
offer the more sophisticated Grade I course.

Midwifery was also taught at Queen Elizabeth,
but it was entirely different from Abiriba. In
1944 the Christian Council decided that the country
needed a first-class training hospital, financed by
the government and managed by the missions. The
government was interested and offered to put one of
its planned new hospitals at the disposal of the
churches on terms to be negotiated. The
negotiations were long and sometimes difficult, and
it was entirely appropriate that Akanu Ibiam
usually was the Presbyterian representative. the
hospital opened in 1955 on the outskirts of
Umuahia, and during its short life as a church

institution, it was one of the best hospitals in the Eastern Region.

Queen Elizabeth Hospital was a joint venture of the usual three churches, Anglican, Methodist, and Presbyterian, and the government of the Eastern Region. Because of its different financial structure, it was free of most of the financial headaches that plagued the other hospitals, and with three churches to draw on, it was much better staffed, with four or five doctors and two or three senior nurses, in addition to a business manager and usually a pharmacist. The Presbyterians had supported the venture from the beginning, but were very cautious about committing themselves to either money or staff. They had, they said, a larger medical establishment than any of the other churches, and keeping their own hospitals staffed was difficult enough. They agreed to supply one doctor; from 1955 to 1965 this was Tom Burnet, one of the most senior of the new young men. For a number of years he was the medical superintendent.

If developments in medicine led to the birth of a new institution at Umuahia, they destroyed one at Itu. Circumstances, and Macdonald's conviction that treating the whole man--both body and spirit-- was the best way to handle leprosy, led to the founding of the leper colony, but the colony's viability depended on the ingenuity of John Paterson and his successors. Their work, in turn, depended on an extensive labour force. For twenty years there were enough lepers and they stayed long enough to keep the place afloat. But in the late 1940s the sulphones came on the market, and Macdonald began to use them in a small way with very encouraging results. It was an expensive treatment, costing £7 a year for the drug alone compared to £5 for all patient costs with hydnocarpous oil. But when the new drugs had proved themselves, the government began supplying them free.

Too much can be made of the impact of sulphones on leprosy. Macdonald discharged over 800 patients in 1950, one of his big years, and only 13 of them were on the new drugs. But the men who succeeded Macdonald used almost nothing else, and they cut the average treatment time of a strong patient, the kind who was most useful to the colony, from four or five years to two or three. Itu was soon discharging far more patients than it was taking in, and those who were left were often people able to make very little contribution to the colony's economic stability. Its financial position got steadily worse; the colony was dying of its own success.

To make matters worse, the nature of leprosy treatment itself was changing. The disease had been considered extremely infectious both by the community and the medical profession, but by the 1950s opinion was coming around to the view that a large number of lepers could be treated as ordinary out-patients. In 1956 the colony was asked to cooperate with the government in a program of leprosy control through clinics in the lower Cross River valley. The clinics grew at a respectable rate; in 1965 there were twenty-two with a total of 385 patients, while the colony, which at one time had 4,000 residents, was down to 462, with the new patients all serious cases. In 1961 R. M.

Macdonald began casting around for alternative uses
for the very extensive property the colony held.
In 1963 the colony's board of directors settled on
a farm settlement scheme which it hoped would help
both the colony and the young men in the area. The
initial money came from Christian Aid, a British
development agency, but the scheme was just getting
underway when the civil war intervened.

While the Itu Leper Colony was succumbing to
its own success, the general hospitals were
expanding to the limit of their usefulness. At Itu
the principal expansion was to accommodate the
nurses' training, but at Uburu business was growing
by leaps and bounds. Ibiam's five years from 1952
to 1957 saw the hospital almost completely rebuilt,
and as at Abiriba, he pioneered in obstetrics.
Attendance at the prenatal clinic he started in
1954 doubled in three years; the number of people
served by the dispensary doubled between 1952 and
1958 and again between 1963 and 1966.[15] The number
of Itu's hospital's out-patient numbers expanded
even more dramatically, from 1,382 to 8,458. But
costs rose even faster. Uburu's budget in 1961 was
£4,200; in 1966 it was £23,333, of which only
£5,200 was government grant. The rest had to come
from patients' fees. Although some of this sharp
increase was due to inflation, the cost of medical
care, especially in drugs and staff salaries, was
rising faster than the cost of living. In 1966
Uburu hospital found it could not pay the wages
recommended by the government without raising fees
beyond the level the administration believed the
clientele could reasonably be expected to pay. The

only solution was to apply for joint status, a decision taken as far back as 1961.

For an ordinary mission hospital, the government paid a fixed bed-occupancy grant, and the difference had to be made up in fees. Under joint status the hospital drew up a budget which, when approved by the ministry, committed the government to paying the difference between income from fees and the budgeted expenditure. The system had been first introduced at Queen Elizabeth, and subsequently at Abiriba. The two remaining hospitals, Uburu and Itu, opened negotiations with the government, and by the outbreak of the civil war, both had been successful.

A different financial system would have improved the running of the hospitals considerably, but a more significant development of the period was a growing conviction that the general hospitals were not really the way to proceed. It was common knowledge among the doctors that a high percentage of their work was with diseases either caused by or complicated by the environment--malaria, intestinal parasites, and some form of malnutrition.[16] In 1927 an article appeared in the International Review of Missions arguing the case for preventive rather than curative medicine as the focus for medical missions. In Britain during the early years of the twentieth century, the article pointed out, public health measures had played a large part in cutting infant mortality in half.[17] But only in the late 1950s did the medical staff begin to put their minds seriously to changing their emphasis, and they had not worked out any procedures before the fortuitous appearance of the Dutch.

The dispute between Indonesia and the Netherlands over Papua, New Guinea, led to the cessation of visas for Dutch missionaries. Indonesia had been the principal mission field of the Netherlands Reformed Church and, rather than close down, the church decided to look for alternative outlets. Already Scotland had recruited Dutch medical personnel to fill medical vacancies, so it was entirely natural that the Presbyterian Church of Nigeria should have been one of the places that quickly established a new relationship with the Netherlands church. In 1961 agreement had been reached in principle between the Dutch, the synod, and the Ministry of Health for the extension of "the work of Uburu hospital by means of a government sponsored Rural Health Scheme based on Uburu and Itigidi hospitals."[18]

Itigidi hospital was the creation of Dr. S. I. Imoke, an Itigidi man who had trained at the medical school in Yaba outside Lagos. He remained the owner, while the church managed the hospital. Negotiations were almost concluded when the Dutch appeared, sending to Nigeria a series of people, notably Herman Middlekoop, who had been a government doctor in Indonesia and who came with considerable experience in rural health.

Middlekoop's contribution to the Presbyterian cause was to show how rural health programs could be carried on. He started with something everyone knew, that children from conception to age five were a particularly vulnerable group. The approach, therefore, was to concentrate on prenatal and child-care clinics, with nutrition and vaccinations, using a card developed by a

Dr. Morely which the mother kept and on which were recorded vaccinations, growth rate, and other relevant information. Essential to the system were the Grade II midwives, who went through the routine procedures and screened out those who should see the doctor. With ten such women one doctor could handle a clinic of 600 in a single day. Itigidi's child-welfare clinics blossomed from 5,000 to 27,000 between 1962 and 1967.[19]

Although Itigidi was the clearest example of the new direction in medical work, the pattern was followed in the other hospitals, especially at Uburu. Itu opened a number of clinics, but for reasons which are not altogether clear, the Ibibios were much more cautious in accepting this approach than the people in Ogoja. In Ogoja, of course, a framework was already there. Logan and A. C. Macdonald had expanded Hastings' few clinics into a network all across southern Ogoja, including two substations across the river in the hands of expatriate leprosy workers. Although leprosy was a more serious disease in Ogoja than further south, the new treatments were keeping it under control, and the leprosy workers had the opportunity, with some retraining, to move into other forms of health care as well. Appropriately, the Southern Ogoja Leprosy Service changed its name to the Presbyterian Rural Health Service.

At this point, John Paterson reappeared. He had left the mission after his dispute with the Macdonalds, worked for awhile with the government introducing rice cultivation into the country south of Abakaliki, and spent some time in Malawi. When he returned to the mission, he built the base

hospital at the Southern Ogoja Leprosy Service and
then transferred to Yakurr, one of the out-stations
on the east side of the Cross River. With money
from development agencies abroad to pay his
patients, Paterson developed an extensive nursery
at Yakurr. Using plants from his own nursery, and
with the cooperation of Presbyterian and other
schoolteachers, he began promoting nutrition. A
particular kind of cherry with a high vitamin C
content was planted in so many school yards and
villages that it came to be known as Paterson's
Cherry. Another project was the cultivation of
mulberries which he had started originally for the
berries, but although the plant grew furiously, the
fruit was disappointing. However, one of the
chiefs in Ugep mentioned that his wife had tried
the leaves in the traditional stews and found them
delicious. Paterson promptly tested the leaves and
found they had a 4.5 percent protein content. A
more sophisticated test in Oslo showed 8 percent.
In a country with a chronic protein deficiency,
this was a significant find.[20]

If the environment was known to be a
significant factor in Nigerian disease, it seems at
first sight strange that the medical profession
took so long to shift its emphasis towards
preventive medicine. But dealing with the
environment meant dealing with diet, adequate water
supplies, and sewage disposal, problems which
required the talents of engineers rather than
doctors. The medical profession has traditionally
been trained to cure rather than prevent disease.
As long as curative medicine was a feasible
program, the doctor simply did what they were

trained to do and what the community expected of them. Yet the change of emphasis is also an illustration of the dictum that people only do the wise thing when the other alternatives have been exhausted. As traditional medicine became more sophisticated and expensive, the hospitals which relied so heavily on fees simply reached the limit of their possibilities; the search for joint status was one result and the move into rural health the other. The church was fortunate in finding men like Middlekoop and Paterson to show the way, and fortunate also in Paterson's case that the work was able to attract the support of the new money that was becoming available in Europe for development projects.

The importance of a man like Paterson in the new program raised another possibility which the church had perhaps not fully realized when the war came. Paterson had been trained as a builder, but taught himself both agriculture and nutrition. He was a self-educated man. But the medical work had always been dominated by the doctors, expatriate experts with a sophisticated and expensive education. As long as doctors could command a high salary because of their education, the church could not afford to employ Nigerians, and the medical work remained dominated by missionaries whose salaries were normally paid from abroad. The late start in training nurses meant that fully qualified women did not begin to appear before the 1960s and none of them reached senior positions in the Presbyterian hospitals before the outbreak of the war. Expatriate domination, plus the concentration of the medical work in a few places, meant that the hospitals never became part of the church in the way that the schools did.

Virtually all the church's leadership had gone through the schools. Many of them had been or were still teachers. They had risen through the ranks on the basis of a relatively limited education and years of experience. On the other hand, before the beginning of nurses' training, senior positions in medical work were effectively closed to the Nigerian staff. Potentially the shift towards a more decentralized kind of medicine, first in the leprosy clinics and later in rural health, meant the creation of a situation in medicine analogous to that in the schools. Because a system of clinics meant a much more extensive use of partially trained staff and because the mastery of nutrition, water supplies, and sewage disposal does not require the same protracted and expensive education that a doctor needs, the new developments in medicine meant that Nigerians could rise through the ranks, as the teachers had, with relatively limited education and hard work. Further, because people like Middlekoop made a determined effort to relate the work of the clinics to the congregations, medical work became something in which ordinary Christians could take a significant part. Preventing and healing disease is an obvious Christian service in the Cross River valley. The coming of preventive medicine meant that the church, as well as the missionary doctors, could take it up.

Chapter 7

TO HEAL THE SICK

[1] Somerville to Hewan, July 7, 1855.

[2] The Record, June 1864.

[3] United Presbyterian Mission Board, Minutes, February 4, 1882.

[4] The Record, February 1900.

[5] United Presbyterian Mission Board, Minutes, January 28, 1896. Such at least is a reasonable inference from the debate reported from the presbytery meeting of December 2, 1895.

[6] Conversation with E. L. Lloyd, 1977.

[7] D. E. Umo, in They Were Cleansed, 39.

[8] Conversation with John Paterson, 1977.

[9] D. E. Umo, in They Were Cleansed, 42.

[10] D. O. Afikpo to Resident, Ogoja, May 30, 1940; Ogprof, 2/1/1789.

[11] The correspondence is in Ogprof, 2/1/1789. See also Ogprof, 10/1/31, Annual Report Afikpo Division, 1944.

[12] Conversation with Akanu Ibiam, 1977.

13 Ibid.

14 Marjorie Ross, <u>New Life in Uburu</u>; and conversation with Clyne Shepherd, 1977.

15 <u>New Life in Uburu</u>, p. 32.   The Presbyterian Hospital, Uburu, Report, March 31, 1967 and Medical Board, May 1963.

16 Anne McMahon, <u>Hill of Healing</u>, 19; and conversation with E. L. Lloyd.

17 Ruth Young, "Preventive Medicine and Medical Missions," <u>International Review of Missions</u> 16, 1927, 556-566.

18 Standing Committee, Minutes, May 1961.

19 Conversation with Herman Middlekoop, 1977.

20 Conversation with John Paterson, 1977.

Chapter 8

THE MOTHERS IN ISRAEL

Work among the women in Calabar began as soon as the missionaries had settled in. At its third meeting in July 1847, the Old Calabar Mission Committee "took into consideration and arranged" the activities of the "female servants" of the mission. At first the work fell to the missionary wives, but the first full-time woman missionary, Euphemia Miller, arrived in 1849.

From the beginning, the women divided their time between the girls in school and the wives of the Calabar aristocracy.[1] This two-pronged approach remained standard procedure in the mission for over 100 years, with varying degrees of success. The initial response was not very encouraging. The women of Calabar were "spiritually and bodily naked" and showed little inclination to change their ways. The most disappointing were the daughters of the free born, for they left school early before any serious impression could be made, married and settled down to raise another generation of equally conservative Calabar women. When it appeared that neither assiduous visiting nor the day schools were making much impression, Hugh Goldie proposed a third approach. In 1862 he asked for permission to open a boarding school for girls.[2]

It was not an expensive development. Already
the mission houses in both Duke Town and Creek Town
had become accustomed to taking in children from
the community. Goldie's idea was simply an
extension of an existing practice. The woman
missionaries in Creek Town--Mary Edgerley, S. H.
Edgerley's sister, and Goldie's two sisters-in-law,
Euphemia and Mary Johnston--simply extended their
household to make it a small boarding school. In
1864 they had nineteen girls: four free, five
half-free, five slaves, three emancipados, and two
twins. Of these girls only the four free children
were from the class for which the school was
originally intended. Euphemia Johnston thus made a
virtue of necessity when she remarked that it was
advisable to train the free girls with their social
inferiors. However, the real trouble was with the
program itself--a combination of Christian
education and domestic science.

> Besides a religious education these children
> are trained to industrial habits--to wash,
> mend and wear their own clothes. The elder
> ones besides some domestic work are also
> taught dressmaking, which is now coming into
> requisition, owing to the great improvement
> which in later years has taken place in dress;
> the females seeking and being allowed to ear
> clothing.[3]

The school aimed to train the girls in the
nurture and admonition of the Lord and in the arts
of a Victorian household. But as long as Calabar
society remained substantially intact, no free man
needed or wanted a Victorian wife. Because the
education offered by the Creek Town boarding school
was not a particularly marketable commodity, its
impact on the community was negligible. On the

other hand, within the church where many of the
girls found their husbands, its impact was no doubt
more significant.

The mission houses, especially in the more
sophisticated Creek Town form, were the precursors
of the girls' schools. The other side of the work,
the district work, began in the 1850s with visits
to women in their homes, especially the
aristocratic houses and sometimes the twin mothers'
village. By the 1870s, the visits had developed
into classes: "I have a large class of women,
twice every Sabbath," Euphemia Sutherland reported,
"the most of whom can take their turn reading to
the class; one of these women, a church member
teaches another large class of women."[4]

Until the coming of the British this double
pattern of boarding schools and vernacular Bible
classes continued with little change of emphasis or
staff. The Victorian women--the Johnston sisters,
Mary Edgerley, Euphemia Miller Sutherland, and Mary
Slessor--were very long-lived. Unlike the men,
they took little or no interest in training an
African staff. A few appointments, like Asuquo
Ekanemn's daughter, were made, but they were
neither numerous nor permanent, and they did not
involve much training.[5]

But an indigenous staff was present, even if
only in a small way. Thus before the coming of the
British, the principal themes of the colonial
period had appeared: the training of wives in
institutions, the vernacular Bible classes, and the
development of an African staff. It was not a
particularly popular program, but the advent of the

Empire set in motion changes in society that made a
British-trained wife a more desirable commodity.
As early as 1886 Mary Slessor observed: "The
people in [Creek Town] . . . are becoming quite
civilized and decent. They are getting houses of a
better stamp, they have candles and paraffin lamps,
clocks, pictures etc., and have begun to wear hats
and boots and nice things. . . ."[6]

As the British presence became more noticeable
in Nigeria, an education to manage this more
prestigious kind of household became somewhat more
attractive. If the boarding schools of the
precolonial period were little more than an
extension of the missionary's household, in the
colonial period they became serious institutions.

THE WOMEN OF THE MISSION

The first girls' boarding school in the
colonial period was at Hope Waddell, but when the
boys needed the space the girls moved over to Creek
Town, forming in 1898 the first of the separate
institutions for girls, the Creek Town Girls'
Institute. This school, unlike its predecessor in
Mary Edgerley's garden, "was to impart a good
ordinary and thorough religious education."[7] It
was the same program as in the day schools, except
that this one was mainly for boarders. But the
staff could not resist the temptation to add to the
standard curriculum domestic science, hygiene,
farming, first aid, and European and African
cooking. It was a sensible program, but a school
which depended as heavily on mission wards as this
one did could not last forever. By 1932 numbers

had fallen so sharply that in the absence of significant support for the school in Creek Town the mission closed it.

The second institution was more successful. In 1904 Mary Chalmers sent the Council a proposal for a boarding school in Calabar. After five years working with the women in Duke Town, she had become concerned about the lack of facilities for training girls and proposed to start a school simply by building, at her own expense, a corrugated iron fence around Orange Grove, that part of the original mission property where the women lived. Scotland offered the princely sum of five pounds to repair the outhouses and Edgerley Memorial School was born, offering the young women of Calabar a sound general and religious education.[8]

Though Mary Chalmers had little formal education, she was a level-headed and strong-minded woman, everyone's picture of the missionary school mistress. For twenty years she expanded her school on a shoe string, clearing out the space under her house, converting storage rooms into classrooms, and adding mud-and-thatch buildings as the need arose. In 1907 she had 200 girls; in 1926 she had 100 with a staff of four--herself and another European, and two teachers from the Hope Waddell Institution--and a few pupil-teachers. In May of that year, she finally gave up on expedients and asked for six or seven thousand pounds to replace the whole school. After more than the usual difficulties, the school moved to a new site on the other side of town and reopened in 1931.

The difference between Creek Town and Edgerley
was one of emphasis. Creek Town was supposed to be
an ordinary school with some domestic science,
while Edgerley was to be an industrial school for
girls. But as things worked out, the two were
perhaps not very different. Edgerley offered the
usual primary school curriculum, but the girls ran
the establishment, doing their own shopping and
cooking, making soap and marmalade from local
materials, and running a small laundering service.
Outside the school they lent a hand with the
district work, helping with the vernacular classes
and visiting in homes and prisons. It was Mary
Edgerley's work writ large.

Edgerley's success indicated a real demand for
marriage training, but if work with girls was to
prosper, trained Nigerian teachers of the same sex
were essential. In 1916 a proposal for a girls'
normal college appeared before the Council and four
years later classes were started at Creek Town. It
was a small school with one teacher and about a
dozen students, and it spent most of its first
fifteen years looking for a place to stay. After a
few years in Creek Town it went to Akpap, from
Akpap to Ikot Obong, from Ikot Obong to Hope
Waddell, from Hope Waddell to Creek Town and, when
the Girls' Institute closed, the school flitted
back to Ikot Obong. Finally in 1934 an inspired
suggestion came from the Education Conference; the
Council opened negotiations with the Methodists for
a joint college, and, from that point things began
to look up. The Anglicans joined the project, and
after a false start at Owerri, land was secured

outside Umuahia, a railway town in Methodist country but convenient for both Anglicans and Presbyterians. In 1937 classes were held in Arochuku until the new buildings were ready.

Women's Training College in Umuahia was thus the first of the joint institutions and very much an experiment. Given the formidable problems of running such a cooperative college, success dependent largely on the determination of the staff to make the experiment work. All three churches nominated excellent people, and the Presbyterian, Alice Lyon, became the first principal. It was, said J. M. Lewars, one of the finest things she ever did. By the time she left the college in 1939 to marry John Paterson there could be no doubt that such ventures were feasible.

The Women's Training College was a pioneer in another sense. It was the first venture into professional training for women, a field which was to become much more prominent in the nationalist period. But for the missionaries, the college was a logical extension of their primary school and marriage training program, not a venture into something new. Their principal interest remained the preparation of girls for marriage, as can be seen in Edgerley and to some extent in Creek Town, as well as in the two northern schools, Slessor Memorial and the Ohafia Girls' School.

Slessor Memorial began in 1917 with the appointment to Arochuku of three women, Mrs. Arnot, Susan McKennell, and Marion Gilmour who soon left for Ohafia. The other two stayed on at Aro for over thirty years. Susan McKennell was mainly

responsible for the district work, and the school
fell to Mrs. Arnot, called Ezinne, the good mother.
Like Mary Chalmers, she felt that the training of
girls for marriage was of paramount importance,
overshadowing by necessity the literary side of her
work. She had three kinds of girls: unschooled
brides sent by their fiancés for finishing, girls
whose parents preferred the Slessor Memorial
curriculum to that of the ordinary day schools, and
a sprinkling of waifs and strays, the mission
wards. Mrs. Arnot offered classes up to Standard
III, vernacular literacy, and some knowledge of
English, but the main emphasis was on housekeeping,
hygiene, and improved farming, including poultry-
keeping, for an Igbo woman was normally expected to
support or at least contribute significantly to the
support of herself and her children. In the 1930s
Slessor Memorial had seventy girls, and Mrs. Arnot
thought that was enough.[9]

The establishment of promising churches in
Ohafia naturally suggested that the women might
extend their work further north. In 1922 a site
had been prepared in Asaga, the most Christian of
the Ohafia villages, and Marion Gilmour was
detached from Slessor Memorial to organize the new
school. Like her colleagues, she remained at her
posting for about thirty years, and like them, she
ran the same kind of literacy and home-making
program.

These four schools, with the partial exception
of Creek Town, are logical extensions of the
classes in Mary Edgerley's backyard in the more
receptive atmosphere of the colonial period. But

the schools were never entirely distinguished from
the district work. Women tended to shift from one
to the other, and the girls in Edgerley Memorial
were expected to lend a hand with the visiting and
the vernacular classes. But in Ibibio country the
schools did not develop to the same extent, and it
was here that the district work developed the
furthest and became the model for the postwar
reforms.

In the wake of Mary Slessor's activities, the
women inherited full responsibility for the church
and school system in Akpap and Enyong. Mina Amess
and Martha Peacock were virtually district
missionaries until the last of their schools were
taken over by the men in the 1920s. As soon as she
was free from school administration, Martha Peacock
turned her attention to women's work, enrolling the
women of Asang in vernacular classes. In 1923 she
extended her work to Obio Usiere and from there
along the creek until she had nine or ten classes
once a week. It was hard going. The classes had
to be organized with considerable skill to avoid
market days and still allow time to get from one to
the other. Travel was not easy. While they had
the use of the mission launch, the <u>Pearl</u> (or <u>Peril</u>
in the missionary dialect), and canoes, the creek
was inclined to flood, and unless the villages were
scrupulous about keeping the paths clean, walking
could be almost as difficult as travelling by
water.

But the primary problem was staff. The
council felt that two women had to be kept on the
station at all times, and sickness or furloughs cut

into their classes with alarming frequency. Naturally the Council called for reinforcements, but by this time the Depression had set in and Scotland was trying to retrench rather than expand. The Council's instinct was to look for ways to pass the bills over to Nigeria, and a committee with the imposing title of "The Committee on Devolution" was formed to investigate and report.

Alice Beveridge and J. K. Macgregor were the key members of this committee, and for the women's work they recommended the formation of a corps of "Bible Women" to handle the classes, leaving the missionaries free for supervision and training.[10] Most of the Committee's recommendations were too radical for 1933, but Alice Beveridge was in the fortunate position of being able to put her own suggestions to the test. In 1934 she and her colleagues began a series of classes in the art of teaching a Bible lesson, the routine of class organization, keeping accounts, writing letters. With the support of the ministers in their area, they extended their work from Enyong to the rest of Ibibio country, and by 1939 they were ready with a proposal for the next stage, the training of full-time, salaried professional women workers.[11]

The salaries were the problem; neither Scotland nor Nigeria was willing or able to pay these women, and without some indication of where the money was coming from, there was no point in proceeding with the plan. The training of women workers did not get off the ground. Except for the graduates of the Women's Training College, who were just beginning to appear, and one or two others,

the women's work at the outbreak of the Second
World War remained entirely in expatriate hands,
and the expatriate staff--after reaching a peak of
twenty in the early 1930s--was beginning to fall
off.

In the years between the two world wars the
number of men and women missionaries in church and
school work was roughly the same, but the women
were entirely absorbed in managing a limited amount
of district work and the four schools. Two reasons
may be suggested for this relatively limited sphere
of influence. The first is the cultural lag
between men and women. Nurses' training, for
example, was delayed in part by a lack of young
women with enough education to train,[12] and until
they stayed in school long enough and in sufficient
numbers, there was little hope of building up a
Nigerian staff. But at the same time the women,
especially in the schools, were attempting a much
more ambitious program than the men. It would be
too much to say that they were trying to turn their
pupils into Scottish housewives, but the reform of
domestic manners which they envisaged was
sufficient in their opinion to require the close
supervision of a relatively small number of
students.[13] Without a steady flow of trained
Nigerian women, they would have to do most of the
work themselves.

COMING OF AGE

It was an arrangement that could not last.
The number of women on the staff continued to fall.
Even if it hadn't, neither missionary theory nor

nationalist Nigeria could accept the continued
domination of the women's work by expatriates. The
war undoubtedly held things up, for while the
reform of Edgerley Memorial was discussed as early
as 1942, it was only in 1945 that the school took
in a post-primary class. In the same year the
mission opened negotiations for a joint secondary
school for girls.[14]

Thus the schools moved first. Despite chronic
staff difficulties, Edgerley continued to offer
post-primary courses and the secondary department
of Duke Town school continued to grow. But the
most dramatic development was at Ibiaku, where
after some four years of negotiation a secondary
boarding school for girls was opened in cooperation
with the Methodists. Once Ibiaku was running,
Edgerley Memorial settled down as a Secondary
Modern School, offering a two-year post-primary
course with a bias towards domestic science but
also giving the students an opportunity in either
teaching or nursing. In 1951 Ohafia Girls School
followed suit, and in 1952 Slessor Memorial dropped
its marriage preparation course (for lack of
customers) and became simply a girls' boarding
school with a training college for women next door.
Finally, in the 1960s the church took up a
secondary school project in Afikpo, the Akanu Ibiam
Secondary School for Girls.

All this post-primary education indicates a
significant change in emphasis. Both the
nineteenth-century missionaries and the women of
the twentieth century took for granted that a
woman's vocation was housekeeping; therefore, any

program among girls would centre on marriage training. The boarding schools, even when they became Modern Schools, reveal this approach. But as the system became more Nigerianized in the 1950s, it was altered to fit Nigerian ideas of what education for girls was all about. Mrs. E. N. Inyang, the first Nigerian principal at Edgerley, suggested that her students take the nursing entrance examinations, and when they passed with flying colours, a new avenue of professional education for graduates of Modern Schools was opened.[15] It was Nigerian pressure that led to the secondary school for girls at Afikpo. Behind this concern for higher education for girls lay, of course, the pressure of Roman Catholic competition. But behind the competition itself lay demand. Nigerian girls wanted a better education and they wanted it, not as an alternative to marriage, but as preparation for it.

It was common in polygamous households for the woman to be responsible for her own support and that of her children. Some women farmed, others went into trade. The market woman, whether she was simply selling her own produce or turning over several thousand pounds a month as manager of a retail chain, was a common sight in southern Nigeria. A professional education was simply an alternative means of achieving the same end, of preparing oneself for a woman's traditional role in marriage, and no doubt being able to claim a better dowry. The girls who went on to nursing or teaching did not expect a life of single blessedness; they married and had children. But they saw marriage in their own way, and when they recognized education as a better means of supporting themselves within marriage, they demanded--and the pressures of ecclesiastical competition ensured that they got--precisely what they wanted.

The appearance of professional church workers has a somewhat different history. The original plan foundered in the late 1930s for lack of money and remained for almost ten years a subject of discussion rather than action, except for a limited amount of in-service training at Ikot Obong. As late as 1946, the council could still think in terms of as many district women missionaries as Scotland could find and finance. But that particular motion was a pipe dream, as the Council probably realized. In 1947 the synod envisaged a program of training for educated women--nurses and teachers--to enable them to take the lead as volunteers in the women's classes. The Council, which was still in charge of women's work, replied with a proposal to train full-time workers. A joint committee was formed and in 1949 the Synod accepted, at the suggestion of the women missionaries, the principle of an order of deaconesses within the church.[16] But as before money was hard to find; only in 1951 was it finally agreed that Scotland would finance the training of the first class on the understanding that henceforth the training and the support of women workers would be a synod responsibility.

The 1951 proposal was rather ambitious, envisaging two levels of staff training. The higher level, the assistant woman district worker, was to be a certified teacher of several years' experience, while the woman evangelist needed only to be a primary school graduate with experience in women's work. The assistant district worker program failed for lack of candidates, but in 1952 six women of the second class started training at the old theological college in Arochuku.

The key figure in the new departure was C. H. Denham, a relative newcomer. Opposition to the plan was not a problem; everyone, missionaries and ministers alike, wanted trained women. Miss Denham's difficulties were practical ones: organizational, financial, and above all recruitment. It was not easy to find suitable candidates, for talented and reliable women without family responsibilities were few and far between. Nevertheless, in the fifteen years of the plan she trained fifteen women. The first class contained some people who had worked at Ikot Obong, but the second class was younger, women in their twenties and thirties, primary school graduates, virtually all of whom had been married, but most were widowed, or divorced usually because of the lack of children. The centre of the course was Bible study, around which Miss Denham built a range of practical activities--health and hygiene, a bit of farming, and a great deal of daily experience in the routine of church work, preaching, Sunday School teaching, and class management--the things the women would have to do in the parishes.[17] It was a technical rather than an academic program. Fortunately, they did not stop there. In 1963 Ako

Oku, a member of the second class, went to Britain
for further study and returned to become the first
of the senior staff appointments among the women.

Parallel to the revival of staff training was
the return of the Women's Guild. An organization
known as the Esop Iban, the women's meeting, had
appeared in the 1930s in Efik-Ibibio country, and
by the 1940s it was spreading into Igbo country.
Unfortunately, the Efik-Ibibio leadership mislaid
in Calabar some hundreds of pounds the women had
collected. The Igbo women promptly lost interest
in the organization. Miss Denham was intrigued by
this curiosity, traced the money through the
mission accounts and found some 400, the balance
left over after feasting the Scottish delegation at
the time of the mission centennial in 1946.[18] With
this discovery, the primary obstacle to a church-
wide women's organization was removed. The Esop
Iban was reborn with a neutral English name, the
Women's Guild.

The guild took over the work the women
missionaries had started or encouraged. The women
met regularly for Bible study, prayer, and
fellowship. They visited the sick and the elderly
and organized the provision of firewood and water
for those who could no longer manage for
themselves. It was a fellowship of Christian
women, with a certain amount of social service on
the side.[19] When she wasn't training full-time
staff at Arochuku, Miss Denham was on the road
organizing the training of volunteers, a work which
enlisted the assistance of a number of missionary

wives and, in the early days, the new Canadian women.

The appearance of the Canadians added a new dimension to the program. The first pair, Agnes Gollan and Joan Rochemont, arrived in 1955. Joan Rochemont left in 1957 and was replaced at the beginning of 1959 by Dorothy Bulmer. The veteran and the newcomer then set off for their new house in Ohafia with a new mandate: the organization of work among girls. The Christian Girls' Club was one of the more permanent contributions of the Canadians. It was an organization for young teenage girls with many of the same objectives and functions as the Women's Guild. The project began to take shape as early as 1956, but only in 1961 was the experimental stage declared over and serious organization begun.[20] Within a year the Christian Girls' Club had eighty branches and 1,000 members. Not only was it one of the more successful of the Canadian endeavours, but it was about the only case in which a coherent alternative to Christian education through the schools was developed.

When the Canadians made youth work one of their priorities they were simply picking up a concern which had been around for some years. Besides the two deaconesses, Earle Roberts and his wife had been working on a reform of the Sunday School curriculum for some years after 1957. However, he was transferred to the Forward Movement in 1962. Walter MacLean went into student work late the same year, but he spent his time in Enugu and Nsukka. Youth work in the traditional

Presbyterian area, therefore, tended to founder for
lack of leadership, except for the very valuable
contribution of charismatic young men like Nwosu
Udoh. But because the Christian Girls' Club had
the benefit of consistent professional leadership
from the beginning, it rapidly developed a sound
organization and program.

    The years after the Second World War saw a
shift within the women's work comparable to that
which took place in medicine. As new staff and new
techniques transformed the medical work, the
women's work was remade by new staff and new
demand. With one exception, the generation of
women missionaries was gone by the early 1950s, and
that exception was Frances Cameron, a professional
teacher at the Women's Training College and
subsequently at Ibiaku. By 1953 the generation
which had run the boarding schools and the district
work had been replaced, on the one hand, by a
handful of deaconesses and, on the other hand, by a
somewhat larger number of teachers, both Nigerian
and Scottish. In the same years, the Nigerian
perception of what they wanted for themselves and
their daughters was changing. They were no longer
happy with marriage preparation courses on the
missionary pattern, but looked rather for
professional training and organizations for
fellowship. These were not new concerns;
professional training had begun with the Girls'
Normal School in 1920, and the Esop Iban appeared
in the 1930s. But the emphasis was new, and
because the generation which had built and operated

the older system was gone, the church responded almost unconsciously to the new demand.

Demand was the decisive factor. Post-primary education for girls was pressed on the church from the Nigerian, not the missionary, side. If the Women's Guild and the Christian Girls' Club were unusually successful, it was because Nigerian women wanted them. The church's leadership in the 1960s may have seemed almost oppressively expatriate, but it was a leadership which operated successfully only within the limits of Nigerian concern.

Chapter 8

THE MOTHERS IN ISRAEL

[1] The Record, December 1857; Hope Waddell, Twenty-Nine Years in the West Indies and Central Africa, 346-347; The Record, January 1858.

[2] United Presbyterian Mission Board, Minutes, March 25, 1862.

[3] Euphemia Johnston, The Record, December 1866.

[4] Euphemia Johnston, The Record, March 1878.

[5] Buchanan to Beedie, October 27, 1899; Old Calabar Mission Committee, Minutes, February 5, 1890.

[6] The Record, November 1886.

[7] Buchanan to Thomson, April 7, 1899.

[8] The fence cost 30, a considerable sum in 1907 for a single missionary.

[9] General Assembly of the Church of Scotland, Acts and Proceedings, 1932. See also A. S. Arnot, "Home Making in Calabar," Other Lands 18, no. 33 (1939), 46-48.

[10] Council, Report of the Devolution Committee, 1933.

[11] Council, May 1939.

[12] Conversation with Dr. Clyne Shepherd, 1977.

[13] Arnot, "Home Making."

[14] Education Conference, Minutes, May 1945.

[15] Notes on a conversation with Mrs. Inyang, 1977.

[16] Synod, 1947, 1948, 1949.

[17] Conversation with C. H. Denham, 1977.

[18] Ibid.

[19] Notes on a conversation with Elder Mrs. S. U. Olugu and others, 1977.

[20] Agnes Gollan, Annual Report, 1961.

Chapter 9

THE CHURCH AND CIVIL POWER

When the *Waree* dropped anchor before Duke Town in 1846, the missionaries found a community almost entirely devoted to the Atlantic trade. It was not a typical West African tribe, but a Delta state which had refined the institutions of fishing people to make them applicable to the more complex problems of a commercial town. However, while the Efiks had managed to make the change from a fishing to a trading people without losing their identity or social cohesion, they had not been able to bring the Europeans in the river under their control. The British, in the interests of suppressing the slave trade, had posted a naval squadron on the coast, and the Europeans found the temptation to invite the representative of the British crown to settle their disputes with the Efik aristocracy too strong to resist. In 1846, therefore, there were three centres of power in the Cross River Delta: the Ekpe society; the European merchants; and the British consul, conveniently located in Fernando Po.

A fair statement of the missionary attitude towards the consul can be found in the formal address presented to Consul Hutchinson on the occasion of his first visit to the river:

> As agents of a Christian mission we cannot, of course, expect or desire any display of the physical power with which you are armed as an

aid to us in the work of evangelizing and civilizing the tribes among whom we labor; but as the Representative of England, you possess a vast moral influence over the native tribes inhabiting this portion of Africa and this influence we feel assured you will, with all prudence, employ towards the abolition of many inhuman practices which still prevail among them.[1]

The objective of the missionary enterprise is given as evangelization and civilization; along with the preaching of the gospel was to go a process of social reform. Acceptance of Christ inevitably means a measure of alienation from one's society, and the Victorians naturally used an idealized version of their own society as the standard against which their surroundings were judged. The Presbyterians in the precolonial period were persistent in the pursuit of social reform, and since reform involves the use of the civil power, it is understandable that they attempted to keep the representative of British power on their side. It was not simply a matter of finding allies wherever they could. One of the themes of missionary propaganda was the moral responsibility of Great Britain to West Africa. The British had taken the lead in ruining Africa through the slave trade; hence, it was a British responsibility to rebuild where once they had destroyed.[2]

However, the missionaries disclaimed any interest in the consul's physical power as an agency of social reform. In 1863 Andrew Somerville argued on the basis of Indian experience that missionaries should make it abundantly plain that they had nothing to do with British warships.[3]

Unfortunately, the meetings at which the
missionaries expected the consul to use his
influence were held on the deck of a man-of-war.
British influence could not be separated from
British power, and without the use of one or more
of the power centres in Calabar, reform was
impossible. Missionary strategy in any instance
was to use a combination of power centres, and they
differed among themselves as to the precise
combination of Efik authority, shipping, and the
consul to employ.

SOCIAL REFORM IN OLD CALABAR

The various points at which the mission
attempted to reform Calabar society cannot be
discussed in detail. Instead, three cases will be
chosen that indicate the kinds of reforms attempted
and suggest the methods used. The first deals with
the right of asylum,. the second with human
sacrifice, and the third with commercial monopoly.

In 1856 three people in Henshaw Town were
accused of witchcraft and ordered to "chop nut," a
form of trial by ordeal in which the accused drank
a mixture of water and the esere bean. If they
vomited, they were declared innocent; if, as was
more likely, they died, they were declared guilty.
The three who had been accused promptly took refuge
in Duke Town mission house and Anderson refused the
case to Hutchinson. Hutchinson agreed to support
Anderson's granting of asylum, even though there
was no treaty governing such cases, and instructed
the chiefs of Calabar to leave the refugees alone.[4]
For a time the chiefs obeyed, but then pressure for

the prisoners' release from Anderson's custody was resumed. When Anderson refused, the Ekpe society "blew Egbo" on the mission house, effectively cutting it off from all dealings with the town. A deathly hush settled over all ecclesiastical activities until Hutchinson appeared to settle the case. While they were waiting, the chiefs of Calabar began to question the right of the mission to hold land.

In June Hutchinson appeared and the principals assembled on the decks of his man-of-war for the palaver. After some discussion it was agreed that to take refuge in a mission house amounted to an appeal to the consul, and that refugees could not be surrendered except to him. To seek the protection of a missionary was to seek the protection of the Royal Navy, a dangerous idea to say the least,[5] but one which the mission accepted without demur. But of equal significance was Hope Waddell's reaction to the suggestion that the mission had no right to its land, a subject in which he was at least as interested as he was in the question of the refugees. In rebutting the Efik case, he argued primarily on the basis of indigenous practice. The mission had been invited to Calabar by the Efik people, and the invitation guaranteed them the use of land. When Hope Waddell arrived in Calabar, he went with an official of the Ekpe society to take formal possession of the property.[6] Although he also brought in his connection with Great Britain, it was a secondary line of argument; his main contention was based on his understanding of Efik law. To argue on these

grounds was typical of Hope Waddell. "Native
instrumentality and cooperation," he wrote, "are
indispensable to native social reformation."[7] Such
was also his position in the case of the most
celebrated of missionary reforms, the abolition of
human sacrifices and its unfortunate sequel in the
affair of Old Town.

In 1847 King Eyamba of Duke Town died and the
ritual murders designed to provide the king with a
decent retinue in the next world were on a scale in
keeping with the king's status in the community.
At the time the missionaries protested, but to no
avail. In 1850 two lesser but still important
Calabar aristocrats died, and the process began
again. This time Anderson resolved to use stronger
measures and turned to the shipping. On this point
merchants and missionaries could agree, and a
pressure group was formed to end the practice.
King Eyo attached himself to the party at once and,
at the palaver, the merchants threatened Duke Town
with a commercial boycott if the practice was not
abolished.[8] The alliance carried the day. An Ekpe
law banning the custom was duly passed, with Duke
Town and Creek Town standing surety for each other.
Unfortunately Old Town was not included because
Willy Tom Robins, the principal chief, was not on
hand to sign his name. This point was apparently
cleared up later in the year. Subsequent treaties
confirmed the law, but as far as Hope Waddell was
concerned, the prohibition rested, not on a treaty,
but on an Efik statute.

It is true that the reform was carried through
under and immediate threat of commercial boycott

and a more remote possibility of consular intervention. Hope Waddell did not object to the boycott: "Reform may originate and carried forward [sic] by instruction, admonitions and persuasive motives from without, but not by compulsion. . . ."[9] Economic sanctions were permissible, but military action was not, and neither was acceptable until all the resources of native law had been used. Such, at least, seems to have been Hope Waddell's attitude in the Old Town affair.

When Willy Tom Robins, the principal chief in Old Town, died in 1854, a number of people were killed. Samuel Edgerley, the missionary in Old Town, whose approach to Efik religion was marked more by zeal than by discretion, promptly made the sacrifices public. Somewhat embarrassed by Old Town's indiscretion, the Ekpe society declared that the funeral ceremonies could not be completed until the culprits had been surrendered. Given the importance of a decent funeral in Calabar, Hope Waddell thought this was a good beginning, but it failed to produce the guilty parties. The European shippers then decided to use the unlawful human sacrifices as a lever in their dealings with the Efik commercial community. In December 1854 they called a meeting to which the missionaries were not invited, and offered the gentlemen of Calabar two alternatives: exile the headmen or burn the town. The Africans replied with a third suggestion: a fine of twenty slaves.

Hope Waddell thought that all three proposals were wrong. Exile was unjust because at least one of the headmen was too old and infirm to kill

anyone; burning the town would punish the innocent
with the guilty; and a fine, since the slaves would
be paid over to the Ekpe society, would give the
judges an interest in the crime. His suggestion
was the exile of the culprits on pain of flogging
and confiscation of goods if they appeared in town.

In the meantime the merchants had sent for the
consul, and in a few weeks Consul Lynslager
appeared in a Royal Navy gunboat, the Antelope.
When the proposal to destroy the town was made,
Hope Waddell and Edgerley both protested, and Hope
Waddell again suggested exile, something that could
be managed under Ekpe law. But the meeting went
against them; Eyo and Duke Ephraim were given two
days to find the culprits or the town would be
destroyed.[10] Given the amount of forest in the
neighbourhood, there was no way the men could be
found in two days. On January 19, the   Antelope
opened fire, and what we left after the bombardment
was destroyed by a party of marines. Lynslager
then forbade the rebuilding of the town and sailed
off down the river.

Old Town blamed Edgerley for its misfortunes
and expelled him. But this side of the dispute was
largely personal; Anderson reached an agreement
with Old Town to accept another missionary if the
mission would try to get the town rebuilt.[11] The
missionaries referred the case to Edinburgh and
Edinburgh took it up in London. Clarendon, the
foreign secretary, could see no reason why the town
should not be restored and instructed Hutchinson,
the new consul, to get on with the job. In January
1956 a new treaty was signed with Old Town on

condition of, among a list, the protection of missionaries within the town. This provision was inserted at the insistence of the British government; the missionaries neither asked nor desired it: "We knew that, if our brother could not live there without treaty stipulation for his safety, he could do little with it."[12]

Hope Waddell believed that the primary motive behind the whole affair was commercial. The trust system, a form of credit in goods, ensured that the Calabar traders were permanently in debt to the Europeans, and the British traders had never been able to use the Royal Navy to collect their debts. Old Town, which was commercially insignificant, could be destroyed without harming trade and stand as an example to more important communities. Without accepting all Hope Waddell's argument, it is difficult to take seriously the facade of humanitarianism that the shippers used, since they deliberately excluded the missionaries from the meeting which came up with the idea of destroying the town. The destruction of Old Town was a project conceived of and executed by shippers, without benefit of missionary support, and against their expressed views as stated by Hope Waddell, Edgerley, and to a lesser extent Anderson. Hope Waddell regarded the bombardment as illegal and unwise. The law abolishing human sacrifices was a native law and the Ekpe society, with encouragement if necessary, was quite capable of enforcing it. As well, an indigenous statute would have a much more permanent result than any attempt to impose the reform by force.[13]

But the missionaries cannot go blameless. Samuel Edgerley was a headstrong and rather tactless individual with a history of unnecessary attacks on Efik religion. Hope Waddell admitted that he was too emphatic about the possibility of a man-of-war being used when he took Old Town to task for the events at Willy Tom's funeral. Further, when Lynslager arrived in the vier, he sent round a note asking for complaints to be dealt with while he was there. Hope Waddell had none. Anderson wanted the consul to use his influence in connection with the trial by ordeal, and Edgerley listed a dozen points in dispute between himself and Old Town, concluding "that I have no protection from any party in the country from any violence or outrage, and therefore as a British subject, most respectfully claim the protection of Her Britannic Majesty's Consul for this river."[14] Hope Waddell wanted nothing; Anderson wanted influence; Edgerley wanted protection. Even among the half dozen or so missionaries, there were differences about how much the consul should be used. Hope Waddell preferred to rely on traditional authority; his colleagues in the less congenial atmosphere across the river were more ready to send for the consul. But even they rarely asked for more than influence. Edgerley's more aggressive approach was not shared by his colleagues.

Edgerley died in 1857, but his mantle fell on William Cooper Thomson, who was posted in 1858 to Ikunetu. It was the same year that Ikorofiong was opened, with the restrictions on the use of the buildings which have already been noted. Calabar people were uneasy about the prospect of Europeans living so close to their sources of palm oil. In 1861 Thomson made three trips into the interior, one to Uwet and two to Umon, none of which had the authorization of the chiefs of Calabar and, in the third case, was against their expressed wish. The missionaries repudiated Thomson's conduct and the Board backed them up. A missionary should respect the wishes of a native ruler unless it were a case of conscience. But not only had Thomson disregarded the views of the Calabar aristocracy in a matter which was not one of major ethical concern, but he had actually broken his own word.[15] The following year Thomson went with Consul Burton to Itu. He was captured by an armed band of Duke Town slaves and Burton was forced to retreat down the river to secure his release. Duke Town was in an uproar, but Anderson backed his Duke Town friends against his colleague. Burton decided not to press the matter and, for the time being, Thomson fell silent. The following year he tried another tack: if he could not take the British to Umon he would take Umon to the British. With the assistance of a slave belonging to Henshaw Tom Foster, a church member, he arranged to deliver a cargo of oil to Calabar in an Umon canoe. Henshaw Tom was fined £300 and the case was closed. This time Thomson had had enough. Thoroughly disillusioned by his failure to break the Calabar monopoly and troubled by ill health, both his own and his wife's, he resigned a few years later.

In this case a reform which was not a moral question but which the missionaries favoured was

rejected. The missionaries had given their word
that they would respect the Calabar monopoly
because their success and probably their residence
in Calabar depended on the support of the Efik
aristocracy. Given a choice between breaking a
monopoly and preserving the mission, they chose the
mission.

In precolonial Calabar, the missionaries acted
as a pressure group working for a series of well-
defined reforms. Normally they dealt directly with
traditional authority, but in serious cases the
consul was involved, not always willingly, in
arbitration. The British government's function,
therefore, was judicial rather than administrative.
It did not initiate social reform; it simply
arranged for the settlement of disputes out of
which reforms sometimes came. But in the last
years of the century the British began taking
serious initiatives on their own, and before long
the church's function in social reform had changed
beyond all recognition.

THE COMING OF THE EMPIRE

By the mid-1870s a good deal of reform had
been introduced. Human sacrifice had been
effectively abolished throughout Calabar. Within
Creek Town, infanticide had become a capital
offense; a village for twin mothers had been
established outside the town; and as the years went
by its inhabitants gradually gained the freedom
enjoyed by residents of Creek Town itself. In
Creek Town substitutionary punishment, or allowing
a slave to be punished instead of his master, had

been abolished, and although trial by ordeal was not, the practice declined. In Duke Town, on the other hand, the aristocracy would have nothing to do with a village for twin mothers, not would they act seriously against trial by ordeal or substitutionary punishment. In fact, the missionaries were in the middle of one of their periodic campaigns for reform when Consul Hopkins appeared with a treaty ready for a signature and calling for a series of reforms which the missionaries wanted, but which were not all very high on their list of priorities. The treaty of 1878 was not engineered by the mission. Hopkins appeared on instructions from London, and his arrival happened to coincide with a Presbytery campaign. The Foreign Office was not thinking particularly about the reformation of manners in Calabar, but about events in Europe and elsewhere in Africa. The scramble for Africa was getting underway, and in 1884 Consul Hewett appeared before Duke Town with a pocket full of treaty forms. When he left a few days later Calabar had become a protectorate.

The missionaries were not involved with these momentous events. They were the consequence of developments far removed from the concern, and possibly even the knowledge, of the handful of Presbyterians in the Cross River delta. The British took over Calabar because they were concerned to maintain their hold on the trade of the lower Niger, and Calabar was close enough to be taken seriously. They would have gone into the

Cameroons as well, but the Germans beat them by
five days.

The missionaries accepted the protectorate
with equanimity. Hope Waddell had toyed with the
idea as far back as 1851, but the missionaries had
never pressed for it. Goldie was hardly
enthusiastic:

> In August two gunboats came up the river,
> bringing Consul Hewett with treaties ready for
> the signatures of the chiefs, pledging them to
> accept the British protectorate. The
> signatures of those of Creek Town were at once
> given, the principal of whom would have
> preferred annexation. The heads of Duke Town
> also gave their names, with the petty tribes
> in the neighborhood, on being assured that
> their normal relations would not be disturbed.
> A sanction such as power can give to its acts
> of spoliation was given by the Treaty of
> Berlin. . . .[16]

But there was nothing Hugh Goldie could do
about it. In any case, the protectorate might be
useful. On the one hand, it secured the mission
against the risk of French occupation. The
Catholic powers in Fernando Po, for example, had
been less tolerant of the Protestants than the
British, and a leading Presbyterian like Eyo VII
considered this tolerance a major reason for
accepting British protection. But probably closer
to Goldie's heart was the hope that a wisely
managed Protectorate would further the work of
social reform: "The resident consular officials
will no doubt have such influence, beyond what
properly belongs to their office among all these
tribes, and if men of prudence and kindly bearing
will be able greatly to promote their
advancement."[17]

The protectorate had a long childhood. It formally began in 1884, but serious administration did not begin until 1891. It was another twenty years before the Presbyterian area was firmly in British hands. In these years, the primary factor in the missionary attitude towards the British presence was whether or not it promoted social reform. This point can be illustrated by two contrasting incidents.

Early in 1890 Consul Annesley called a meeting, inviting the missionaries, to discuss ways and means of dealing with Ndem Eno, an Enyong man who was trying with some success to monopolize the Cross River trade. Annesley proposed to send a force of Calabar militia, a suggestion which the missionaries opposed as being both futile and bloody. They proposed instead a peaceful expedition and palaver, and if that failed, a stoppage of trade.[18] Annesley declined to accept their advice. He not only failed to improve the situation but actually made it worse. The missionaries protested vigorously in the pages of The Record, and the Board took the matter up with Salisbury, the British Foreign Secretary. Their actions were somewhat belated, for their meeting with Salisbury also included Major Claude Macdonald, who was already on his way to establishing more effective administration in the Oil Rivers.

Claude Macdonald's handling of the chronic wars on the Cross River contrasted sharply with that of his predecessor. In 1893, for example, the people of Okurike fell out with their nominal

sovereigns, the Akunakuna. Okurike waylaid an
Akunakuna canoe paddled by Afikpo men and killed
five of the paddlers. The Akunakuna returned the
heads to Afikpo with apologies and offered to pay a
fine, at the same time disclaiming all
responsibility. The Afikpo demanded the murderers
and, when they did not appear, captured several
hundred Akunakuna people. Trade came to a dead
stop. James Luke, the missionary among the
Akunakuna, concerned that there was a war on, asked
Macdonald to intervene. He did so, found Okurike
guilty, and demanded the release of the culprits.
When Okurike refused, Macdonald burned the town.
The guilty party was then surrendered and taken to
Afikpo for hanging. Luke commented that the whole
affair left a good impression of the "equity, care
and firmness of Sir Claude's administration."[19]

Macdonald acted as an arbitrator; Annesley, at
least in missionary eyes, acted as an agent of the
Calabar aristocracy. R. M. Beedie, a missionary
who had spent some time in Ikorofiong, said he had
seen Calabar people acting in a manner which would
justify their hanging on the nearest tree. "Were
only Calabar people to be protected?" he asked.
Macdonald, on the other hand, heard both sides of
the case before acting. Once having given a
decision, he saw that it was enforced. The
missionaries were so impressed by Claude Macdonald
that they invited him to become a member of the
missionary committee, an invitation which he
accepted, but it seems he did not come to any
meetings.

The presence of a competent and progressive British official in Calabar presented the old problem of relations with the civil power, but in a new way. It was tempting to become so enthusiastic about British policy that the mission risked losing its independence. Thus when in 1901 Peter Rattray, the secretary of the Mission Council, reported that he had made arrangements to lease the mission's riverboats to the government for the duration of the Arochuku Expedition, the Council accepted the action but warned that Rattray "should be careful not to compromise the Mission in connection with war in any way that would be injurious to the work."[20] Rattray took the hint. Though he worked for the expedition as a medical officer, it was under Red Cross terms of service, and the red cross was prominently displayed on the boats. It is doubtful whether the Aros were impressed but at least the mission had tried. Maintaining one's independence is difficult when the government's objectives are seen to be both right in themselves and useful to the work.

At the same time, the imperial presence presented new problems. When Mary Slessor was appointed a judge of the consular courts, the presbytery named a committee to discuss the question with her. Slessor argued that she did not think being a judge compromised her position as a missionary and, in any case, she did not intend to resume the work after the end of her tour. The Presbytery recorded in the minutes its pleasure and the appointment was temporary but added that it was "unanimously of the opinion that acting in an

official or semi-official capacity in court is
calculated to compromise her position and interfere
with her usefulness."21

The significance of this decision is that it
reveals the Presbytery's inability to adjust its
thinking to new circumstances. If Mary Slessor
were regarded as primarily a preacher, then given
the assumptions of Scottish dissent sooner or later
she would have to choose between her responsibilities as a preacher and her responsibilities as a
judge. But Slessor's importance lay in her ability
as a reforming chief, and the first function of a
chief is to settle disputes. Her position then was
closer to that of a Christian prince than that of a
preacher. The Presbytery seems to have failed to
see what her real significance was, or if they did
see it, to grasp that being a reforming chief
rather than a reforming preacher was a legitimate
missionary function. The Slessor incident
indicated that the coming of the Empire not only
put old problems in new ways, but also posed new
problems which would be rather difficult to handle.

CHURCH AND STATE IN THE COLONIAL PERIOD

At first the coming of the Empire did not seem
to make much difference. James Luke remarked that
the mission regarded the presence or absence of the
consul with indifference.22 The consuls paid no
attention to him, nor he to the consuls. While
Luke may have been exaggerating, certainly one of
the most striking things about both church and
government archives is the lack of cross-
references. The reason is close at hand. The

government took over from the church the work of
social reform; in this area the objectives of
church and state were roughly the same. First,
since the government was more interested in court
statistics and miles of motorable road than it was
in conversion, or even in education, the
missionaries and the District Officers had little
to do with each other. In 1913-1914 a dispute
broke out between the people of Nenwe and their
warrant, or government-appointed chief. As the
nearest missionary, Hitchcock became involved and
was almost charged in court himself, but since the
whole affair was impossible to clear up, the
government let it drop. But that incident occurred
shortly after pacification, and as the government
settled into a routine, relations with the church
became almost non-existent.

It would be misleading to say that relations
entirely ceased. District officers and
missionaries were from the same country and were
relatively isolated from normal social contacts.
In particular, young administrative officers posted
to Itu or Ohafia came to have a very high regard
for senior missionaries like Cruickshank and
Collins. The District Officers were frequent
visitors to the Ohafia manse, but Collins did not
record what they discussed. A. K. Mincher, who
succeeded him, found this tradition rather
embarrassing, for Ohafia people believed that he,
like Collins, had the ear of the government. The
second generation of district missionaries, those
who came after 1930, made a point of keeping their
distance. It had to be made clear "that you were

not the D.O.'s agent, or his brother."[23]   But some
kind of contact was useful, and once the District
Missionary recognized that the District Officer had
certain responsibilities whether he liked them or
not, a measure of distance could be maintained
without interfering with personal relationships.

Conflicts between the church and traditional
authority were much more frequent. Most of these
were dealt with outside the church and never appear
in the records, but one or two which have come to
light in oral tradition are worth mentioning as
examples of the kind of dispute that was common
throughout southeastern Nigeria.

In 1926 the Christians in Ediba fell out with
the chiefs over a relatively minor issue. This
dispute was settled without much difficulty, but it
became the prelude to a more serious case two years
later. In 1928 a young Aro man, Isaac Uwakwenta,
was called to the ministry at Ediba, where he had
served his probation. Soon after his call, he was
alerted to the fact that some of the members were
suspected of dealing in slaves. He called a
congregational meeting and pointed out that the
Christians were in a bad position as a result of
the 1926 affair and that it would be wise for them
to behave. The participants at the meeting agreed
that anyone found dealing in slaves would be
disciplined. In accordance with that decision,
when one member was found buying a slave, he was
suspended. The man then took the case to the
chiefs, claiming that Uwakwenta was out to make
trouble for all slave buyers. Since the custom was
important in Ediba, the chiefs chose to force a

showdown with the church. Eventually the case involved the lieutenant governor, but because slavery was by this time illegal, it was settled in the church's favour.[24]

The church's numerous disputes with legal secret societies did not always end so satisfactorily. In general the church held that if people wished to belong to secret societies, they were free to do so; however, church members could not belong, and the societies should not hinder anyone from going about lawful business. Most district officers would probably have agreed in principle, and they would sometimes uphold a decision in the traditional courts, but quietly suggest to the missionary that the case be appealed.[25]

For the administration, cases of this nature were simply civil disputes between two sections of the community, but they are analogous to the nineteenth-century situation in which the consul arbitrated between the church and traditional authority. But traditional authority did not see it that way, regarding any government interference in the way justice was administered as an intervention on behalf of the Christians. The government did not intend to support the church, but the way it approached such cases inadvertently assisted the Christian community in its disputes with traditional authority.

Some disputes never went to court but were settled through the normal procedures, with the church people taken a major part. In Abiriba, for example, a dispute broke out in the late 1930s

between the chiefs and some of the younger members
of the community over the handling of certain gifts
presented to the chiefs at one of the major stages
in the life of an age-grade. An age-grade is an
organization involving all the men born in a
village within a given number of years, three or
four years in some cases, longer in others. The
age-grade was and still is an important village
institution, for the community chores were often
allotted to this grade or that. One grade would be
responsible for clearing the paths, another for
guarding the village. In this case it had been
suggested that the traditional gifts, instead of
simply going to the chiefs, be divided three ways:
one part to the chiefs, one part to a community
project, and one part to an education fund. At
first the chiefs agreed, but when they realized
what the proposal might mean to their incomes, in
effect, to their pensions, they changed their
minds, much to the displeasure of some of the
younger members of the community.

The church at that time was served by three
outstanding men: Awa Ubagha in the congregation;
Usang Iso in the school; and Akanu Ibiam in the
hospital. They arranged for a meeting between the
"sons abroad," those who had left home to seek
their fortunes in the cities, and the chiefs. The
palaver was held at the traditional meeting place.
When all had spoken, Iso suggested that the three
church people consult together. Ubagha was chosen
as their spokesman. In a powerful speech that
scattered praise and blame with studied
impartiality, he proposed that the plan be adopted

but that first the "sons abroad" should bring a
goat and some gin to the meeting place so that,
after due respect had been paid to the ancestors,
the chiefs might feast. It was a suggestion
acceptable on all sides and was the beginning of a
more or less consistent policy of sending young men
off for education at the town's expense.[26]

These disputes illustrate not only how the
church dealt with civil authority, but also how
much the field had narrowed. The great issues of
the nineteenth century--substitutionary punishment,
trial by ordeal, ritual murder, slavery, and twin
murder--had been taken up by the government. The
church was left with ensuring its freedom of
worship and regulating marriage among church
members. Slavery, of course, persisted, as the
Uwakwenta case shows, and the church continued twin
rescue-work in a quiet way until the 1950s. But
the traditional issues were largely dealt with
elsewhere.

The traditional issues were also the obvious
ones. In Victorian eyes, substitutionary
punishment and trial by ordeal were cruel and
inhuman practices. But the problems of British
colonial government were much more subtle. The
first system of local government, government by
warrant chiefs, was notoriously corrupt, but
corruption is hard to prove. The church maintained
a studious silence. Subsequent constitutional
reforms seemed to raise problems for political
scientists rather than theologians. The church did
not feel called upon to comment. Only with the
coming of the most momentous reform of all,

independence itself, did the church's leadership
show signs of returning to the nineteenth-century
concern for social reform.

INDEPENDENCE AND AFTER

The Presbyterian attitude towards independence
was rather like Hugh Goldie's comment on the
protectorate. It was a matter which Presbyterians
did not entirely approve but could do nothing
about. They do not seem to have had any difficulty
with the principle. In 1951 the Christian Council
decided, and the Presbyterians agreed, that Nigeria
had a "natural right to self-government." But like
the Christian Council, the Presbyterians were
concerned that, without men of integrity,
parliamentary democracy in Nigeria simply would not
function. They didn't say much about the subject
at the time, but when they did they tended to
stress personal responsibility. In 1947 one of the
missionaries published an article called "Democracy
Without Religion," in which he observed: "A nation
does not learn overnight to think of power as the
servant and not the master of justice. People do
not acquire in a single generation that sense of
responsibility, that sense of stewardship, that
integrity without which corruption and greed will
speedily threaten all attempts to run their own
affairs."[27]

In the same vein, A. K. Mincher, in a rather
dispassionate discussion of the nationalist
movement during 1953, was concerned to stress the
presence, along with men of undoubted integrity, of
a disturbing number of rascals and demagogues in

the nationalist movement.[28] The synod returned to the same theme in its independence minute: "The Presbyterian Church of Nigeria appreciates the independence of Nigeria and prays that the Christian people will walk righteously in an independent Nigeria, for righteousness alone exalts a nation."[29]

As the country was told repeatedly before October 1, 1960: "Independence means more Responsibility." It was a slogan with which the church did not dissent and beyond which the church did not go. In itself the slogan was valid and important, but a social analysis which does not go beyond personal responsibility is actually no social analysis at all.

The church never attempted a theological understanding of society. The reforms of the nineteenth century arose out of an instinctive compassion for the weaker members of the Efik community. The church did not develop a theological rationale for social reform because it did not feel it had to; its objectives seemed self-evident. Therefore, when the British took over the country and achieved most of the objectives of nineteenth-century social reform, establishing a society run by something akin to British notions of law and order, the church's leadership felt it had nothing to say. Because the obvious barbarisms had been abolished and since the church had no theological tools to analyze what was happening in colonial Nigeria, its work in the social reform field simply lapsed. Similarly, when things began to go wrong in the nationalist period, the church had no ideas with which to work except that old evangelical standby, personal integrity. But the deterioration of Nigerian politics which set in after 1964 involved not just corruption but also the nature and use of political power in a country where tribalism and politics were inextricably combined. The Presbyterian church took no interest in such subjects, and the crisis that overtook Nigeria in 1966 found the church utterly wanting.

By 1966 every major city in Nigeria contained large numbers of easterners, especially Igbos, who had migrated in search of work or to establish private businesses. In May of that year and again in November serious rioting broke out in the northern cities, rioting aimed at easterners in general and Igbos in particular. Refugees poured into the east and by the end of the year, it was estimated that they numbered a million, many of them destitute. Because the trains from the north unloaded hundreds of frightened and wounded people at the Enugu railway station, the Enugu congregation was one of the first to become involved in relief. Most people were soon taken care of by their families, but the Christian Council organized a Refugee Fund which raised £11,000 by the end of the year. The Presbyterian contribution to the fund was £1,600, most of which had come from Canada, but as in the other churches, the contributions by Presbyterian congregations and families to particular individuals was undoubtedly a great deal more. Like the reforms of the nineteenth century, it was a spontaneous response to human need, and like the Victorian reforms, it was not accompanied by any serious reflection on what was happening.

In its comment on the national situation, the first since 1960, the church expressed its sympathy to those who had suffered loss and called on the government, presumably that of the eastern region, "to explore every avenue to reopen normal lines of communication and dialogue in all levels of government and civilian life," hoping that "humanitarian interests should prevail over political or sectional advantage, thus providing a basis for unity rather than grounds for further divisions."[30] It was a cautious, moderate statement at a time when caution and moderation were badly needed. In January 1966 easterners had been enthusiastic about national unity, but the riots of May and November had brought public opinion almost full circle. Innocuous though the statement may seem, to call for discussion of humanitarian concern and unity in January 1967 was to take a reasonably well-defined political stance.

But it was also instinctive. Like its work among the refugees, the church's comment on the national situation was a reflex action straight out of the evangelical tradition. Neither social comment nor social action is ever entirely rational and detached. But this comment did not rest on any kind of analysis, for the analysis had never begun. In 1966 the Development Plan called for the formation of "an articulate body of Christian opinion which can speak with authority on the problems of the country." The task force dealing with this item decided on a series of pamphlets

selling at sixpence apiece, but the men who could
write with authority were so busy dealing with the
crisis at hand that the pamphlets never appeared.
The articulation of Christian opinion did not get
off the ground.

Because the church's approach to social reform
was instinctive rather than reflective, it was ill-
equipped to deal with a society in which it felt at
home. Social reform was a major theme in the
nineteenth century, and a minor one in the
nationalist period. In the colonial years, it was
hardly mentioned. Despite the warrant chiefs,
British government in Nigeria was reasonably just
and reasonably efficient, and it was administered
by men who thought in much the same terms as the
missionaries. Since the missionaries provided most
of the church's leadership, it was entirely natural
for the church to fall into line with the colonial
regime. Only indirectly, through education, were
the churches an agency of social change in the
colonial period. In the 1960s preaching and
teaching that made no direct reference to the
burning issues of the day, social as well as
personal ones, became painfully obvious. But
traditional evangelical theology was no guide; the
Presbyterians and the other churches remained
silent at a time when the country needed them
desperately.

Chapter 9

THE CHURCH AND CIVIL POWER

[1] Old Calabar Mission Committee, Minutes, January 22, 1856.

Although individuals may have toyed with alternatives, the missionary body as a whole does not seem to have gone beyond requesting the consul's help in social reform. Here I differ from both Ayandele and Ajayi. Ayandele (The Missionary Impact on Modern Nigeria, 8) suggests that Hope Waddell refused to leave Scotland until he had an assurance of British protection. I find no evidence that Waddell made such protection a condition of his departure for Africa. It is difficult to see how he could, for the initiative for this mission had come not, from Scotland, but from Hope Waddell and his friends in Jamaica long before this point was raised. The request to the Admiralty seems to have been an afterthought brought up late in the proceedings. As the day for departure approached Waddell may have been suffering from a mild case of cold feet.

Similarly, I find Ajayi's interpretation of Hope Waddell's reaction to the French visit in 1848 too strong (Christian Missions in Nigeria, 60; cf. Twenty-Nine Years, 350-352). The board's memorial does not ask for a protectorate, it merely points out the danger to commerce and mission from French penetration. The board may have had a protectorate in mind, but the evidence can also be interpreted as a request for a defensive manoeuvre, designed to keep the French out rather than to get the British further in. This would be quite normal for a missionary body, for it not unreasonably believed that a French presence would mean Catholic missionaries. Its motive then would be ecclesiastical rather than political. Such an interpretation is consistent with the fact that Hope Waddell disclaims any knowledge of the suggestion that the British standard should be raised (Twenty-Nine Years, 373).

[2] Hugh Goldie, The Record, December 1874. See also A. Robb, The Record, October 1872.

3 Somerville to W. C. Thomson, March 22, 1863.

4   Correspondence   between   Anderson   and
Hutchinson, Parliamentary Papers, 1856, vol. 62,
109ff. Hope Waddell, Diaries, May 1856.

5 Hope Waddell, Diaries, June 14, 1856. Ajayi
(Christian Missions, 119-120) argues that this
incident was a case of using the consul to force a
reform that could not be accomplished in any other
way, and that it was carried through under threat
of bombardment. He is right on the first point and
wrong on the second. The suggestion of a
bombardment was not in connection with the refugee
question, and in any case, the missionaries argued
against it (Hope Waddell, Diaries, June 14, 17,
1857).

6 Waddell, Twenty-Nine Years, 580-581.

7 Waddell to Somerville, January 22, 1855
(copied in his diary).

8 Society for the Abolition of Inhuman
Practices, Minutes, April 30, 1850.

9 Waddell to Somerville, January 22, 1855.

10 Ibid.

11 Old Calabar Mission Committee, Minutes,
March 23, 1855. The committee had started
proceedings to get the town rebuilt at the previous
meeting, February 6, 1855, on condition that the
people agree to abandon "the inhuman practices
which brought this affliction on them."

12 Hope Waddell, Twenty-Nine Years, 555.

[13] Waddell to Somerville, January 22, 1855;
and Waddell, Twenty-Nine Years, 553-554. It seems
likely that the Duke Town missionaries took a
somewhat stiffer attitude towards Old Town than did
Hope Waddell. If the bombardment was wrong in the
first place, there seems no justification for
saying that permission to rebuild the town should
be conditional upon abolishing human sacrifice.
Similarly, Lynslager reported that both Edgerley
and Anderson told him they considered the
bombardment a well-merited punishment, "but as
missionaries of the church, they were bound to
protest against such proceedings" (Parliamentary
Papers, 35). It is far from clear what that comment
was supposed to mean, and in any case, Lynslager
was not exactly an unprejudiced observer. At the
very least it does suggest that Anderson and
Edgerley were less sympathetic towards Old Town
than Hope Waddell.

[14] Edgerley to Lynslager, January 16, 1855,
Parliamentary Papers, vol. 56, 164.

[15] Somerville to missionaries, June 21, 1861.

[16] Hugh Goldie, Calabar and its Mission, 253.

[17] Hugh Goldie, The Record, January 1885.

[18] The correspondence is in FO 84/2020,
February/March 1890.

[19] The Record, January 1894.

[20] Old Calabar Mission Committee, Minutes,
September 12, 1901.

[21] Presbyterian Church of Biafra, Minutes,
April 19, 1898.

22 James Luke, Pioneering in Mary Slessor's Country, 79.

23 A. G. Somerville, in conversation with district missionaries, 1977.

24 Notes on a conversation with Isaac Uwakwenta, 1965.

25 Neil Bernard, in conversation with the district missionaries; also notes on a conversation with A. O. Anicho, 1977. See Calprof 14/6/20/7 for a case from Arochuku which was settled out of court, as it were, between missionaries and administration.

26 Notes on a conversation with Usang Iso, 1977. For a similar case in Ohafia, see G. Johnston, "Ohafia, 1911-1940," 150-152.

27 N. M. Bowman, "Democracy Without Religion," Life and Work 28, no. 4 (October 1947), 111.

28 A. K. Mincher, "Nigeria in the News: Background to the Self Government Discussion," Other Lands 34, no. 3 (October 1953).

29 Presbyterian Church of Nigeria, Minutes, June 1960.

30 Presbyterian Church of Nigeria, Minutes, January 1967.

Chapter 10

THE AUTHORITY OF THE WORD

The church's concern for social reform led to
its involving the imperial authorities in the
internal affairs of Calabar, but not all reforms
required consular intervention. Many could be
managed within the framework of traditional
authority, and some that did not require any
massive changes in social organization could be
handled as questions of discipline.

SLAVERY IN CALABAR

Slavery was central to the lives of both
missionaries and Efiks. The men who had served in
Jamaica--Anderson, Goldie, Samuel, Edgerley, and
Hope Waddell--had either known plantation slavery
in its last days or worked with people who had
recently been emancipated. In Calabar slavery
pervaded every aspect of economic and social life.
A man was either a slave or a slaveholder or both.
Although some slaves had managed to establish
themselves as people of substance in the community,
the majority were often in difficult straits, poor,
weak, and subject to either arbitrary punishment or
death. For the missionaries, the system was unjust
for no other reason than that it wronged human
beings, men and women for whom Christ died. As a
starting point such sentiments cannot be faulted,

but the church failed to go beyond sentiment to a
theological understanding of the system.

Thus on the Sunday morning following the
abolition of human sacrifices, Hope Waddell
exhorted the slaves in his congregation to take
advantage of the new situation. Since they could
no longer be killed to accompany their masters to
the next world, they should settle down, work hard,
and prosper, for they had a future and God would
bless their labours.[1] On another occasion he and
King Eyo waxed eloquent on the responsibilities of
masters to their slaves, arguing that it was
shameful that slaves should work hard for so
little, that they should be severely punished for
small crimes, or that the best should be the ones
in greatest danger of losing their lives in cases
of substitutionary punishment.[2] Again, when the
farm slaves first appeared as a force to be
reckoned with, the missionaries showed little sign
of appreciating what was happening.

These people were the farmers of Calabar. Why
they were there is somewhat obscure, for the Efiks
were not traditionally farmers but fishermen and
subsequently traders. But once the settlements
were established, they served a dual purpose,
providing foodstuffs for the towns and a pool of
self-supporting retainers for the heads of houses.
Though they were technically slaves, they were
actually, as Hope Waddell put it, "more or less
free," being closely connected with the house which
had purchased them or their parents, but living a
largely independent existence as peasant farmers.
In 1850 the Akpabuyo farmers, most of whom were
connected with the Duke house, combined in a

covenant known as "chopping blood," because the pact was sealed with a drop of blood. The original objective was to protect themselves against the exactions of the Duke Town gentry and, to that extent, it was a class alliance. But when in January 1851, 200 armed men appeared in the streets of Duke Town, they came not so much to protect class interests as to intimidate the suspected poisoners of King Archibong, the head of their house who had been seriously ill.[3]

Since the slave population outnumbered the free by some twenty to one, this development caused a major panic among those who had a stake in the status quo. The European traders were the most alarmed, sending for the consul and declaring at Eyo's weekly dinner party that they would like to see heads roll by the dozen. Eyo himself was more discreet, contenting himself with the proclamation of a law forbidding such combinations on pain of death, or if the parties to the pact were free, the substitution of a head slave.

The missionaries seem to have been the odd men out. Hope Waddell was annoyed with both Eyo and the Europeans because they talked of violent action against men who had combined in pursuit of a perfectly legitimate end, self-protection, and who passed their time in noisy but harmless pursuits like dancing in the streets. Anderson in Duke Town was more directly concerned, but since he saw no danger to mission life or property, he declined all invitations to move out.[4] Anderson turned out to be right, the "blood men" departed without causing any damage but leaving the Europeans looking rather foolish.

When Consul Beecroft came, he arranged a treaty with the chiefs and the blood men which was a fairly conservative document conceding to the slaves only a confirmation of the law abolishing human sacrifices and a right of appeal to the consul in case it were infringed. On the other hand, the aristocrats got extensive restrictions on slave alliances and, in their turn, a right of appeal to the consul if the articles of the treaty were broken. The missionaries had nothing to do with this document, and none of them was very enthusiastic about it. They were a little more positive about the sudden appearance of the farm slaves as a political force: "It will be seen . . . that the plantation slaves are treated like men, not as chattels, nor even as outlaws, but as men forming an important portion of the inhabitants of the community."[5]

However, as Goldie pointed out, this did not signify the establishment of a free community, since many of the slaves were slaveholders themselves. In other words, the missionaries continued to interpret these events within the categories of the antislavery tradition. Their reaction to subsequent appearances of the blood men was similar. Anderson's primary concern in the invasions of 1852, 1871, and 1874 was the prevention of a series of "chop nut," trials by ordeal. Although the missionaries are the major sources for these events, they show little sign of appreciating the combination of house and class interests which the blood men represent. For them the movement was a good thing because it established a greater measure of freedom for the slaves, and a bad thing because it was inclined to demand trials by ordeal. No doubt the missionaries were right as far as they went, but their approach reveals once again the inadequacy of the evangelical tradition in the face of a social question of any real complexity.

THE CHRISTIAN AS SLAVEHOLDER

When it came to treating slaveholding as a matter of church discipline, the missionaries showed a good deal more imagination. At the end of 1853, Anderson reported to the Old Calabar Mission Committee that he had a number of young men who were interested in joining the church, but since they were slaveholders, he doubted whether he should admit them. Given the antislavery background of the missionaries, it comes as something of a surprise that the committee, instead of taking a stiff line against slaveholders being members of the church, commented that the question was extremely difficult and asked the Board of Missions for advice. When Somerville asked for more information, he probably learned more than he wanted to know, for in January 1855 everyone came to the Mission Committee armed with discourses on the subject, which were all sent off to Britain.

The missionaries began with a distinction between plantation slavery as practised in the United States and slavery in Calabar. In the United States slaves had a prescribed social and economic status; however, the slaves and not their masters were responsible for their conduct at law. In Calabar the reverse was true. There was no way slaves could escape their legal status, although it

was common for a slave to rise to a comfortable
place on the social scale. A few even became the
equals of all but the most powerful freemen--
indistinguishable from the gentry by all who did
not know their origins. Degrading though the
system was, the potential social mobility of the
slaves was a mitigating factor. Further, to ask
owners to free their slaves before becoming church
members was to ask the impossible. In Efik law a
slave could not be freed. Owners would be
responsible for slaves over whose conduct they had
renounced control. Because Calabar slavery was so
different from American slavery, the action of the
United Presbyterian Church in Scotland of cutting
off friendly relations with the American churches
which accepted slavery could not be taken as a
precedent.[6]

But the system could not be accepted just as
it was, for it did provide for the absolute
authority of the master over the slave. If this
aspect of the system could be reformed, at least
for Christians, slaveholders could be accepted as
members either until such time as the system was
abolished altogether or until freeing slaves became
legally possible. Accordingly, in March 1855 the
committee adopted a series of conditions under
which slaveholders could be admitted to full
membership. Christian slaveholders were to treat
their slaves with justice and mercy, respect
property lawfully acquired, encourage education and
proper marriage, and work for the conversion of
slave labour into free labour. The clause that
caused the most difficulty was one that forebade
sale of slaves except for crimes which would

endanger their lives under Efik law. Edinburgh questioned allowing masters the right of sale, but agreed to accept the provision when it was pointed out that the clause was meant to apply only in those cases where the death penalty was involved and that it was actually merciful, for it substituted banishment for death.[7]

Somerville went to a great deal of trouble to prepare his case and was gratified to see the proposal go through the synod of 1856 without difficulty. It seems to have been a workable solution, for the question disappears almost entirely from the minutes except for a few cases which show it was still in force as late as the 1890s. Eventually the problem solved itself, for the colonial government abolished slavery in 1915.[8] Unfortunately, the other problems of the nineteenth century were not disposed of so easily.

THE DEMON RUM

Some evangelical critics have argued that the British abolished the trade in slaves in order to make room for the trade in gin. Although this was an improvement in some respects, it was not exactly what the abolishionists had in mind. The first reference to this problem appears in the presbytery minutes of September 1859, when the presbytery discussed an overture from the Duke Town session calling for a strong statement against the trade in and use of strong drinks and a prohibition of trade in spirits for church members.

The presbytery declined to make trade in "ardent spirits" a question of discipline, but did agree that it was a question requiring serious

attention. Goldie came to the next meeting with a
paper on the subject which was later printed as a
tract. A few years later, he published a long
article on the subject in The Record, full of lurid
tales about the havoc wrought by the use of
imported gin and insisting that Scotland did more
to ruin missions by the trade through its own
merchants than it did to support the missions
through the church.[9] Thus by 1870 the main lines
of the Presbyterian approach to the trade in
"ardent spirits" had been established. The church
would make neither use of nor trade in alcohol a
matter of discipline, but would treat it as a
matter for education in Nigeria and agitation in
Europe.

The campaign against gin did not really get
underway until 1888, when Cruickshank introduced
into the presbytery a long motion deploring the
social consequences of this "enemy of missions" and
urging the Mission Board to take action. The board
was sympathetic but cautious, agreeing only to take
the "first suitable opportunity" to bring the
matter before Her Majesty's Government. The
establishment of the protectorate suggested a line
of attack, for if some kind of international
agreement could not be reached in Europe, it was
possible that the protectorate might introduce a
prohibitive duty. Claude Macdonald, however,
declined to take the problem as seriously as did
the missionaries. In his view, the trade in
spirits was a crucial item in West African trade,
and to abolish it would bring on a major disruption
of commercial activity on the coast, if not
paralyze it altogether. Nor did he think it would

achieve the desired result, for palm wine, under
certain circumstances of fermentation, was just as
intoxicating as the imported beverages. Besides,
he did not think the problem was all that serious:
"I have seen more drunkenness in some of the larger
towns of Great Britain in the course of one hour
than I have in the eight years I have been
connected with Africa, East and West." He did not
pretend that the liquor traffic was anything but
bad, simply that it was not as bad as some of the
practices the protectorate was stamping out by
using the revenue gained from import duties on
spirits.[10] The editor of The Record commented that
Macdonald was a fine fellow, but that in this case,
he didn't know what he was talking about. A person
living in the spacious quarters of Government House
could not know as much about the actual conditions
of life in Nigeria as the missionaries who lived
with the people.

     In 1897 a suitable opportunity finally
appeared: the Brussels International Act of 1892
came up for revision. The board assembled its
ammunition, obtained from Presbyterians, Bishop
Tugwell of the Anglicans, and from none other than
Frederick Lugard who published a moving appeal for
a prohibitive duty. Chamberlain, the colonial
secretary, proved to be sympathetic. He promised
to press for a minimum duty of four shillings a
gallon a liberty to do what he liked within the
territories under British protection. He got three
shillings instead of the four he desired, plus
liberty of action. The presbytery was more pleased
than it should have been, for the Nigerian
government, with a long and virtually open border

on two sides that invited smugglers, was sure to
resist a prohibitive duty. In 1908 the problem was
still attracting the presbytery's attention, and a
motion making trade in spirits a matter for
discipline was lost nine to seven.[11] The following
year the British government became sufficiently
concerned to appoint a commission. It met in
Calabar during May, hearing, among others, Mary
Slessor, Arthur Wilkie, Alexander Cruickshank, and
Eyo Effiom, an elder who had prospered in business
without selling gin.

The commission's findings repeated the
arguments used earlier by Claude Macdonald. On the
moral issue, the commissioners held that the
dangers of the trade were exaggerated. Wilkie
commented that the missionaries, not the
commissioners, knew what was really happening, and
The Record questioned the commission from the
start. It was absurd to expect a government
commission to recommend the abolition of a major
portion of that government's revenue. On the other
hand, the missionaries, especially Mary Slessor,
may have overstated their case, giving evidence
that was too lurid to be believed.[12]

The commission of 1909 was the high point of
the Presbyterian campaign. As the Presbyterians
came into contact with other missions, the gin-
trade question tended to become one for joint
action. Perhaps to their surprise, the
Presbyterians found that they were among the more
liberal. The Qua Ibo Mission required of its
members total abstinence from trade in spirits, not
as a condition of baptism, but as a test of
sincerity, a distinction that is not altogether

clear. The conference in 1911 contented itself
with noting the Qua Ibo position and urging all
churches to instruct the young in the evils of
strong drink and form temperance societies pledged
to abstinence from "Foreign Intoxicating Liquor."[13]

After 1911, the campaign slowed down partly
because the government restricted imports during
the war and partly because it steadily increased
the duty to twenty-seven shillings and sixpence per
proof gallon in 1929. The quality of the imports
as well as the quantity increased. Although the
vigorous protests of earlier years had died down,
interest never completely died. In 1932 the
Christian Council was worried about liquor
advertisements in railway stations. References to
temperance in the Presbyterian sources may have
disappeared, but Presbyterians continued to take an
active part in the Christian Council, where such
things were more likely to be discussed. In 1944,
at the instigation of the Methodists, the Eastern
Regional Committee sent a memo to the government
with particular reference to illicit distilling,
the produce of which was known locally as OHMS, Our
Home-Made Stuff. In 1947 the Christian Council
protested vigorously and fruitlessly against the
establishment of a brewery in Nigeria. By the
1950s the council was concerned with more pressing
questions, such as urbanization, the decline of
rural life, bribery, and unemployment. Temperance,
once a major issue, tended to become the concern of
a relatively small minority. It was not that the
church had come to favour intemperance, but simply
that it was no longer regarded as a major issue.

The church was undoubtedly right. Despite the passionate sincerity of people like Wilkie and Mary Slessor, it is difficult not to agree with Claude Macdonald. The trade which was supposed to be ruining Africans by the thousands sixty years ago has left little more than a few scars: "It is probable that a number of Africans, including Christians, drink more than is good for them. But alcohol and alcoholism would not now, I think, be reckoned among the major problems of Tropical Africa."[14]

If it is not now a major problem, it probably never was, at least to the extent suggested by the prohibitionists.

The church was prepared to campaign, and campaign vigorously, against both alcohol and slavery but not to insist on abstention from either as a condition of membership. It was sound Reformed theology, for in the Presbyterian tradition, people are saved by grace, not by works, and to insist on a particular line of conduct as a condition of membership in the church is to suggest that that line of conduct is essential to salvation, that people are saved by a particular work. The church adopted an entirely different approach with regard to polygamy.

ONE MAN, ONE WIFE

Polygamy is perhaps the most vexatious of the problems before the church in Africa. It has been formally rejected by almost every imported denomination and accepted by almost every indigenous church, even though the indigenous churches may sometimes require their ministers to

be monogamous. So persistent has been the
rejection of polygamy by the missions that one
commentator called it almost a mark of the church:
one, holy, catholic, and monogamous.[15] The
continuing debate on the marriage question
suggests, if it does nothing else, that the simple
Victorian solution created as many problems as it
solved. Most Africans continue unconvinced by the
orthodox Christian argument and regard polygamy as
an entirely natural African institution, while the
alternative is a European import in the same class
as literacy and motor cars, though perhaps somewhat
less desirable than either.

The debate was not new when the Scots arrived
in Calabar. Hope Waddell considered it a
sufficiently important question to devote a lengthy
appendix to the subject in this autobiography,
providing a reasoned statement on the problem from
the founder of the mission. His argument has two
main points: polygamy is unscriptural, and
polygamy is pernicious.

In defense of the first argument Hope Waddell
cites the usual biblical evidence that God created
one man and one woman, that the survivors of the
Flood were four men and four women, that both
Christ and Paul assume monogamy and thus outlaw the
alternatives by implication. Against the objection
that many of the Old Testament worthies were
polygamous, he contends that the Bible never hides
the errors of God's people, but that being frank
about a practice does not make it right. He also
picks up an argument that is central in both Jesus
and Paul, that marriage makes a couple "one flesh."
It is impossible, he contends, for this kind of

relationship to exist between one man and several
women at the same time.

Departure from the clear testimony of
scripture has consequences: polygamy is pernicious
because it deprives the woman of any rights,
because in a world where the numbers of men and
women are roughly equal, it means that some men
must go without wives, and because the practice
involves the withdrawal of God's blessing.
Therefore, Waddell concluded, the Christian nations
expand over all the world and the Muslim countries
languish for want of people.[16]

The Victorian missionaries never withdrew from
this categorical rejection of polygamy, but a hard
line meant the rejection not simply of a form of
marriage but of the social system which was built
around it, the communal way of life in family
compounds.[17] Consequently the Presbyterians
rejected the method by which the British Isles were
brought into the church, the acceptance of the
faith by a whole tribe at once, following a
decision taken through the normal constitutional
channels. It was a consequence the Presbyterians
were prepared to accept, for British society was a
good deal more individualistic in the nineteenth
century than it had been in the seventh. But this
same concern for individuals led, by a somewhat
roundabout route, to the antislavery campaigns.
Although the Presbyterians were prepared to
compromise with slavery, they would not with
polygamy.

The senior Presbyterian missionaries had never
seen polygamy at its best. Their first experience
was in Jamaica where marriage patterns were, to say

the least, rather lax. When they came to Calabar they found themselves not in a typical African community but in a Delta state where the few were free and the many were slaves: "While a marriage ceremony is observed by the chiefs when taking to wife a woman of their own rank among most of the population no ceremony exists. They form connections and separate at their pleasure."[18]

In these circumstances it seemed that the axe would have to be laid to the root of the tree. Partial measures would not do; standard which did not appear to exist could not be reformed.

But Anglican missionaries who had never seen the West Indies and who were working in normal African communities took substantially the same position. It was not a Presbyterian but a Victorian attitude. Polygamy seems to have touched the Victorians in a tender spot. It could be argued that Christianity has rarely been entirely scriptural on the subject of sex. There is a strong ascetic strain in Christianity, and for Hope Waddell, King Eyo's household was a vast sink of licentiousness: "Ah, what a low fleshly life he lives, what a miserable corruption of heart and conscience he gives himself up to, with these naked young women about him continually in his house and private yard."[19]

In Efik a girl was nka iferre, the age-set of nakedness, until she was formally initiated into womanhood, and even then she was not likely to wear a great deal. The missionaries were thoroughly shocked. To them nakedness could only mean sensuality, and they reacted with an uncompromising rejection of both polygamy and the traditional undress of Calabar women.

G. M. Young observed that during Victoria's reign only representative institutions and the family escaped searching criticism. Some form of representative government and the monogamous household were, so to speak, the foundations of the social order. Neither existed in Calabar. Polygamy was normal. Slavery was accepted as a necessary evil, even though it was inconsistent with any form of representative government. Slavery, as Hope Waddell ruefully admitted, was something one got used to, even if one didn't like it.[20] Sex, on the other hand, because of its greater intimacy, provoked a different kind of emotional response. Besides, monogamy was possible, while manumission, or the freeing of a slave, was not. To round off the argument, while the scriptures are vague on monogamy, they are decidedly clear on slavery. In the case of Philemon and Onesimus, we find Paul dealing with the relation of a master and a slave without questioning the right of either to belong to the church. On both emotional and scriptural grounds, therefore, the Presbyterians could find some room in their hearts for slavery, but not for polygamy.

THE REGULATION OF MARRIAGE

The first generation of missionaries did not have to decide that Christian marriages should be monogamous--they took it for granted. However, once they had a church and its members married, the presbytery began to develop regulations for the governing of such marriages. The first case appeared in 1859, when Goldie asked for guidance in a case of remarriage of persons divorced under native law and custom. The presbytery agreed they could remarry, provided the initial marriage had been dissolved for such cause "as is allowed by the law of Christ," that is, adultery.[21] By that decision the presbytery established a precedent which has governed the church's life ever since. The legitimacy of Efik marriage is taken for granted, divorce is granted only for adultery, and the scriptural texts are taken as law. Hope Waddell's use of "one flesh" was unusual. That idea is not legislation, but rather a first principle upon which reflection and subsequently legislation can be built. This approach, however, was not used by Waddell's colleagues and successors. Instead, they used texts as pieces of legislation to be followed wherever possible. Only where no clear text could be found was the church free to adopt whatever seemed to be the best practice.

References to marriage are rare in the nineteenth-century minutes. Senior ministers handled the problem in sessions, the governing bodies of the congregations, and could be trusted to know what the rules were, since they had made them up. It was very time consuming. J. K. Macgregor once described the Creek Town Session Minute Book as "a dreary record of fornications and adulteries."[22] Hence, when the first generation began to pass away, the newer men drafted more formal legislation. In 1894 strict rules governing divorce were adopted. Five years later monogamy was formally declared to be the rule, along with the proviso that in normal circumstances Christians should not marry non-Christians.

Declaring a marriage code was relatively simple when all one had to deal with was Efik law. The coming of the British introduced a new complication, however, and following the expansion of the churches at the beginning of the twentieth century, the Presbyterians came into closer contact with churches whose views on the marriage question were significantly different.

The colonial government introduced a new law to stand alongside native law and custom. Under it marriages came to be known as "under the ordinance." At first all marriages in which vows of permanence and exclusion were taken had to be performed under this ordinance, and they thus became subject to British law in respect to all things except inheritance. The presbytery, with some prodding from the Efik community, went to considerable lengths to skirt this provision in order to continue with the practice of blessing a native marriage, which reflected its acceptance of Efik marriages as valid. Eventually the ordinance was altered to allow for the indigenous custom.

The government was not the only body with which the Presbyterians found themselves at variance. The Qua Ibo Mission and the Anglicans insisted on marriage "under the ordinance," while the Methodists had a dual system, requiring marriage under colonial law for those who were church members, but accepting traditional marriages among those who came for baptism. At the conference of 1911, the Presbyterian position found considerable support among the non-Anglicans; it

was agreed to call for the legalization of a
service blessing a native marriage, at which time
further vows could be taken. By 1928 the Anglicans
were hold outs, but they agreed to a compromise
which accepted, for purposes of transfer of church
membership, marriages that were for life and
exclusive, indissoluble except for adultery,
sanctioned in the house of God, legal, and carrying
a bona fine certificate. Thus if a couple raised
as Anglicans wish to become communicants, they had
to be married "under the ordinance," but if they
became communicants by transferring from a
Presbyterian church, a reformed native marriage was
sufficient. It was not consistent, but it seems to
have been a workable compromise.

Presbyterian practice was summarized in a
submission to the synod of 1936:

Marriage should be one man to one woman.

The local custom binding any marriage should
be recognized by the church with the proviso
that it is monogamous.

There is no divorce under ordinary
circumstances except on the ground of
adultery.

Separation by death or adultery entitles each
party concerned to a second marriage.

A polygamist seeking church membership is at
liberty to choose a wife when becoming a
church member, but preference should be given
to his first wife.[23]

A sixth article dealt with a series of special
reasons for divorce, such as lunacy or leprosy.
These articles were sent to presbyteries, returning
to the Synod in 1938 where, after considerable
discussion, they seem to have been adopted. They
represent the mature form of the Presbyterian
marriage code, little had changed after ninety

years. The three principles of the founding
missionaries--monogamy, the legitimacy of native
marriage, and divorce only for adultery--remained
the basis of the code.

The only significant change in the church's
marriage code after 1938 came in the wake of church
union. Given the importance and complexity of the
problem, the negotiators included a section on
marriage in the constitution. The Presbyterians
had no serious objection. Only at one point did
the church feel it had to alter its own code.
Presbyterians had traditionally allowed remarriage
after divorce, but not all the churches were
comfortable with the practice. The section on
marriage, therefore, contained a clause which
forbade the remarriage of a person if the partner
in a previous Christian marriage was still alive,
something which would have been a major departure
from Presbyterian practice. The next paragraph,
however, argued that it was not always wise to
apply the strict letter of the law and set up
procedures to get around the rigidity of the
original rule. The synod of 1962 adopted both
clauses as they stood, altering only the wording to
fit the Presbyterian system. These clauses appear
in the book of canon law, Practice and Procedure, a
lingering relic of a union that failed.

MARRIAGE: AFRICAN AND CHRISTIAN

The very fact that the constitution of the
church of Nigeria included a statement of marriage
indicates not so much the varying practice of the
churches as the difficulty of the problem itself.
Marriage cases took up an inordinate amount of

session time. We have noted that almost the same
comment as J. K. Macgregor's on the Creek Town
minutes could be made of Ohafia session, both
during and after Collins' tenure.[24] However much
the Presbyterian approach appears to be a reform of
traditional marriage, it was in fact the
introduction of a system based on entirely
different principles. African and Presbyterian
marriage practices agreed only that the institution
had something to do with sex.

The basis of African marriage, by and large,
is that it exists for the continuation of the
family. Its purpose is children. If childless,
there is no point in continuing the marriage;
either it can be dissolved or additional wives can
be taken in. The marriage contract rests on
consent, and consent can be withdrawn by either
party. Since in most parts of the Presbyterian
area the bride-price was relatively low, divorce
was not hard to get.[25] Into this rather casual
arrangement came Scottish missionaries with
orthodox evangelical ideas about exclusiveness and
permanence. The preoccupation of sessions with
marriage cases was predictable.

The Church of Scotland tradition held that
marriage was primarily for human companionship.
Children are important but not essential.[26]
Nowhere is the contrast between Nigerian and
Scottish ideas of marriage more clearly shown than
in the fact that until the 1950s, the district
missionaries were either unmarried or childless.
As long as it was considered unwise to have small
children in the tropics, the missionaries had to
choose between their families and their work. It

was a difficult and painful choice, but it was at
least possible. For most Nigerians, a decision to
remain   childless   would   be   inconceivable.
Furthermore, in the Scottish tradition the sexual
relationship was so intimate and profound that a
marriage   was   normally   seen   as   lifelong   and
exclusive. This perhaps touches on the fundamental
reason for the church's rejection of African
marriage.   The   sexual   relationship   was   such   a
profound part of human life that no compromise with
the world was possible.

     J. K. Macgregor came close to adopting a
different view. In 1935 during a review of mission
practice in Africa on the marriage question, he
asked whether it might be possible to allow the
Holy Spirit to take over African custom and make it
into something new.[27] If the answer were yes, then
the polygamous family could be accepted as an
imperfect institution, but one which did allow a
measure of Christian fellowship. In the course of
time   the   church   might   decide   to   abandon   the
practice, polygamy might die a natural death, or
the church might come to a new understanding of
biblical ideas about marriage. Such a policy would
be similar to that adopted with slavery, but
whether for emotional or theological reasons or
possibly both, the church's leadership could not
bring itself to reform polygamy; like idolatry, it
could only be abandoned.

GOSPEL AND RELIGION

     In an article introducing its readers to the
Calabar   Mission,   The   Record   described   the
inhabitants of Africa as degraded idolaters.[28]

After a few years' residence among the Efiks, the missionaries decided things weren't as bad as all that. Goldie accepted without difficulty the Efik word for God, noted with approval the belief that God was the Creator, and treated an Efik creation story, which bore some resemblance to Genesis, as evidence of a previous revelation via Noah and Ham. Africans and missionaries had a broad measure of agreement on the doctrine of creation, and Christian apologetic frequently started at that point.

However, once past creation missionary and Efik came to a parting of the ways. Hope Waddell thought the basic problem was, not idolatry, but "inhuman practices." He soon found that his most effective sermons were those which dealt with the customs of the country rather than salvation. "Calabar people no fit saby that yet," said King Eyo. "Tell them about the fashions." And so he did; Hope Waddell could readily preach a sermon with social implications. In August 1851 he preached on the text "I am the light of the world." His message did not deal with the inner light, but with the darkness in which the people of Calabar languished--they were still destroying twins.[29]

In this particular case, the mission followed through with a practical suggestion. Later in the year King Eyo agreed to the establishment of a special village for twins and their mothers outside the town. But the twin mothers' village had theological implications. Twins, like children who cut their upper teeth first, were regarded as an abnormality and therefore dangerous. The survival of twins without ill-effects on the community

required a revision of the Efik doctrine of
creation. The church made this point by engaging,
not in theological discussion, but in concrete
acts. The church's teaching was action and its
action, teaching. Thus from the earliest days the
church's approach to traditional religion was set
out. It agreed with the Efik idea of God as
Creator, rejected the rest of Calabar theology, and
tried to prove their case, not through argument,
but through a series of symbolic acts, like saving
twins.

While direct attacks on traditional religion
were rare, when Hope Waddell did turn to the
subject, he sounded like a latter-day Isaiah. As
the prophet had mocked the idolatry of Babylon, the
missionary decried the "superstitions" of Calabar.
In November all of Calabar observed *Indok*, a ritual
expulsion of ghosts from the towns. Hope Waddell
parodied this practice, pointing out that the Efiks
and their neighbours, the Quas, did not observe
Indok on the same day. Therefore, after the ghosts
had been driven out of Calabar they went to Qua,
only to be expelled from their new homes the next
week and return to Calabar. As for Creek Town, the
only place the ghosts could go was to the Mission
House, but for six years the missionaries had been
living there without ill-effects. This exposition
got an "immoderate" laugh from the Creek Town
gentry, evidence that the point had struck home.[30]

But such parodies were the exception rather
than the rule; for the most part, the missionaries
ignored traditional religion in their public
preaching. Thus when Anderson persuaded his more
advanced inquirers to sign an anti-idolatry pledge,

he found he had "set the town by its ears."[31] No
doubt   he   had   made   clear   in   his   private
conversations that to accept Christ meant to reject
the gods of the country, but because he did not
dwell on the point in his sermons, the town as a
whole did not grasp the full significance of what
he was saying.   Like Hope Waddell, Anderson could
be publicly critical of "inhuman practices," but
for the most part, he left traditional theology
alone.   Thus James Luke's comment on his own method
is probably true for the nineteenth century as a
whole: "We do not interfere with the religious
practices of the people; but we feel bound to step
in when any form of superstition leads to loss of
life."[32]

    The   tradition   was   carried   forward   by   the
twentieth-century   missionaries.   Robert   Collins
said very little in his preaching about traditional
religion, preferring to concentrate on the positive
presentation of "the supreme God and the love of
Jesus Christ."   Ulu Eme used the same message when
he went to Ikwo forty years later.[33]   More dramatic
activities   were   characteristic   of   converts.   In
Ikwo the sign of conversion was the destruction of
the   cult   objects   in   the   compound.   Very   often
Christians went beyond destroying their own cult
objects to an attack on the sacred objects or
institutions of the village.   Oral tradition in
southeastern Nigeria is littered with stories of
the Christians cutting down sacred trees or killing
sacred animals.   In Arochuku the Christians were
taken to court for witnessing, as non-initiates,
the   activities   of   the   Ekpe   society   and   even
entering the house itself.[34]   In other words, the

church's apologetic was not so much spoken as
demonstrated. The crucial events were not sermons
but acts; people publicly attacked the apparatus
and the customs of traditional religion in order to
demonstrate that the wrath of the gods or the
ancestors had no effect on Christians.

To a great extent, this behaviour was
instinctive rather than reasoned. The Christians
did not say "We will demonstrate the power of
Christ by cutting down this tree." They just cut
it down. Because the traditionalists replied with
court action rather than theological rebuttal, the
church never had to reflect on the implications of
its actions except insofar as they involved the
public peace. Thus the Christians undercut the
foundations of traditional religion without really
articulating either their own reasoning or the
structure of thought they were attacking.

In a sense, the appearance of the independent
churches was the first sign of the inadequacy of
this approach. The mission churches did not really
articulate the Christian message in terms of
traditional thought. The independents, for all
their faults, at least tried to be both biblical
and African. But the independent challenge went
unnoticed, or at least went without response until
the 1960s. It is no longer possible to let the
question lie. The mood of modern Nigeria demands
that the church take seriously its relation to
traditional thought, not simply by "baptizing" this
custom or that, but by delving to the roots of
traditional religion, grasping its first
principles, and developing a theological analysis
in the way the Church Fathers approached the

traditions and thought of the Roman Empire. The church's history has left it ill-equipped for such a task, but ill-equipped or not it is a challenge which must be met, just as the church over these 120 years has faced many challenges and, with greater or lesser enthusiasm and success, responded.

Chapter 10

THE AUTHORITY OF THE WORD

[1] Hope Waddell, Diaries, February 24, 1850.

[2] Ibid., April 1851.

[3] Latham, Old Calabar, 94; and Hope Waddell, Twenty-Nine Years, p. 476.

[4] Waddell, Twenty-Nine Years, 478 and William Anderson, Journal, February 20, 1851.

[5] The Record, August 1851.

[6] Waddell to Somerville, January 22, 1855; and The Record, February 1855.

[7] Old Calabar Mission Committee, Minutes, March 15, 1855.

[8] By the Native House Rules (Repeal) Ordinance, 1915. December 31, 1914, no. 15.

[9] The Record, August 1869.

[10] The Record, May 1895.

[11] Presbyterian Church of Biafra, Minutes, June 9, 1908.

[12] The Record, April 1910.

[13] Parliamentary Papers, vol. 56, 35.

14 S. C. Neill, Colonialism and Christian Missions, 320, no. 1.

15 H. W. Turner, "Monogamy: A Mark of the Church," International Review of Missions 55, no. 219 (1966), 313-321.

16 Waddell, Twenty-Nine Years, 487, 668-669. For the "one flesh" argument, see Genesis 2:24, Mark 10:8, 1 Corinthians 6:16.

17 Ajayi, Christian Missions, 107-108.

18 Hugh Goldie, Calabar and its Missions, 23.

19 Waddell, Diaries, November 2, 1854.

20 Waddell, Twenty-Nine Years, iv-v.

21 Presbyterian Church of Biafra, Minutes, January 5, 1859.

22 The authorship of this remark is uncertain. It was found on a slip of paper in the leaves of the nineteenth-century minute book.

23 Presbyterian Church of Biafra, Minutes, 1936. It is probable but not certain that these articles were those approved in 1938, but the 1938 minutes do not give the text of that on which they voted. Practice and Procedure makes no mention of them, but the provisions for admission and suspension from church membership which Practice and Procedure includes are clearly derived from these articles, or others very like them.

24 Ohafia Session, Minutes; and conversation with Agwu Oji, 1977.

25 A bride-price is a payment by the
bridegroom to the bride's family in cash or kind or
both. A divorce usually cannot be arranged without
repayment. In some parts of Igboland it is very
high, but the Presbyterian area, particularly
Ohafia, prefers a lower rate.

26 _The Book of Common Order_, pp. 154-155.

27 J. K. Macgregor, "Christian Missions and
Marriage Usage in Africa," _International Review of
Missions_ 24 (1935), 390-391.

28 _The Record_, January 1846.

29 Waddell, Diaries, August 1851. See also
Waddell, _Twenty-Nine Years_, 376-377.

30 Waddell, Diaries, November 30, 1851. See
also Waddell, _Twenty-Nine Years_, 397-398 for the
abolition by a similar technique of _Ekpenyong_.

31 _The Record_, October 1851.

32 James Luke, _Pioneering in Mary Slessor's
Country_, 75.

33 Conversation with Agwu Oji, 1977. Notes on
conversations with Ocha Mbila and Ulu Eme, 1977.

34 _Calprof_, 14/6/20/7.

Chapter 11

THE PROPHETS AND THE PEOPLE

In May 1977 I happened to be in Lagos
Presbyterian Church when the moderator of the synod
came by on a western tour. As is the custom on
such occasions, the congregation gave a reception,
and when the refreshments had been served,
presented the moderator with a speech of welcome,
containing in this case a series of complaints the
congregation had against the synod. The guest
replied with wit and wisdom. When things go wrong,
he asked, do you blame yourselves, do you blame the
synod, or, as he continued gesturing at me, do you
blame the white man? When I protested innocence,
the room dissolved in laughter. Both the moderator
and I had recently attended a ministers' retreat at
which the sins of the pioneers, real and imagined,
were amply discussed. Within the Presbyterian
church there exists a real confusion about their
inheritance. Who, in earlier days, had been
responsible for what?

The initial impetus in the church's life was a
package of prophetic ideas and prophetic acts
brought to Calabar by the first generation of
missionaries. Insofar as the ideas and practices
were acceptable in Calabar, they became established
and once established they became part of tradition,
tradition that might continue to be prophetic but
still tradition handed down from one generation to

the next. Against this constant in the church's
life, Nigerians within and without the church
responded, and tradition, with varying degrees of
flexibility, responded to the response. The
history of this church is the history of the
interplay between tradition and response. Without
the presence of the missionaries the church would
not have been available; without the Nigerian
response it would not have come into existence, nor
would it be what it is today.

It is this analysis, this understanding of the
church's history as the interplay between the
missionary tradition and the Nigerian response,
that explains the title. The decisive event in the
church's history was the British conquest. When
the maxim guns overturned the old order, people
began looking for answers to questions they had
never asked before. Because the missionary
tradition offered reasonably satisfactory answers,
the church changed from an appendage of the mission
to a potentially viable Nigerian institution, and
in the nationalist period, the potential began to
become a reality. Yet despite these profound
changes, certain elements in the church's life have
remained constant.

In the nineteenth century the pioneers
established certain practices which may be
described as the missionary or prophetic tradition.
The Christian presence was always both church and
school. The work among women offered a fellowship
of adults and marriage preparation for the young.
Although beginning late, curative medicine was well
established by the turn of the century. The church
was active in social reform. It did a reasonable

job of ministerial training and admitted Nigerian
leaders into the central councils of the church
without discrimination. It was open from the
beginning to cooperation with other denominations.

In the nineteenth century the response to this
missionary tradition, with the partial exception of
the house of Eyo, was not very enthusiastic. But
the trauma of the British conquest brought major
changes to the life of the church. The tradition
came to be seen as the answer to the problems
created by the conquest. The church grew by leaps
and bounds; the schools were changed from literacy
and Bible classes to units in a system of public
instruction. The work among girls grew from
rudimentary classes in a missionary's house to a
system of boarding schools. Fifteen years later
the women became formally organized and began the
training of staff. Cooperation with other
denominations, somewhat theoretical in the
nineteenth century, became a real possibility,
bearing fruit in a series of ecumenical
conferences, the joint institutions, and the
abortive search for union.

The British conquest also brought changes in
missionary thinking. It gave the new generation an
unbounded confidence in its ability to manage the
affairs of the church. Consequently, control of
the church's life was assumed by the Mission
Council rather than by the presbytery, and
ministerial training lapsed for lack of interest.
In the early years of the twentieth century,
therefore, certain aspects of the tradition were
submerged. However, they did not disappear--
Nigerian pressure brought them back to life. Staff

training was resumed at Arochuku. It reached a
more sophisticated level at Trinity College, and
with the advent of the Advanced Training Fund,
began to attain the levels reached by the
missionaries. From the mid-1930s the exclusive
control of the church by the missionaries was
increasingly challenged, until in 1960 the Mission
Council disappeared and the various functions of
the church were integrated under the synod.

Two aspects of the church's life do not fit
this pattern so neatly, but illustrate the thesis
in a different way. First, medicine differed from
education in that the services offered were subject
to considerable change. The schools provided a
fairly standard product from 1846 to 1966, although
they became more sophisticated as time went on.
But the hospitals could only offer what the medical
profession in Europe made available. Thus they
achieved their first successes in surgery, but it
was not until the appearance of new treatments for
yaws and leprosy in the 1920s and antibiotics in
the 1940s that the hospitals really began to grow.
Nigerians could demand a better kind of education
because they knew it was available. They could
only respond to new treatments as they were
discovered.

Second, social reform, a major part of the
tradition in the nineteenth century, withered away
in the colonial period and only began to reappear
in rudimentary form in the nationalist years.
Because social criticism was instinctive rather
than based on a solid theological analysis, it did
not survive when the church found itself in a
society in which it felt at home. Only when the

missionaries began to feel alienated from society in the nationalist period did they resume any kind of critical comment on the world around them.

In both these cases the missionary tradition was inadequate; however, if the tradition was inadequate so were the resources of Nigerian society. The diseases which baffled the Scottish doctors were equally puzzling to the practitioners of African medicine. If the tradition the Scottish missionaries brought to Nigeria has never been strong on social criticism, neither was Nigerian thought. As the Scottish tradition stressed personal salvation, so many of the clans in the Cross River valley stressed personal achievement. As the Ohafia proverb puts it, "Only the returning warrior can dance to the big drum." Only he who has proved himself in battle can receive honour on his return. In other words, there was little in the Nigerian inheritance to offset the inadequacies of the Scottish tradition.

To return to the original question--who in the past was to blame for our present troubles?--the answer must be that everyone was responsible. The missionary tradition offered certain services to Nigeria, which Nigerians could accept or reject. As A. G. Somerville remarked, "You can't carry on a school, no matter how much you may want to, if you have no customers." The inheritance of the church is a joint product of a prophetic tradition and a peoples' response. It falls to this generation to ensure that the outcome of the jostling of tradition and response continues to be prophetic.

INDEX

Abam: warriors, 34; founding of church in, 45

Abiriba: founding of church in, 43-45, 58-59; hospital in, 203-204; dispute in, 261-263

Agricultural Missions: in Ikwo, 52-53. NORCAP; C. Hutchison; J. Paterson

Akunakuna, 24-25, 36; dispute with Okurike, 255-256

Amakofia: founding of church in, 42

Amaseri: progress of church in, 45; resistance to Christianity, 64-65

Anderson, William, 15-16; dispute with colleagues, 74; dispute with Alexander Ross, 77-79; on the right of asylum, 244-246; on human sacrifice, 246; on Europeans trading above Calabar, 251; on the "blood men," 275-277; on idolatry, 296-297

Anglican Church and Mission: in Bonny, 18; and Arochuku, 41-42, 138; in Calabar, 139; and church union, 144-146

Apiapum: founding of church in, 47

Arnot, Mrs. A. S., 227-228

Aro, 32-35

Arochuku: expedition, 35-36, 257; oracle in, 34-35; founding of church in, 40-42; settlements, 135-136; church and the Ekpe society, 297. Anglican Church

Bahumuno. *See* Ediba

Baptists: in Fernando Po, 132; in Calabar, 132-133

Beattie, J. A. T., 94

Beecroft, J., 10

Blood men, 274-277

Bookshop: relation to Synod, 96. *See also* the Hope Waddell Training Institute

Bonny: founding a mission in, 17-18; Anglicans in, 18

Buchanan, J.: and missionaries for Unwana and Akunakuna, 25; and the reorganization of the mission, 80-81; and Hope Waddell Training Institute, 163-165

Builders (the mission): origins of, 162; outside Calabar, 176. *See also* Education

Buxton, T. F., 8

Calabar, 2; church in, 2; opening of mission in, 11; origins of, 11; slave trade in, 12; social structure, 12-14; political structure, 242

Calabar Mission Council, 4, 36; dismantling of, 5, 93-94; founding of, 85; functions, 86

Canadian missionaries. *See* Presbyterian Church in Canada

Chalmers, M.: and higher education for Africans, 118; and Edgerley Memorial School, 225-226

Christian Council of Nigeria: precursors, 143; and the liquor traffic, 283

Christian Girls Club, 237

Christie, W. M.: moves to Okposi, 48; on church government, 94

Church growth: in the nineteenth century, 26-28; in Ibibio country, 39-40; in Igboland, 40-46, 47-53; on the east bank of the Cross River, 46-47; in the cities, 54-57; reasons for, 57-67

Church union: negotiations towards, 144-145; collapse of, 146-147

Collins, R.: moves to Ohafia, 43; and Abiriba, 43-45; his message, 297

Colonial: mentality,   3,   117-120;   regime,   4;
    period, 5. *See also* Empire

Comity Agreements: and the cities, 54-55, 139-142;
    history of, 134-138; nature of, 138-139

Conquest (the British):   consequences   for   the
    church, 57-59. *See also* Arochuku Expedition

Consul (the British): and the right of asylum,
    244-246; and Old Town, 248-250; and interior
    trade, 250-251; and the Cross River wars, 255-256

Creek Town, 3; in the nineteenth century, 75-76;
    social reforms in, 257

Cross River, 16; trade along, 18-19, 250-251; wars
    on, 255-256

Cruickshank, A: and founding of churches in
    Ibibioland, 38-39; letter to FMC (1902), 57; on
    the liquor traffic, 280

Dean, J. T.:   theological tutor, 113-115; and
    church union, 143

Denham, C. H., 235-236

Devolution, 86, 92

District Missionaries: development of, 83; as
    theologians, 98-99; disappearance of, 179-180

Doctors. *See* Medicine

Dodds, F. W., 45; and R. Collins, 136

Duke Town, 3; social reform in, 253

Duke Town Church: in the nineteenth century, 76;
    and theological education, 116-117

Ecoma, Ejemot, 46-47, 112

Edda: progress of church in, 45-46; resistance to
    Christianity, 64-65

Ediba: founding of church in,   47; dispute in,
260-261

Edgerley, M, 222-223

Edgerley, S.:   arrival in Calabar, 10; dispute with
colleagues, 74; missionary in Old Town, 247-250

Edgerley, S. H.:   at Creek Town, 21; as explorer,
22; at Umon, 24-25; as theological tutor, 106,
109; as amateur physician, 192

Ediene: founding of church in, 39-40

Education: for   girls,   4;   nineteenth century
rationale for,   160;   Efik response to,   161;
secondary, 167, 169-170, 174-175, 182; secondary
education for   girls,   232-233;   primary,   168,
170-171, 173; supervisor of, 171; financing of,
183-184; government takeover of, 184

Education Authority: formation of, 91-92; as part
of Synod, 93-94, 96

Education Conference: formation of, 89-90.   See
also Education Authority

Education (technical):   origins of, 162; development of, 165; decline of, 175-176

Education: theological. See theological education

Efik, 12; marriage, 288-290

Efiong, O., 88, 117; and Education Conference, 89

Ekanem, A.:   at Okoyong, 22; as translator, 107

Ekoi, 22

Eme, N.:   as Synod Clerk, 95; study in Canada, 126

Eme, Ulu: moves to Ikwo, 51; evangelistic method,
51-52

Empire (the British), 3; missionary attitude to,
243-244;   the   Protectorate   (1878),   253-254;
relation to mission, 258-260, 263-264.   See also
Colonial

Enugu: founding of church in, 56; relief work in,
  266

Enyong: Creek, 33; founding of church in, 39; war
  with Calabar, 193, 255; women's work in, 229-230

Esega, Chief Eja, 46-47

Esien, E. E., 95; as supervising teacher, 180

Expansion.   Church growth

Eyo Honesty II, 3, 14-15, 19; on the "blood men,"
  275; his household, 287

Eyo VII: and Umon, 24, 26; and the Protectorate,
  254

Eyamba II: and the founding of the mission, 10

Ezza: progress of church in, 48-50

Foreign Mission Board. *See* United Presbyterian
  Church of Scotland; United Secession Church of
  Scotland

Foreign Mission Committee: *See* United Free Church
  of Scotland; Church of Scotland

Gardiner, W. A. J.:   moves to Unwana, 26

George, W., 107

Girls' Schools.   *See* schools

Goldie, H.:   at Ikunetu, 19; at Creek Town, 21; on
  mission policy, 27; and girls' boarding school,
  221; on the Protectorate, 254; on the "blood
  men," 276; on the liquor traffic, 280; on African
  theology, 295

Government.   *See* Empire (the British)

Hart, S. M., 169-170

Hastings, H.: moves to Uburu, 48, 196; treatment of leprosy, 201-203; training of staff, 208

Hitchcock, J. W.: moves to Uburu, 47-48

Hope Waddell Training Institution: relation to Mission Council, 84, 86; relation to Synod, 96; origins of, 162-163; early problems, 163-165; relation to Foreign Missions Committee, 165; under J. K. MacGregor, 165-168; developments after 1946, 172-177

Hugh Goldie College: founding of, 115; last class, 122; training of women at, 235

Hutchison, Charles: at Ikwo, 52

Ibiam, A.: Principal of HWTI, 180; and the Advanced Training Fund, 181; accomplishments, 189, note, 18; at Abiriba, 203-206; and the training of nurses, 204-205; relation to missionaries, 205-206; and Queen Elizabeth Hospital, 209; at Uburu, 212

Ibiono: founding of church in, 42

Igbere: founding of church in, 45

Ikom: founding of church in, 47

Ikorofiong: founding of church in, 19; source of teachers, 38-39; nineteenth century ministers, 76

Ikot Ana: founding of church in, 24-25

Ikot Ekpene: ecumenical conference about, 134-135

Ikot Obong: Mary Slessor moves to, 40

Ikunetu: opening of mission in, 19; in the nineteenth century, 76

Ikwo: progress of church in, 48-53, 65

Imoke, S. I.: at Itigidi hospital, 214

Independent churches, 150-152, 154-155

Inyang, N. E., 95; Principal of Edgerley Memorial School, 190

Iso, U., 95; as supervising teacher, 180; as Secretary of the Education Authority, 180, 186

Itigidi, 36; founding of church in, 46-47; hospital in, 214

Itu: opening of station at, 36-37

Itu Leper Colony: founding of, 198-199; development of, 200-201; decline of, 201-203

Iwerre: founding of church in, 42

Izzi: progress of church in, 48-50

Jamaica, 2; Scottish mission in, 8; mission to Africa, 8-9; missionaries from, 25; source of mission teachers, 169

Johnston, E.: and boarding school for girls, 222-223

Johnson, E. H.: and theological education, 125; contribution to Nigerian church, 131, note 27

Kaduna: sending of minister to, 55-56

Lagos: founding of church in, 56

Leper Colonies: Itu, 198-199, 200-201; in Ogoja, 203; decline of Itu, 210-211

Leprosy, 199, 211

Leprosy Clinics: near Itu, 211. See also Southern Ogoja Leprosy Service

Lewars, J. M., 94; and Education Authority, 92; and theological education, 121-122, 126; supervisor of schools, 171

Liquor traffic: and the Calabar churches, 139; and
  the Presbyterians, 279-283; ecumenical action on,
  282-283

Long Juju. *See* Arochuku oracle

Luke, J., 25; at Hope Waddell, 165; on the Empire,
  258; on African theology, 297

Macdonald, A. B.: arrival at Itu, 196; treatment
  of yaws, 196-197; treatment of leprosy, 198-201

Macdonald, Sir Claude, 32; and the Okurike war,
  255-256; approved by missionaries, 256; on the
  liquor traffic, 280-281

Macdonald, R. M., 94; and the Education Conference,
  89; and Education Authority, 92; and the "open
  towns," 142; and the "Spirit Age," 152; and the
  independent churches, 152; and the Mennonites,
  153; and Itu Leper Colony, 211-212

Macgregor, J. K.: and Education Conference, 89;
  Principal of Hope Waddell Training Institution,
  165-168; educational   philosophy,   185;   on
  marriage, 294

Macrae, N. C.: as Principal of Hope Waddell
  Training Institution, 123

Marriage: training of girls for, 221-223, 224-226,
  227-229; Presbyterian   attitude   to,   286-288;
  Presbyterian regulations about, 288-290, 291-292;
  regulations   in   other   churches,   290-291;
  missionary attitudes to, 292-294

Medicine: medical work, 5; Medical Board, 96;
  rationale for nineteenth century mission doctors,
  191; in Old Town, 192; in Unwana, 193-194; in
  Calabar, 194; in Uburu, early years, 195; in Itu,
  early years, 195; European vs. traditional
  medicine, 197-198; the chemo-therapeutic revolution,   207;   joint   status   hospitals,   213;
  preventive medicine, 213-215. *See also* Leprosy;
  Yaws; Itu; Uburu; Abiriba; Itigidi, Nurses

Mennonites: and the independent churches, 152-153;
  at Abiriba, 153

Methodist, Church and Mission: in Archibong, 133;
   in Jamestown, 133-134; in Ikot Ekpene, 134-135;
   in Fernando, 135; boundary agreements, 136-137;
   in Calabar, 139-140; and church union, 146-147.
   See also F. W. Dodds

Middlekoop, H.: member of Synod, 97; at Itigidi,
   214-215

Midwives, midwifery. *See* Rural Health; Obstetrics

Mincher, A. K., 94; and Education Authority, 92

Ministers, Nigerian, 88; in the nineteenth century,
   105-107; active in Synod, 88-89; ordinations of
   (1918), 112; at Trinity College, 123-124; other
   forms of training, 124-126

Missionaries: district,   84-85;   as   members   of
   Sessions, 88-89; education of, 104-105, 112;
   attitude to Africans, 108, 111, 117-120; and the
   Protectorate, 254-258; and the Empire, 258-260,
   263-264; and Independence, 264-265.   *See also*
   Marriage; Slavery; African theology

Mission Districts, 84-86, 97

Netherlands Reformed Church, 214

Niger: the Expedition, 10; the Mission, 79-80

NORCAP, 52-53

Nurses: in the colonial period, 207; training of,
   204-205, 207-209, 231

Nya, Chief Onoyom Iya, 39

Obstetrics: and the Ibiams, 204; at Abiriba, 209;
   at Queen Elizabeth Hospital, 209; at Uburu, 212;
   at Itigidi, 215

Ohafia: founding of church in, 42-43, 58; girls'
   school in, 228; Canadian missionaries in, 237

Okoyong: founding of church in, 22-24

Okposi: progress of church in, 48

Old Calabar Mission Committee, 73-75; reconstituted, 80-81; dissolution, 83

Old Town: founding of church in, 11; as a medical station, 192; human sacrifice in, 247-250

Onuk, E.: and the opening of churches in the cities, 55-56; study in Scotland, 126

Ordained Assistant Ministers. *See* Ministers

Otisi, A., 44-45

Otisi, N. A., 95, 97

Otisi, O. A., 95

Otuma, Chief Nwancha, 5, 51-52

Paterson, J.: at last Council meeting, 94; at Itu Leper Colony, 200; in Ogoja, 215-216

Peacock, Martha: at Ikot Obong, 40, 229

Polygamy. *See* Marriage

Port Harcourt: founding of church in, 56

Presbyterian Church in Canada: supplies ministers for city churches, 56; and theological education, 130-131, note 27; and youth work, 237-238; and the crisis of 1966, 266

Presbyterian Church of Biafra: founding of, 74-75; functioning of (1858-1881), 75-80; formation of Synod of, 87; development of, 87-88; constitution of Synod, 90-91

Presbyterian Church of Nigeria: and the "open towns," 55-56; integration of mission into, 93-94; description of, 95-100; lack of political theology, 265-266; and the crisis of 1966, 266-268

Qua, 12

Qua Ibo Mission: and Ikot Ekpene, 134; and the
    "Spirit Age," 151; origins, 157, note 5

Queen Elizabeth Hospital, 209-210

Race, 3, 110-111; in the Presbyterian Church of
    Biafra, 76

Rankin, J.:   moves to Arochuku, 41-42

Religion, African.   *See* Theology, African

Robb, A.:   in Jamaica, 25; as theological tutor,
    105, 108

Roman Catholic Church: and the "Spirit Age," 151;
    lack of cooperation with, 155; at the University
    of Nigeria, 159, note 33; competition in educa-
    tion, 174, 184, 185; competition in medicine,
    202; competition in girls' schools, 233

Ross, A.:   dispute with William Anderson, 77-79

Rural Health: at Itigidi, 214-215; in Ogoja,
    215-216

Scholarships, 5; for theological studies, 125-127;
    for teachers, 175; the Advanced Training Fund,
    181

Schools, Boarding: Hope Waddell Training Institu-
    tion, 161-168, 172-177; for girls, 221-223; Creek
    Town Girls' Institute, 224-225; Edgerley Memorial
    School, 225-226; Ohafia Girls' School, 228

Scottish Missionary Society: mission to Jamaica,
    8, 10

Secret Societies: and the church, 64-65, 261

Shepherd, C.:   member of Synod, 97

Slave Trade: continuing after 1808, 8; in Calabar,
    12

Slaves: in Jamaica, 8; mission policy towards, 73–
74; the "blood men," 274–277

Slavery: in Jamaica, abolition of, 8; in Calabar,
13; missionary approach to, 273–274, 277–279

Slessor, M.:   at Okoyong, 22–23; on the Enyong
Creek, 36–37; and Arochuku, 41; as a consular
magistrate, 257–258

Slessor Memorial School, 227–228; first Nigerian
principal, 180

Somerville, A.:   on mission policy, 74–75; on
education, 160; on medical missions, 191; on
slave holders as church members, 277, 279

Somerville, A. G.:   and integration, 93–94; as
Clerk of Synod, 93, 95; on theological education,
125; on the limits of missionary initiative, 302

"Spirit Age," 151–152

Spirits.   *See* liquor traffic

Standing Committee: responsibilities of, 96

Teachers, Nigerian: difficulties with, 173; and
school management, 177–180; as principals, 180

Teacher Training: in the nineteenth century, 106,
111; at Hope Waddell Training Institution, 166;
at Afikpo, 174; expansion of, 181–182; for women,
226–227

Theological Education, 4, 5; in the nineteenth
century, 105–107; under J. T. Dean, 113–115;
Nigerian criticism of, 115–117; limitations of,
117–120; twentieth century standards, 121, 130,
note 22; alternate forms of, 124–126

Theology, African: and the British Conquest, 58–
67; missionary approach to, 295–297; twins and
twin mothers, 295–296

Trade, traders: and human sacrifices, 246–247; and
Old Town, 247–249

Trading: in palm oil, 14; on the Cross River,
    18-19,   20-21,   30,   note   13;   prohibited   to
    missionaries   at   Ikorofiong,   19;   controversy
    about, 20; by Europeans at Calabar, 250-251

Trinity College: founding of, 121-122; development
    of, 122-123; Presbyterians in, 123-124

Twins, twin mothers. *See* Theology, African

Uburu: founding of mission in,   48; progress of
    church in, 53

Uburu Hospital: financial problems of, 212-213

Ukpabio, E. E.:   in Creek Town, 21; at Adiabo, 22;
    as head of station, 81; as theological student,
    106-107

Umon, 20-21, 24

United Free Church of Scotland: and the "Wee
    Frees," 37; Foreign Missions Committee, 37-38;
    Women's Foreign Mission Committee, 37

United Presbyterian Church in the United States of
    America, 56

United Presbyterian Church of Scotland, 27; and Old
    Calabar   Mission   Committee,   74-75;   and   the
    Anderson-Ross dispute, 77-79

United Secession Church of Scotland, 11

Unwana: founding of mission in, 25-26; progress of
    church in, 45, 66; resistance to Christianity,
    64-65; as a medical station, 193

Utit, E., 75, 112

Ututu: founding of church in, 42

Uwa, A. E., 25-26, 85

Uwakwenta I, 95; and Ediba dispute, 260

Venn, Henry: missionary theorist, 72-73; and the
   Niger Mission, 110

Waddell, G. B., 11

Waddell, H. M., 5, 10, 15; disputes with other
   missionaries, 74; on other missions, 132; primary
   school curriculum, 160-161; on social reform,
   245-247, 249; on human sacrifice, 246; on the
   Protectorate, 234; on slavery, 234, 288; on the
   "blood men," 275; on polygamy, 284-285; on
   African religion, 295-296

West Indies, 2

Wilkie, A. W.: and Arochuku, 41; and the liquor
   traffic, 139, 282; and church union, 143

Women: early work among, 223-224; work among in
   the twentieth century, 229-231; training of
   workers, 230-231, 234-236. See also Schools;
   Teacher training; Women's Guild; Women's Training
   College; Christian Girls' Club

Women's Guild, 236-237

Women's Training College, Umuahia: founding of,
   226-227

Yakurr: founding of church in, 47; Paterson's
   nursery at, 216

Yaws: campaigns against, 196-198

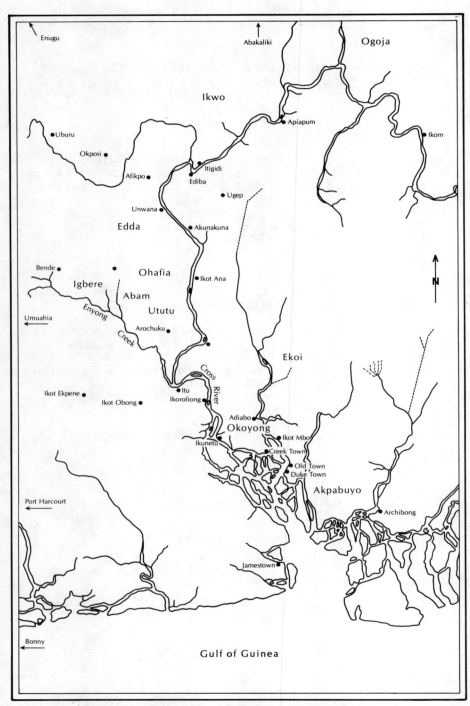

PRINCIPAL CENTRES OF THE PRESBYTERIAN CHURCH OF
NIGERIA, 1846-1966